VISUAL QUICKSTART GUIDE

PHOTOSHOP
ELEMENTS 7

FOR WINDOWS

Jeff Carlson

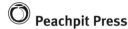
Peachpit Press

Visual QuickStart Guide
Photoshop Elements 7 for Windows
Jeff Carlson

Peachpit Press
1249 Eighth Street
Berkeley, CA 94710
(510) 524-2178
(510) 524-2221 (fax)

Find us on the Web at: www.peachpit.com
To report errors, please send a note to errata@peachpit.com
Peachpit Press is a division of Pearson Education

Editor: Susan Rimerman
Copyeditor: Liane Thomas
Proofreader: Dan Foster
Indexer: Karin Arrigoni
Production Editor: Cory Borman
Composition: Jeff Carlson
Cover Design: Peachpit Press

Notice of rights

Notice of liability

Trademarks

ISBN 13: 978-0-321-56596-9
ISBN 10:   0-321-56596-7

9 8 7 6 5 4 3 2 1

Printed and bound in the United States of America

Dedication:

For Emma V.

And for Eliana, who waited.

Special Thanks to:

For their hard work and positive attitudes, my gratitude goes out to Liane Thomas, Susan Rimerman, Dan Foster, Karin Arrigoni, and Cory Borman. They've been a great team on this edition of the book.

Thank you to Roman Skuratovskiy at Edelman, and Roma Dhall, Ginny Sidell, and Bob Gager at Adobe for their assistance in getting me the software and information I needed.

The content in these pages also owes a great debt to Glenn Fleishman, Agen G. N. Schmitz, Jeff Tolbert, and Laurence Chen, who assisted with the last edition just before the birth of my daughter.

Thanks to my officemates Kim Ricketts and Hillary Vonckx for camaraderie and support.

I also want to thank Craig Hoeschen for providing great material to work with: the editions prior to version 5.

My gratitude also extends to Parie Hines, Cindy Dorsey, Steve Horn, Jill Thompson, and Scott and Lisa Johnson for their permissions to use photos of their adorable kids.

Lastly, my appreciation and love to Kim and Ellie for making me a happy man.

TABLE OF CONTENTS

TABLE OF CONTENTS

TABLE OF CONTENTS

ix

INTRODUCTION

Welcome to Photoshop Elements, Adobe's powerful, easy-to-use, image-editing software. Photoshop Elements gives hobbyists, as well as professional photographers and artists, many of the same tools and features found in Adobe Photoshop (long the industry standard), but packaged in a more accessible, intuitive workspace. Photoshop Elements' friendly user interface, combined with its bargain-basement price, has made it an instant hit with the new wave of amateur digital photographers lured by the recent proliferation of sophisticated, low-cost digital cameras and scanners.

Photoshop Elements 7 provides new tools and enhancements that not only help stretch the bounds of your creativity, but also help to make your quick photo corrections and creative retouching even simpler and more fun than before.

In the next few pages, I'll cover some of Photoshop Elements' key features (both old and new) and share a few thoughts to help you get the most from this book. Then you can be on your way to mastering Photoshop Elements' simple, fun, and sophisticated image-editing tools.

Introducing Photoshop Elements

Photoshop Elements makes it easy to retouch your digital photos; apply special effects, filters, and styles; prepare images for the Web; and even create wide-screen panoramas from a series of individual photos. And Photoshop Elements provides several features geared specifically to the beginning user. Of particular note are a comprehensive Help system featuring a glossary of common, digital image-editing terms; and a unique, engaging palette that helps guide you step by step through a variety of fun and useful tasks: from basic photo retouching to creating special digital effects.

The Glossary, accessible from within Photoshop Elements' Help, provides easy-to-understand definitions of nearly 200 terms. Although this glossary is specifically written for use with Photoshop Elements, it also serves as a good general digital photography and image-editing resource. Alongside the software-specific topics like brush type and canvas size, you'll find excellent working definitions of concepts as diverse as bit depth, PostScript, and RGB color.

What's new in version 7

For most of its existence, Elements has been "Photoshop Light," a scaled-back version of Adobe's image-editing behemoth. With version 5.0, however, the company slightly retooled Elements to be the only program you need to manage and edit your library of digital photos, and version 6.0 reinforced that.

Version 7.0 opens Elements to the broader networked world. Built-in integration with Adobe's Photoshop.com Web site makes it easy to publish online albums directly. But that's just the surface. Photoshop.com is

"Photoshop on the Web," which means you can organize *and edit* your photos on any computer running a modern Web browser. Photoshop.com doesn't offer the sophistication of Elements' tools, but it provides a lot more than you might expect from an online version of an application.

And yet, what excites me most about Photoshop.com is the capability to automatically back up your Elements photo albums. Digital photos truly are irreplaceable, and most people are just one hard-drive failure away from losing all of their digital memories. Elements now transparently uploads copies of the photos you choose to Photoshop.com, and keeps them synchronized; if you edit a photo online, the change is reflected in your Elements catalog.

The new Smart Brush tool lets you paint an area and apply preset effects to it. For example, punch up drab skies with the Blue Skies tool—without first making a selection, creating an adjustment layer, tweaking the settings, and so on.

I'm also partial to the new Photomerge Scene Cleaner feature, which lets you easily and cleanly remove objects (such as the errant tourist walking into frame). You can also now locate photos in the Organizer using the text search field.

If you've worked with Photoshop Elements in the past, you should feel right at home in version 7.0. Although the interface changed appearance in version 6.0 (adopting the slate look used by Photoshop Lightroom), most of the tools, palettes, and menus remain in easy-to-locate areas of the desktop. The toolbox, options bar, palette bin, and photo bin still figure prominently, as does the powerful Organizer.

Personalizing Photoshop Elements

Because no two users work quite the same way, Photoshop Elements gives you the freedom to customize its tools and palettes to suit your own personal work habits, expertise, and aesthetic. You can create favorite sets of brush types, swatch libraries, and patterned fills, and you can set preferences for save options, transparency, ruler units, and grid color. Slightly more advanced options help you to set the ways the program manages memory, and the ways it works with your monitor and printer to display and print color. Additionally, since it supports Adobe's plug-in file format, Photoshop Elements can be a constantly changing and evolving tool, as you add new plug-ins for everything from custom filter effects to digital camera image browsers.

Setting preferences

Preferences are settings that let you control and modify the way Photoshop Elements looks, works, and behaves. The Preferences dialog is divided into a series of windows, each one focusing on a specific aspect of the application: general display properties, file saving options, cursor display and behavior, transparency settings, rulers and units of measurement, grid appearance and behavior, cache levels for managing memory, display settings for the file browser, and more. You can change preferences at any time by choosing Preferences from the Edit menu.

About presets

Presets are collections of brush styles, swatch colors, gradient fills, and patterns organized into sets, or libraries. At any time during your work session, you can load different preset libraries using either the Preset Manager or the palette menus on the options bar or Swatches palette.

About plug-ins

Photoshop Elements makes great use of Adobe's extendable plug-ins format. Plug-in modules are little software programs that add functionality to the main application. For instance, the different filters and effects you access from Photoshop Elements' Filter menu are all plug-in modules. Plug-ins are stored inside a Plug-ins folder, where additional plug-ins can be added at any time.

Plug-ins are worth special mention because you aren't limited to just those included with Photoshop Elements. In cooperation with Adobe, developers of both software and hardware have created compatible plug-ins that install and run seamlessly with Photoshop Elements. If you've recently purchased a digital camera or scanner, its browser or scanning software may very well include plug-ins to help the devices communicate with Photoshop Elements.

✔ Tip

- To download additional plug-ins from Adobe, first make sure your computer is connected to the Internet. In Photoshop Elements, choose Help > Photoshop Elements Online to view an updated collection of plug-ins and other downloads available for purchase.

How to Use This Book

This Visual QuickStart Guide, like others in the series, is a task-based reference. Each chapter focuses on a specific area of the application and presents it in a series of concise, illustrated steps. I encourage you to follow along using your own images. I believe the best way to learn is by doing, and this Visual QuickStart Guide is the perfect vehicle for that style of learning.

This book is meant to be a reference work, and although it's not expected that you'll read through it in sequence from front to back, I've made an attempt to order the chapters in a logical fashion. The first chapter takes you on a tour of the work area and provides a foundation for the basics of importing photos and image editing. From there you dive into managing your photo library using the Organizer. Then you explore color, selections, layers, effects, painting, and typography, and then learn a variety of techniques for saving and printing images, including special formatting options for distributing images over the Web.

This book is suitable for the beginner just starting in digital photography and image creation, as well as hobbyists, photo enthusiasts, intermediate-level photographers, illustrators, and designers.

Keyboard shortcuts

Many of the commands accessed from Photoshop Elements' menu bar have a keyboard equivalent (or shortcut) that appears beside each command name in the menu. Keyboard shortcuts are great time-savers and prevent you from having to constantly refocus your energy and attention as you jump from image window to menu bar and back again. When this book introduces a command, the keyboard shortcut is also listed. For example, the keyboard shortcut for the Copy command is displayed as Ctrl+C. You'll find a complete list of Photoshop Elements' keyboard shortcuts in the appendices.

THE BASICS

Before you start working in Photoshop Elements, take a look around the work area to familiarize yourself with the program's tools and menus. When you first launch Photoshop Elements, you immediately see the Welcome screen, which allows you to quickly organize and edit your files, make photo creations, or share your pictures with friends and family.

The work area includes the document window, where you'll view your images, along with many of the tools, menus, and palettes you'll use as you get better acquainted with the program.

This chapter also gets you started with importing photos from your digital camera, opening images already on your hard disk, and scanning printed photos.

Understanding the Work Area

The Photoshop Elements work area is designed to make the tools easy to find and use. Just as with a well-organized workbench, the menus, palettes, and tools are intuitively arranged in a way that makes them easy to find when you need them.

The Welcome screen

When you first start Photoshop Elements, the Welcome screen automatically appears on your desktop (**Figure 1.1**). Think of the Welcome screen as a handy launching pad for organizing your photo library; editing and enhancing photos; creating slide shows, photobooks, and other materials; and sharing your pictures online or on media such as CD or DVD discs.

The Organizer and the Editor

Photoshop Elements is made up of two separate components: the Organizer and the Editor, which can be (and often are) open simultaneously. The conventions in this chapter primarily apply to the Editor; the Organizer's unique interface items are covered in Chapter 2.

✔ Tips

- If you have a Photoshop.com membership, go ahead and enter it at the Welcome screen—but it's not necessary at this point. I cover Photoshop.com integration later in this chapter.

- Clicking the close button (x) in the upper-right corner of the Welcome screen closes the window without taking any action.

- Click the Home icon in the Organizer or the Editor to return to the Welcome screen at any time (**Figure 1.2**).

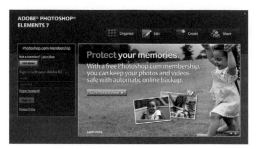

Figure 1.1 The Photoshop Elements Welcome screen provides a simple and fast way to organize, edit, and share your images.

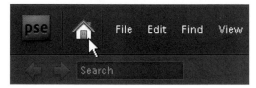

Figure 1.2 The Home icon brings up the Welcome screen from anywhere within the program.

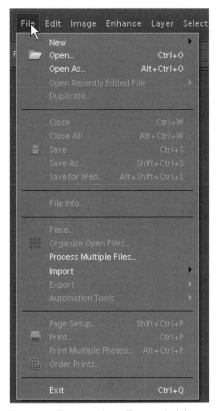

Figure 1.3 The menu bar offers myriad drop-down menus, with commands you choose to help perform tasks.

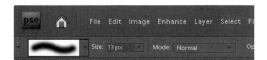

Figure 1.4 The options bar changes its display depending on the tool you select in the toolbox.

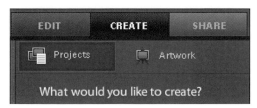

Figure 1.5 The Task Pane gives you easy access to some of Photoshop Elements' most common operations, such as creating, browsing, and printing files.

Menus, tools, and panels

The **menu bar** offers drop-down menus for performing common tasks, editing images, and organizing your work area. Each menu is organized by topic. For example, the File menu offers commands for opening, importing, saving, and batch processing your images (**Figure 1.3**).

The **options bar**, running above the work area, provides unique settings and options for each tool in the toolbox. For instance, when you're using the Marquee selection tool, you can choose to add to or subtract from the current selection; and when you're using a Brush tool, you can adjust settings like brush size and opacity (**Figure 1.4**).

The **Task Pane** (also referred to as the **Palette Bin** in the Editor) groups common tasks and controls into the right edge of the window (**Figure 1.5**). Clicking a colored heading displays the panels for organizing, editing, creating, and sharing. To temporarily hide this area and make more room for working, click the Palette Bin button at the bottom of the area in the Editor, or choose Window > Hide Task Pane in the Organizer.

✔ Tip

- If you're upgrading from Elements 5, you'll see that the shortcuts bar, which included buttons for common commands, no longer appears. Instead, it has been replaced by the Task Pane.

The **toolbox** may be the single most important component of the work area. It contains most of the tools you'll use for selecting, moving, cropping, retouching, and enhancing your images. The tools are arranged in the general order you'll be using them, with the most commonly used selection tools near the top, and the painting, drawing, and color correction tools toward the bottom. The toolbar is docked on the left edge of the work area where the tools are displayed in a single, long column (vertical space permitting). If you prefer, the toolbar can be pulled a short distance from the left edge, where it will display the tools in a two-column format (**Figure 1.6**).

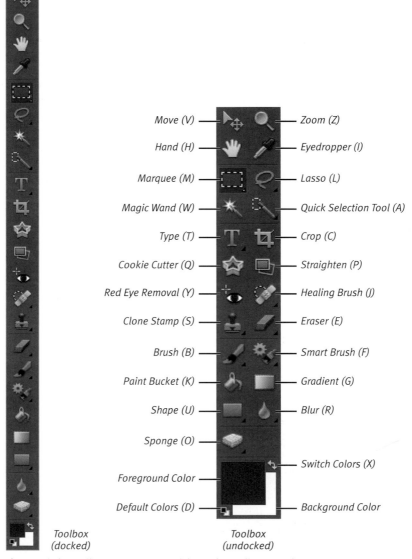

Move (V) — Zoom (Z)
Hand (H) — Eyedropper (I)
Marquee (M) — Lasso (L)
Magic Wand (W) — Quick Selection Tool (A)
Type (T) — Crop (C)
Cookie Cutter (Q) — Straighten (P)
Red Eye Removal (Y) — Healing Brush (J)
Clone Stamp (S) — Eraser (E)
Brush (B) — Smart Brush (F)
Paint Bucket (K) — Gradient (G)
Shape (U) — Blur (R)
Sponge (O) —
Switch Colors (X)
Foreground Color —
Default Colors (D) — Background Color

Toolbox
(docked)

Toolbox
(undocked)

Figure 1.6 The toolbox contains most of the tools you'll use to edit your images.

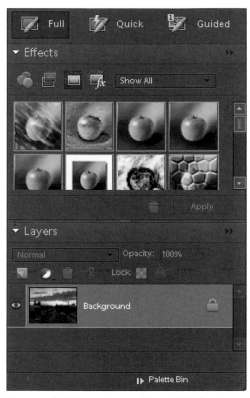

Figure 1.7 Palettes can be used from within the Palette Bin (as shown) or moved to your work area.

The **Palette Bin**, located on the right side of the desktop, contains the Effects and Layers palettes (**Figure 1.7**). Any of the other palettes can also be stored in the Palette Bin, though by default they appear in the main work area when you open them from the Window menu.

You can work with palettes from within the Palette Bin or you can drag them to the main work area. Palettes can also be grouped together or docked to one another, depending on your individual working and organizational styles.

The **Project Bin**, located at the bottom of the desktop, serves as a convenient holding area for all of your open images. In addition to providing a visual reference for any open image files, the bin allows you to perform several basic editing functions. Click to select any photo thumbnail in the Project Bin, and right-click to display a pop-up menu. From the thumbnail menu you can get file information, minimize or close the file, duplicate it, and even rotate it in 90 degree increments (**Figure 1.8**).

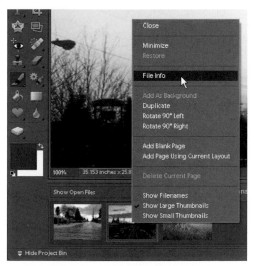

Figure 1.8 The Project Bin is a holding area where you can access all of your open images.

Opening and Closing Files

Photoshop Elements provides several methods of opening photos, depending on whether you're working in the Organizer or the Editor.

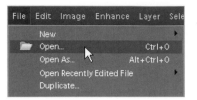

Figure 1.9 Choose Open from the File menu to open an image file on disk.

The Organizer's Get Photos and Video menu item includes commands for importing images from cameras, scanners, and other sources. In the Editor, you can open files using the Open command in the File menu, which displays the Open dialog box. The Open dialog box includes features for limiting your search to specific file formats and displaying an image preview.

To open a file from the Open dialog box:

1. To find and open a file, choose Open from the File menu (**Figure 1.9**), or press Ctrl+O. The Open dialog box appears (**Figure 1.10**).

2. Browse to the folder that contains your images (**Figure 1.11**).

3. To open the file you want, *do one of the following:*

   ▲ Double-click the file.

   ▲ Select the file and click the Open button.

   The image opens in its own document window.

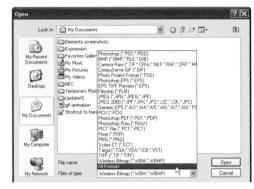

Figure 1.10 The Open dialog lets you browse for specific file types.

To close a file:

◆ Click the close button on the title bar for the active window.

◆ From the File menu, choose Close, or press Ctrl+W.

✔ Tip

■ If several files are open, you can close them all at once by choosing Close All from the File menu or by pressing Alt+Ctrl+W.

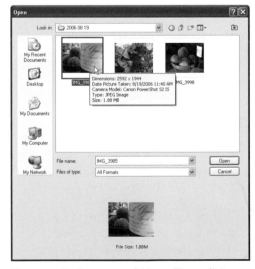

Figure 1.11 Navigate to any folder or file to edit it. Notice that you can view some basic information about the image just by hovering the mouse pointer over the file's icon.

OPENING AND CLOSING FILES

Importing Images

Digital cameras have revolutionized photography and are one of the main forces driving the need for products like Photoshop Elements. Over the past several years, prices have dropped and quality has risen dramatically. Typically, these cameras come with their own software to help you browse and manage photos—but don't even bother breaking the seal on the disc's envelope. You can access your camera from within Photoshop Elements and then download your images, or download photos from the camera to your hard drive and then open them in Elements.

You can also capture frames from digital videos, using the Frame From Video command. To capture video frames, you'll need to make sure your video is in a format that can be recognized, such as AVI, MPEG, or QuickTime.

Scanners offer another way to get images into Elements. They're ideal for digitizing family photos and other paper documents. As long as you can fit the image or object onto your flatbed scanner, you can scan almost anything: letters, buttons, fabric, leaves, or a page of clip art. You can also scan an image from within Elements, as long as your scanner's appropriate plug-in is located inside the Import-Export folder. This folder is inside the Plug-ins folder, which is located within the Photoshop Elements application folder on your hard drive.

Compact Storage Cards

Almost all digital cameras ship with some sort of *compact storage card*—it's a thin, plastic card that stores your camera's digital data. The most common variety is the CompactFlash card; other compact storage cards include SmartMedia, Secure Digital Card (SD), and the MultiMedia Card (MMC). Sony uses its own proprietary storage format called a Memory Stick.

As you snap photos, your digital camera's compact storage card acts as a holding space for all your images. When you delete (or transfer and then delete) images from your camera, that memory space is freed up on your storage card, giving you more room for additional photos.

Most digital cameras include a cable that connects your camera to your computer for easy photo transferring. An alternate way to get photos into your computer is via a *storage card reader,* which you connect via a USB cable. Once you've installed the card reader software on your computer, just insert your compact storage card into the card reader to import your photos from your camera to your computer with a minimum of fuss.

To import images from a digital camera (Standard dialog):

1. Connect your digital camera to your computer using the instructions provided by the camera manufacturer.

   If the Photo Downloader launches automatically, skip to step 3. If you don't see the Photo Downloader dialog, continue to step 2.

2. If you're in the Editor, click the Organizer button in the upper-right corner to launch the Organizer (**Figure 1.12**).

   If you're in the Organizer already, go to the File menu, choose Get Photos and Videos, and then choose From Camera or Card Reader (**Figure 1.13**) or press Ctrl+G.

   The Photo Downloader dialog opens in its Standard mode (**Figure 1.14**). For more importing options, see "To import images from a digital camera (Advanced dialog)" just ahead in this chapter.

3. Your camera will likely be selected in the Get Photos from drop-down menu, but if not, choose your camera.

   Listed below the menu are the number of pictures, and their combined size.

4. By default, images are saved to your My Pictures folder; hold your mouse pointer over the truncated path listed next to Location to view the full destination.

   If you want to save the files to a different location, click the Browse button and choose a folder or create a new one. Then click OK to return to the Photo Downloader dialog.

5. The Photo Downloader dialog is set to create new subfolders to store each batch of imported images, named according to the shot dates. From the Create Subfolder(s) drop-down menu, you can

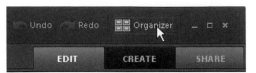

Figure 1.12 The Organizer button launches the Organizer, where you import photos.

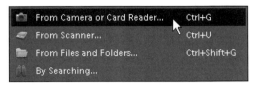

Figure 1.13 Choose From Camera or Card Reader to download photos from your digital camera.

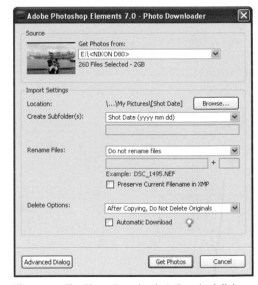

Figure 1.14 The Photo Downloader's Standard dialog makes it easy to import all photos in one fell swoop.

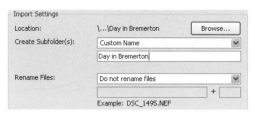

Figure 1.15 To make it easier to find images on disk later, you can specify a custom name for subfolders.

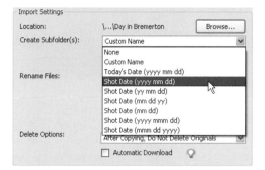

Figure 1.16 Choose a date format for naming subfolders with the images' shot dates.

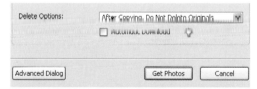

Figure 1.17 You can set Elements to delete the images from the memory card, but I'd rather leave the default setting and erase them later in the camera.

customize this behavior by choosing one of the following options:

▲ None saves the files in the folder specified by Location, normally your My Pictures folder.

▲ Custom Name creates a folder with a name that you enter (**Figure 1.15**).

▲ Today's Date automatically creates a folder named with the current date.

▲ Shot Date creates folders with the date the images were captured; choose your preferred date format from one of the options (**Figure 1.16**).

6. The Rename Files drop-down menu gives you the option of automatically naming the imported files something more descriptive than what your camera assigns. Choose an option from the drop-down menu.

   For example, your camera's default naming scheme is probably something like "IMG_1031.JPG." With a Rename Files option selected, you can name and number a set of photos "Vacation," for instance. Then your photos will automatically be saved and named "Vacation001.jpg," "Vacation002.jpg," and so on.

7. In the Delete Options area, choose what happens to the files on your camera's memory card. Just to be safe, I like to leave the option set to After Copying, Do Not Delete Originals, and then erase the card in-camera later (**Figure 1.17**).

   The Automatic Download option is useful if you want to offload pictures onto the computer without going through the Photo Downloader. Images download automatically when a camera or other device is attached. If you enable this option, you can turn it off later in the program's preferences.

continues on next page

8. Click the Get Photos button to download the selected images to your computer.

Your downloaded photos will first appear in their own Organizer window. Click the Show All button to return to the main Organizer window (**Figure 1.18**).

To import images from a digital camera (Advanced dialog):

1. Follow steps 1 through 8 in the previous sequence, but click the Advanced Dialog button in step 2 to switch to the Advanced dialog (**Figure 1.19**).

2. Click to deselect the check box under any photos you *do not* want to download.

By default, the Photo Downloader assumes you want to download every image in your camera.

3. In the Advanced Options area, choose to enable or disable the following options (**Figure 1.20**):

▲ Automatically Fix Red Eyes attempts to correct red eye problems in your photos as they're downloaded.

▲ Automatically Suggest Photo Stacks groups similar photos together for easy organization and review later (see Chapter 2).

4. Type your name (or the name of whomever took the photos) and a copyright notice in the Apply Metadata fields. This text is embedded with the image files.

5. If you want to rotate an image, select it and click the Rotate Left or Rotate Right buttons at the lower-left corner (**Figure 1.21**). You can also press Ctrl and the left or right arrow keys.

To view your entire photo library, click the Show All button.

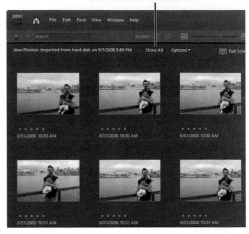

Figure 1.18 Photos downloaded from the camera or memory card appear in the Organizer.

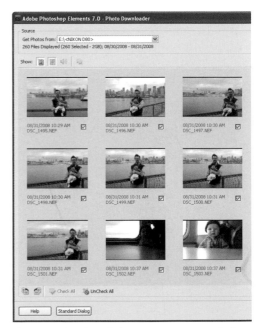

Figure 1.19 Preview all photos on your camera before importing them in the Advanced dialog (left side of window shown here).

IMPORTING IMAGES

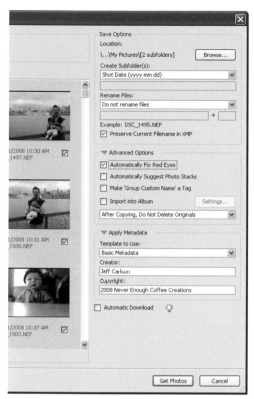

Figure 1.20 Further customize the importing process in the Advanced dialog (right side of window here).

Rotate buttons

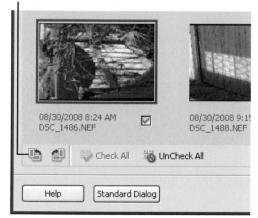

Figure 1.21 Rotate images as they're being imported so you won't have to do it later.

✔ Tips

- When shooting pictures with your digital camera, it's best to use the highest resolution possible. That way, you start out with a high-quality original file. You can always reduce the image resolution or file size later, if necessary.

- If you want to first deselect all of the photos in the Photo Downloader and then select only a few, press Ctrl+A to select all of the photos, then click in the check box of any single photo. All of the photos will be deselected at once. You can follow the same procedure to *select* all photos at once.

- Photoshop Elements can import photos stored in Camera RAW formats, which are the unprocessed versions of the captured images. RAW enables more adjustment possibilities than JPEG (which is processed and compressed in the camera). Elements brings RAW files into the Organizer without editing the image information. When you edit the photo, Elements first brings up the Camera Raw dialog to set initial edits before opening the image in the Editor. For more information, see "Adjusting Camera Raw Photos" in Chapter 7.

- The contents of the Creator and Copyright metadata fields are applied to all photos imported in that batch. If you want different authors for the pictures, for example, either import them in several batches or edit the metadata after they've been added to the catalog (see Chapter 2).

- Elements can also import digital video captured by still cameras. Movies appear in the Organizer like images do; double-clicking one lets you preview the movie in a separate window.

To import images from files or folders:

1. In the Organizer, go to the File menu, highlight Get Photos, and choose From Files and Folders.

   If you insert media that contains pictures, such as a CD, Windows may ask what action you'd like to take (if you haven't specified it already). Click the icon labeled Organize and Edit using Adobe Photoshop Elements 7.0, which opens the Get Photos from Files and Folders dialog (**Figure 1.22**).

2. Select the files you want to import; Shift-click to select a consecutive range of files, or Ctrl-click to select noncontiguous files.

3. If the images are stored on removable media and you want to import only low-resolution versions, disable the Copy Files on Import option and enable the Generate Previews option (see the sidebar for more information).

4. As in the Advanced dialog mentioned on the previous pages, select from the processing options below the preview.

5. Click the Get Photos button to import the photos. If the photos already include keyword tags, you have the option to import them (see Chapter 2).

✔ Tips

- Now that we've gotten those steps out of the way and you understand what's going on, here's a much quicker method: simply drag image files from a folder on your hard disk to the Organizer's window. Elements imports them without fuss.

- If you know some photos exist on your hard disk but can't find them, let Elements hunt for them instead. Under the Get Photos submenu of the File menu, choose By Searching, and click the Search button.

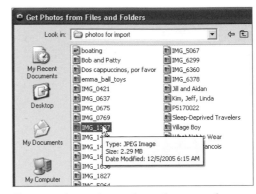

Figure 1.22 Import images from other areas of your hard disk or from removable media such as CDs.

Working with Offline Images

With removable media, you have the option of importing just a lower-resolution file to the hard disk. This feature can save hard disk space, especially if lots of files are stored on a shared network drive or on several CDs or DVDs. Importing them as offline images allows you to view and track your entire catalog of pictures.

Offline images are designated with an icon in the upper-left corner of the image in the Organizer (**Figure 1.23**). You can apply tags, build collections, and perform other tasks. However, if you want to edit the image, Elements asks you to insert the original media. If it's not available, you can still edit the low-res proxy, but the results won't look good. Once you make the original available again, Elements copies the source image to your catalog as an online image.

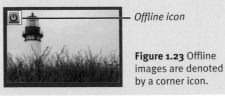

Offline icon

Figure 1.23 Offline images are denoted by a corner icon.

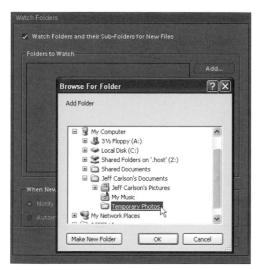

Figure 1.24 Elements can keep an eye on one or more folders and import photos when they're added.

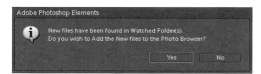

Figure 1.25 This dialog appears when new photos are found in a watched folder.

To import images using Watch Folders:

1. You can specify one or more folders that Elements watches in the background for new files. In the Organizer, choose Watch Folders from the File menu.

2. Click the Add button and navigate to the folder you wish to watch (**Figure 1.24**). Repeat for as many folders as you'd like.

3. Select an action under When New Files are Found in Watched Folders; Elements can notify you when files are found, or add them to the Organizer automatically.

4. Click OK when you're done.

5. When you add photos to your watched folder, Elements asks if you want to import them (if you opted to be notified in step 3) (**Figure 1.25**). Click Yes to add the photos, which are moved from the watched folder to the directory where Elements stores your catalog.

IMPORTING IMAGES

To scan an image into the Organizer:

1. Connect the scanner to your computer using the instructions provided by the scanner manufacturer.

2. In the Organizer, go to the Get Photos menu under the File menu and choose From Scanner.

3. Select your scanner software from the Scanner pop-up menu (**Figure 1.26**).

4. Choose an image format and quality level, and optionally enable the Automatically Fix Red Eyes check box.

5. Click the OK button. Elements hands off the actual scanning duties to the scanner's software for you to complete the scan.

6. When you complete the scan and exit the scanner's software, Elements imports the image to your catalog.

To scan an image into the Editor:

1. Connect the scanner to your computer.

2. In the Editor, go to the File menu and choose your scanner from the Import menu. The scanner's software opens.

3. Scan the image using the scanning software. When it's done, the image appears in the Editor.

4. Save the file (see "Saving Files," later in this chapter).

✔ Tips

■ If you're planning to use only part of an image, you'll save a lot of time by using your scanning software to crop your image *before* importing it into Photoshop Elements (**Figure 1.27**).

■ On the off chance that you want to scan an image in black and white (not grayscale), well, don't. Elements doesn't recognize bitmap images.

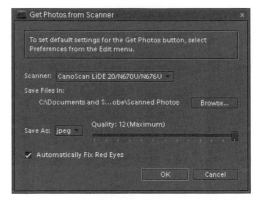

Figure 1.26 Elements works with your scanner's software to import images.

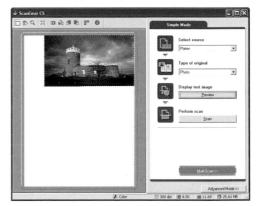

Figure 1.27 Crop your images before importing them. In this figure, Canon's ScanGear software handles the actual scan, but the photo ends up in Elements.

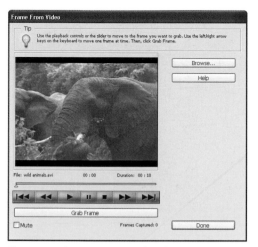

Figure 1.28 The Frame From Video dialog enables you to snag shots from video footage you captured.

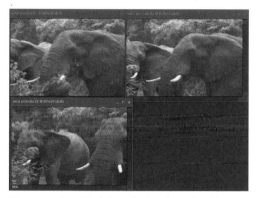

Figure 1.29 I grabbed three frames from the video clip, which appear in the Editor as three separate image files.

To capture frames from video footage:

1. In the Editor, go to the File menu and choose Import > Frame From Video.

   The Frame From Video dialog box appears.

2. Click the Browse button to locate the file you want, and then click Open to see the video footage.

   The video clip appears in the dialog (**Figure 1.28**).

3. To view your footage, click the Play button. When you see the frame you want, click the Grab Frame button.

   To grab the frame you want, you can also use the Pause button to stop the video at the desired frame. Another useful option is to simply move the slider to the correct frame in the video.

4. Grab as many video frames as you want, one by one, and then click Done.

   As you click the Grab Frame button, the images appear as new files in the Editor (**Figure 1.29**).

5. Once you've captured the frames, you can save and edit them just like any other images.

✔ Tips

■ Use the left and right arrow keys to view frames in the video one at a time.

■ You'll likely encounter a greater variety of exposure problems with video frames than with the still shots you take with a digital camera. You can easily fix contrast and tonal problems with a few of Photoshop Elements' correction tools, which you'll explore more in Chapter 6 and in Chapter 7.

IMPORTING IMAGES

Saving Files

As you work on an image in the Editor, it's good practice to save the file to your hard drive regularly. When you save a file, you can choose from a number of file formats. (For detailed information on the formats, see Chapter 13, "Saving and Printing Images.")

If you're interested in posting your photos to the Web, you can choose the Save for Web option. Saving your images for the Web involves its own set of unique operations; these are covered in detail in Chapter 12, "Preparing Images for the Web."

To save a file:

◆ From the File menu, choose Save, or press Ctrl+S.

To save a file in a new format or to a specific location:

1. From the File menu, choose Save As, or press Shift+Ctrl+S. The Save As dialog box appears (**Figure 1.30**).

2. Choose a destination for the file by browsing to a location using the Save In drop-down menu.

3. In the File name text box, type a name for the file. If the option Save in Version Set with Original is selected, Elements adds "_edited-1" to the name (see sidebar).

4. If you want to save the file in a different format, choose one from the Format drop-down menu.

   If you're not sure which format to use, choose either the native Photoshop format (PSD), which is the best all-purpose format, or the JPEG format, which works especially well with digital photos. When saving an image as a JPEG file, choose the highest quality setting possible.

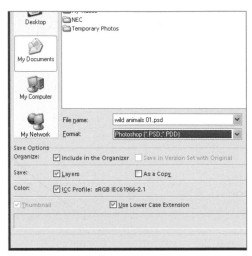

Figure 1.30 The Save As dialog includes several options beyond just naming the new file.

Working with Version Sets

In the digital photography realm, the "negative" is the original image file captured by your camera. On the computer, you're working with those original files. So, for example, if you were to change a photo from color to grayscale and save it, then you've lost the color version forever.

To guard against that, Elements offers the ability to save the file in a version set when you perform a Save As operation. You're saving a new copy, but it's linked to the original image in the Organizer as a revision (**Figure 1.31**); otherwise, the edited version would appear as a completely separate image. Click the expansion arrow icon to the right of the image to view or hide the version set.

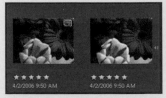

Figure 1.31 A version set tracks image edits.

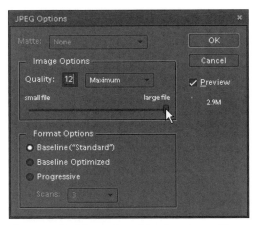

Figure 1.32 Each image format has its own specific settings, such as those shown in this dialog for saving a JPEG file.

5. If you want to be sure not to alter your original file, select the As a Copy option to save a duplicate. This selection protects your original file from changes as you edit the duplicate.

6. To include color profile information, make sure the Color box is selected. For more information on managing color in your images, see Chapter 7, "Changing and Adjusting Colors."

7. When you've finished entering your settings, click Save.

   Depending on the format you chose, you may be prompted to set other options, such as with JPEG files (**Figure 1.32**).

✔ Tips

- Saving using the As a Copy option is a good idea if you're experimenting with various changes and want to ensure that you keep your original version intact. It's also handy if you want to save an image in more than one file format, which is useful if you want to save a high-quality copy for printing and keep a smaller-sized file for e-mailing to friends.

- Photoshop Elements allows you to customize your Save settings. In the Editor, go to the Edit menu and choose Preferences > Saving Files. In the Saving Files dialog box you can control how file extensions are displayed, choose whether to include image previews with your saved files (image previews are small thumbnail images that appear in the Open dialog box when you select a file), and determine in which circumstances you would like to be prompted with the Save As dialog box.

Selecting Tools

The toolbox in the Editor contains all the tools you need for editing and creating your images. You can use them to make selections, paint, draw, and easily perform sophisticated photo-retouch operations. To view information about a tool, rest the pointer over it until a tool tip appears showing the name and keyboard shortcut (if any) for that tool.

To use a tool, first select it from the toolbox. Some tools hide additional tools beneath them, as indicated by a small triangle at the lower right of the tool icon (**Figure 1.33**).

To select a tool from the toolbox:

◆ Click the tool's icon in the toolbox.

   When you move your pointer into the document window, the pointer changes appearance to reflect the tool you have selected (**Figure 1.34**).

To select a hidden tool:

1. On any tool that displays a small triangle, either click and hold down the mouse button, or right-click the tool icon. A menu of the hidden tools appears (**Figure 1.35**).

2. Click to select the tool you want to use.

✔ Tips

■ For easier access to tools, just use keyboard shortcuts. You'll find them in tool tips, on the printed Quick Reference card included in the product box, and in the online help. For example, press T on your keyboard to activate the Type tool. (Note that when you press a letter to select a tool with a hidden tool group, Elements selects the tool from the group that was used most recently.)

■ To cycle through hidden tools, repeatedly press the tool's shortcut key.

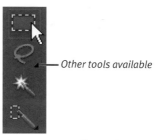

Figure 1.33 A small triangle next to a tool icon indicates additional tools.

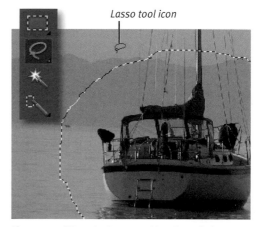

Figure 1.34 When the Lasso tool is selected, the mouse pointer changes to the Lasso tool icon.

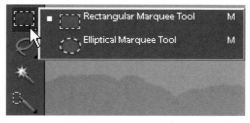

Figure 1.35 Click and hold the mouse button or right-click to view the hidden tools.

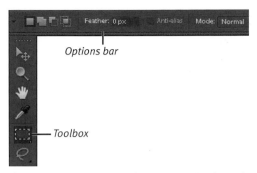

Options bar

Toolbox

Figure 1.36 Use the options bar to customize the tool you've selected, including selecting alternate tools.

Previous View/Next View

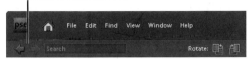

Figure 1.37 The options bar in the Organizer contains commonly used tools.

Using the Options Bar

Think of the options bar as a natural extension of the toolbox. After you select a tool, you can adjust its settings from the options bar. The buttons on the options bar change depending on the tool selected. If you're using the Brush tool, for example, you can use the options bar to select a brush size and opacity setting.

To use the options bar:

1. From the toolbox, select a tool.

2. In the options bar, choose an available option for that tool (**Figure 1.36**).

✔ Tip

- In the Organizer, the options bar includes common tools such as Previous View and Next View, image rotation buttons, a slider for setting the thumbnail size, and others (**Figure 1.37**).

Working with Palettes

Although Photoshop Elements opens with just three palettes displayed in its Palette Bin, a total of nine palettes are available from the Window menu. Each palette can be used entirely on its own or can be combined with other palettes to help organize and streamline your workflow. All the palettes feature handy drop-down menus that allow you to perform additional tasks or customize palette options.

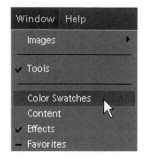

Figure 1.38 Show or hide any palette from the Window menu.

To display a palette:

◆ From the Window menu, choose any palette to display it in your work area (**Figure 1.38**).

To close a palette:

Do one of the following:

◆ If the palette is open in your work area (outside the Palette Bin), click the close box on the palette title bar (**Figure 1.39**).

If the palette is inside the Palette Bin, you must first move it into the work area, and then click its close box.

◆ From the Window menu, choose any open palette; open palettes are indicated by a check mark.

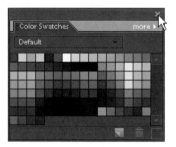

Figure 1.39 To close a palette, click the close icon on the title bar.

To move a palette out of the Palette Bin:

1. Click the tab of the palette that you want to move from the Palette Bin.

2. Drag the tab until the palette is in the desired location in your work area (**Figure 1.40**).

   The palette is now a floating palette on the desktop.

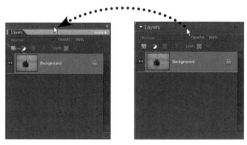

Figure 1.40 To move a palette from the bin, just drag the tab outside the bin, where it becomes a stand-alone palette.

✔ Tip

■ To hide the Palette Bin altogether and gain more workspace, click the Palette Bin button below the bin (**Figure 1.41**).

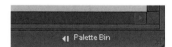

Figure 1.41 Click the Palette Bin button to hide the bin and free up some more working area.

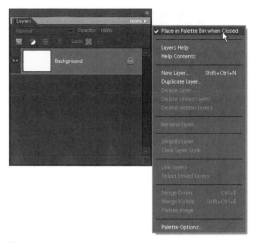

Figure 1.42 Choose to return the palette automatically to the Palette Bin by selecting the command on its More menu.

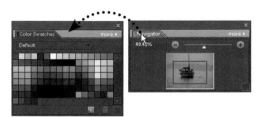

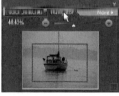

Figure 1.43 Drag a palette tab into another open palette (top) to form a palette group (bottom).

To return a palette to the Palette Bin:

Do one of the following:

◆ Click the palette tab and drag the palette back into the Palette Bin.

◆ From any palette's More menu, choose Place in Palette Bin when Closed, and then click the palette's close box (**Figure 1.42**).

To group palettes:

1. Make sure you can see the tabs of all the palettes you want to group. At least one of the palettes (the target palette) must be outside the Palette Bin.

2. Drag a palette tab into the window of the target palette (**Figure 1.43**).

   A thick line appears around the window of the target palette to let you know that the palettes have been grouped.

   To ungroup a palette, simply select the palette's tab and drag it out of the palette group.

✔ Tips

■ When Place in Palette Bin when Closed is selected for a particular palette, it will always return to the Palette Bin when closed. If you don't want a palette to return to the Palette Bin, choose the Place in Palette Bin when Closed option again to deselect it.

■ If, from the Window menu, you choose to close a single palette residing in a palette group, the entire palette group will close.

WORKING WITH PALETTES

21

To dock palettes:

◆ Drag any palette's tab to the bottom of any palette outside the Palette Bin. Drag the palette by its title bar to successfully dock it to another palette (**Figure 1.44**).

To undock a palette, select one palette's tab and drag it away from the other palette.

To use palette menus:

◆ Click the More button in the upper-right corner of any palette.

The More button looks a little different, depending on whether a palette is located inside or outside the Palette Bin.

To return palettes to their default positions:

◆ From the Window menu, choose Reset Palette Locations.

✔ Tip

■ To collapse a stand-alone palette or a palette group, double-click the palette tab or title bar (**Figure 1.45**). Double-click again to reveal the palette.

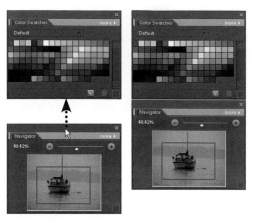

Figure 1.44 Docking one palette below another helps avoid clutter in your work area.

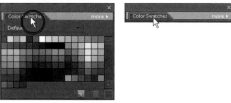

Figure 1.45 Double-click the palette tab to collapse a palette or palette group.

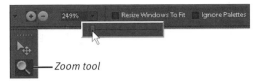

Figure 1.46 With the Zoom tool selected, adjust the magnification level using a slider on the options bar.

Zoom In button

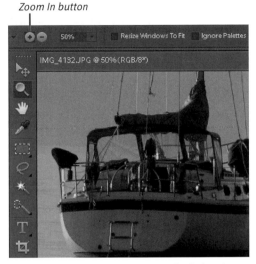

Figure 1.47 To zoom in on an image, check that the Zoom In button is selected on the options bar.

Using the Zoom Tool

It's rare that you'll want to view your images at the same magnification—editing out dust, for example, requires a close-up view. The Zoom tool magnifies and reduces your view, which you can control using a variety of methods.

The current level of magnification is shown in the document status bar and, when the Zoom tool is selected, in the options bar above the document window. In the options bar you can adjust the magnification either with the Zoom slider or by entering a value in the Zoom text box (**Figure 1.46**).

To zoom in:

1. In the toolbox, select the Zoom tool, or press Z on the keyboard. The pointer changes to a magnifying glass when you move it into the document window.

2. Be sure that a plus sign appears in the center of the magnifying glass. If you see a minus sign, click the Zoom In button on the options bar (**Figure 1.47**).

3. Click the area of the image you want to magnify.

   With a starting magnification of 100 percent, each click with the Zoom In tool increases the magnification in 100 percent increments up to 800 percent. From there, the magnification levels jump to 1200 percent, then 1600 percent, and finally to 3200 percent!

USING THE ZOOM TOOL

To zoom out:

1. In the toolbox, select the Zoom tool, or press Z on the keyboard.

2. Click the Zoom Out button on the options bar, and then click in the area of the image that you want to zoom out from (**Figure 1.48**).

   With a starting magnification of 100 percent, each click with the Zoom Out tool reduces the magnification as follows: 66.7 percent; 50 percent; 33.3 percent; 25 percent; 16.7 percent; and so on, down to 1 percent.

To zoom in on a specific area:

1. In the toolbox, select the Zoom tool; if necessary, click the Zoom In button on the options bar to display the Zoom tool with a plus sign.

2. Drag over the area of the image that you want to zoom in on.

   A selection marquee appears around the selected area (**Figure 1.49**). When you release the mouse button, the selected area is magnified and centered in the image window.

3. To move the view to a different area of the image, hold down the spacebar until the hand pointer appears. Then drag to reveal the area you want to see. For more information on navigating through the document window, see "Moving Around in an Image" later in this chapter.

✔ Tip

■ You can also change the magnification level from the zoom-percentage text box in the lower-left corner of the document window. Double-click the text box to select the zoom value, and then type in the new value.

Zoom Out button

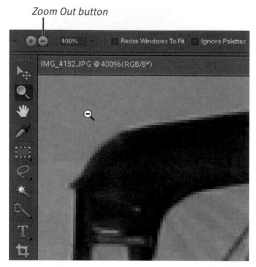

Figure 1.48 To zoom out on an image, check that the Zoom Out button is selected on the options bar.

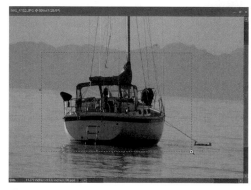

Figure 1.49 Drag with the Zoom tool to zoom in on a specific area of an image.

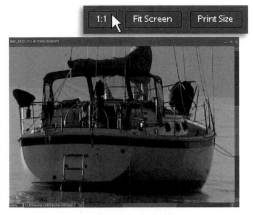

Figure 1.50 Clicking the 1:1 button on the options bar returns the image view to 100 percent.

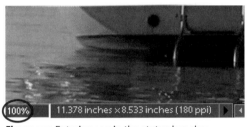

Figure 1.51 Entering 100 in the status bar also changes the image view to 100 percent.

To display an image at 100 percent:

To display an image at 100 percent (also referred to as displaying actual pixels), *do one of the following:*

◆ In the toolbox, double-click the Zoom tool.

◆ In the toolbox, select either the Zoom or Hand tool, and then click the 1:1 button on the options bar (**Figure 1.50**).

◆ From the View menu, choose Actual Pixels, or press Alt+Ctrl+0.

◆ Enter 100 in the Zoom text box in the options bar, and then press Enter.

◆ Enter 100 in the status bar at the bottom of the document window, and then press Enter (**Figure 1.51**).

✔ Tips

■ With any other tool selected in the toolbar, you can toggle to the Zoom tool. Hold down Ctrl+spacebar to zoom in or Alt+spacebar to zoom out.

■ To change the magnification of the entire image, press Ctrl++ (Control and the plus sign) to zoom in or Ctrl+– (Control and the minus sign) to zoom out.

■ Toggle the Zoom tool between zoom in and zoom out by holding down the Alt key before you click.

■ You can automatically resize the document window to fit the image (as much as possible) when zooming in or out. With the Zoom tool selected, click the Resize Windows to Fit check box on the options bar. To maintain a constant window size, deselect the Resize Windows to Fit option.

USING THE ZOOM TOOL

Moving Around in an Image

When working in Photoshop Elements, you'll often want to move your image to make a different area visible in the document window. This can happen when you're zoomed in on one part of an image or when an image is just too large to be completely visible within the document window.

To view a different area of an image:

Do one of the following:

◆ From the toolbox, select the Hand tool and drag to move the image around in the document window (**Figure 1.52**).

◆ Use the scroll arrows at the bottom and right side of the document window to scroll to the left or right and up or down. You can also drag the scroll bars to adjust the view.

To change the view using the Navigator palette:

1. Choose Window > Navigator to open the Navigator palette.

2. Drag the view box in the image thumbnail (**Figure 1.53**).

   The view in the document window changes accordingly.

✔ Tips

■ With any other tool selected in the toolbar, you can press the spacebar to give you temporary access to the Hand tool.

■ Drag the slider in the Navigator palette to adjust the magnification level in the document window.

Drag with the Hand tool...

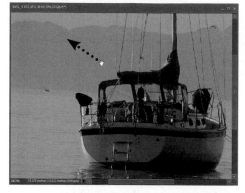

...to move the image.

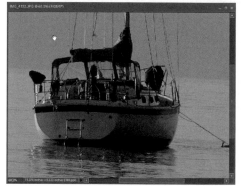

Figure 1.52 To view a different area of the same image, drag with the Hand tool.

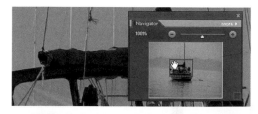

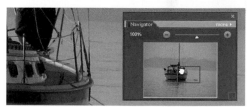

Figure 1.53 You can also use the Navigator palette to view a different area of the same image.

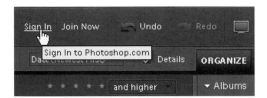

Figure 1.54 Sign in to your Photoshop.com account, or click Join Now to create one.

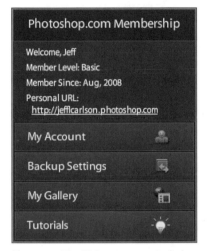

Figure 1.55 The Welcome screen includes links to Photoshop.com actions.

Accessing Photoshop.com

Early in 2008, Adobe introduced Photoshop Express, a Web-only version of Photoshop that let you upload images, edit them in a Web browser, and share them with friends.

Elements 7 integrates directly with the service—referred to as Photoshop.com—enabling you to publish photo albums directly (see Chapter 14). Recognizing the value of digital images, Adobe also added the capability to automatically back up your photos to Photoshop.com, so you have copies in case your computer or hard drive dies (see Chapter 2). And because your photos are online, you can view and edit them from any modern computer, not just the machine where Elements is installed.

A Basic Photoshop.com membership is free and includes 2 GB of online storage. Adobe also sells a Plus membership for $49.95 per year that includes 20 GB of storage and new ongoing tutorials, seasonal artwork, and templates delivered directly to Elements.

You can sign up for a Photoshop.com membership at the Welcome screen. After you've created an account, log in at the Welcome screen or by clicking the Log In link at the top of the Organizer or Editor (**Figure 1.54**).

Once signed in, Elements provides quick access to your settings and online photo gallery at the Welcome screen (**Figure 1.55**). You can also click the "Welcome, *your name*" link at the top of the Organizer or Editor.

✔ Tip

■ For more information on how to use the editing features at Photoshop.com, see my book *The Photoshop Express Beta Pocket Guide* (Peachpit Press, 2008).

Using the Inspiration Browser

As you work, you may notice occasional headlines appear in the lower-right corner of the Organizer or the Editor (**Figure 1.56**). Clicking one of these little morsels leads to the Inspiration Browser, a separate application for viewing tutorials and other content.

To use the Inspiration Browser:

1. Click an Inspiration Browser headline in Elements. A small preview box appears that offers more information about the headline (**Figure 1.57**).

2. Click the link in the preview box to launch the full Inspiration Browser (**Figure 1.58**).

3. Click the Take a Look button to view that tutorial's content. Or, browse for other tutorials.

✔ Tip

■ The first time you launch the Inspiration Browser, you may be asked to agree to terms of service for AIR (Adobe Internet Runtime), which is an Adobe technology for running Internet-enabled applications on the desktop. The Inspiration Browser is an AIR application. What does that mean for you? Essentially nothing—it works as just another application on your computer.

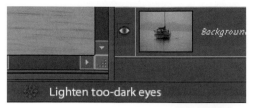

Figure 1.56 Headlines like this one appear at the bottom of the screen, enticing you to click them.

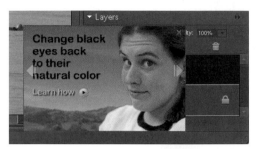

Figure 1.57 Clicking a headline displays a preview box to learn more about the associated tutorial.

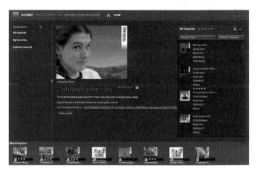

Figure 1.58 The Inspiration Browser offers plenty of free tutorials to help you learn more.

2

THE ORGANIZER

Digital photography can be a bit of a double-edged sword. Ironically, its greatest advantage to the amateur photographer—the ability to quickly and easily capture a large number of images, and then instantly download them to a computer—can also be its greatest source of frustration. Once hundreds of images have been downloaded, photographers find themselves faced with the daunting task of sorting through myriad files, with incomprehensible filenames, to find those dozen or so "keepers" to assemble into an album or post to the Web for friends.

The Organizer workspace comes to the rescue with a relatively simple and wonderfully visual set of tools and functions to help you locate, identify, and organize your photos. And once your photos are organized, you can import categories and collections of images that you assemble directly into projects like slide shows, calendars, flipbooks, and online albums.

Understanding the Organizer Work Area

The Organizer work area is divided into two main components: the Photo Browser and the Organize Bin. The Photo Browser, along with its timeline, is used to find and view thumbnail representations of your photos. The Organize Bin contains the Albums and Keyword Tags palettes you'll use to group and organize your image files (**Figure 2.1**).

The Photo Browser and timeline

At the core of the Organizer is the Photo Browser. Every digital photo or scan downloaded into Photoshop Elements is automatically added to the Photo Browser. Clear, resizable thumbnails in the Photo Browser window make it easy to scan through even a large number of images. (For information on importing images, see Chapter 1.)

The timeline located just above the Photo Browser lets you quickly navigate from one set of images to another. (If you don't see the timeline, choose Timeline from the Window menu, or press Ctrl+L.) For example, when a Date viewing option is selected in the Browser window, the timeline uses date and time information embedded in each image to construct bars (month markers) to represent sets of photos taken within specific months and years. When a month marker is selected in the timeline, that month's photos are displayed at the top of the Photo Browser (**Figure 2.2**).

The Organize Bin

The Organize Bin on the right side of the window holds the Albums and Keyword Tags palettes. Working with the thumbnail images in the Photo Browser, you'll use these to identify, sort, and organize your photos (**Figure 2.3**).

Photo Browser   Timeline   Organize Bin (keyword tags and albums)

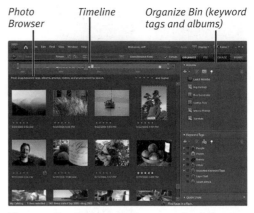

Figure 2.1 The Organizer workspace makes it easy to browse your entire photo collection.

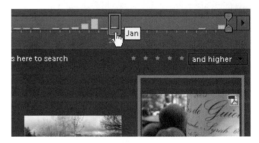

Figure 2.2 Click a month marker in the Organizer timeline to view that month's photos on the Photo Browser.

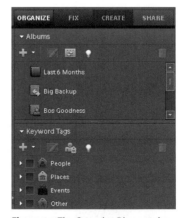

Figure 2.3 The Organize Bin contains palettes for albums and keyword tags.

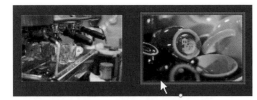

Figure 2.4 A selected thumbnail is bordered with a heavy blue line.

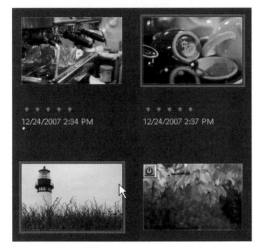

Figure 2.5 Ctrl+click to select thumbnails that are not consecutive.

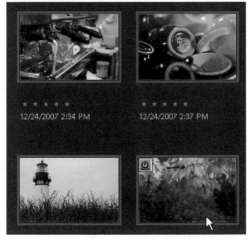

Figure 2.6 Shift+click to select thumbnails that are consecutive.

Working in the Photo Browser

The centerpiece of the Organizer is the Photo Browser, a flexible workspace that provides a number of options for customizing the way you manage and view your image files. Throughout this chapter I'll cover a variety of ways to work in the Photo Browser to label, identify, and organize your photos. But first it's important to know how best to select, sort, and display the image thumbnails within the main Photo Browser window.

To select photo thumbnails:

Do one of the following:

◆ Click to select a thumbnail in the Photo Browser. A heavy blue line appears around it, indicating that the thumbnail is selected (**Figure 2.4**).

◆ Ctrl+click to select several non-adjacent thumbnails at once (**Figure 2.5**).

◆ Shift+click to select a group of thumbnails in sequence (**Figure 2.6**).

◆ From the Edit menu, choose Select All, or press Ctrl+A to select every thumbnail in the Photo Browser.

To deselect photo thumbnails:

Do one of the following:

◆ Ctrl+click to deselect a single thumbnail.

◆ From the Edit menu, choose Deselect, or press Ctrl+Shift+A to deselect every thumbnail in the Photo Browser.

✔ Tip

■ You can tweak the appearance of the Photo Browser. From the View menu, you can choose to display gridlines, filenames, and borders around thumbnails.

To sort photo thumbnails:

◆ From the Arrangement drop-down menu above the Photo Browser, choose a sorting option (**Figure 2.7**):

   ▲ **Date (Newest First)** displays the most recent photos at the top, judged by the images' creation dates.

   ▲ **Date (Oldest First)** displays photos in order, with the oldest at the top.

◆ Click the Display button to choose how photos are grouped:

   ▲ **Thumbnail View** (Ctrl+Alt+1) is the default grid of thumbnail images.

   ▲ **Import Batch** (Ctrl+Alt+2) groups photos into the batches they were imported in. Included is information on when the batch was imported and from what source (**Figure 2.8**).

   ▲ **Folder Location** (Ctrl+Alt+3) displays photos grouped into the folders in which they're stored, and provides detailed file-path information to make it easy to locate the folder and original files on your hard drive.

To resize photo thumbnails:

◆ Above the Photo Browser, drag the thumbnail slider to the right to increase the size of the thumbnails, or to the left to make them smaller (**Figure 2.9**).

◆ Click the Small Thumbnail button to the left of the slider to display the thumbnails at their smallest possible size.

◆ Click the Single Photo View button to the right of the slider to display just one large photo thumbnail at a time.

✔ Tip

■ Double-click on any thumbnail to change to Single Photo View. Double-click the image to return to your most recent multiple thumbnail view settings.

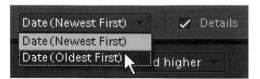

Figure 2.7 Select an option to sort thumbnails in the Photo Browser.

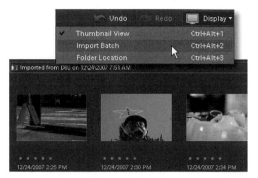

Figure 2.8 When you select the Import Batch option, thumbnails in the Photo Browser are displayed in grouped batch sets.

Small
Thumbnail button   Single Photo
                                    View button

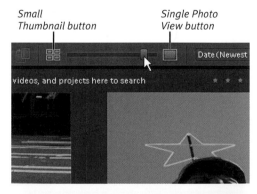

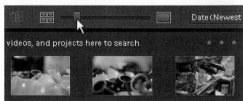

Figure 2.9 When you drag the thumbnail slider to the right, the thumbnails grow larger (top). When you drag the slider to the left, they become smaller (bottom).

Instant Slide Shows with Full Screen View

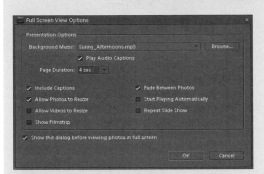

Figure 2.10 Elements ships with a collection of looping music clips that you can use as background tracks for your Full Screen View slide shows.

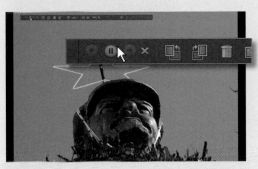

Figure 2.11 Use the control bar in Full Screen View to play and pause your slide show, rotate, and apply Quick Fix effects to your images while you review them.

The Organizer provides an efficient and entertaining way to view a series of images. Full Screen View builds an instant slide show, complete with transitions and a background music track, from thumbnails that you select in the Photo Browser. And Full Screen View not only displays large-format views of your images, but also allows you to rotate and apply automatic color and tonal corrections on the fly as the slide show plays.

To use the Full Screen View feature, first choose which images you want to view by selecting them in the Browser window. (If you don't make any selections, every image in your Photo Browser will be displayed.) Click the Display button and choose View Photos in Full Screen (or press F11).

In the dialog that appears, you can set options for slide duration, captions, and image size, and then choose from one of the supplied background music tracks (**Figure 2.10**). (If you like, you can browse for and select any MP3 file on your computer to use as background music.)

When you're satisfied with your settings, click OK. The screen displays your images in Full Screen View, where you can use a control bar to play the slide show and make minor image corrections (**Figure 2.11**). To return to the Organizer, press Esc.

Displaying and Changing Information for Your Photos

Images you import from a digital camera or scanner carry embedded file information—everything from the date and time a photo was shot or scanned to whether or not the camera's flash fired. The Organizer uses that date and time information to determine the display order of the photo thumbnails in the Photo Browser.

Although you can't change the embedded file information, you can control the order in which images are sorted and displayed. The Adjust Date and Time dialog lets you substitute a new date and time for any image file. Photoshop Elements then ignores the embedded information in favor of the new information you've supplied. Simply change the date and time information of a photo (or group of photos), and the sorting order will automatically change in both the Photo Browser and the timeline.

To adjust the date and time:

1. At the top of the Photo Browser, check that the Details option is selected (**Figure 2.12**) to display date and filename information below the image thumbnails.

2. In the Photo Browser, click to select the thumbnails whose date and time you would like to change.

3. From the Edit menu, choose Adjust Date and Time (or Adjust Date and Time of Selected Items if more than one thumbnail is selected in the Photo Browser), or press Ctrl+J.

4. In the Adjust Date and Time of Selected Items dialog, choose one of the options and click OK (**Figure 2.13**):

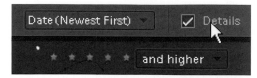

Figure 2.12 The Details option allows you to view title and date information in the Photo Browser.

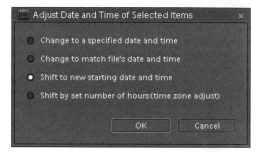

Figure 2.13 The Adjust Date and Time of Selected Items dialog offers different options for changing an image's date and time information.

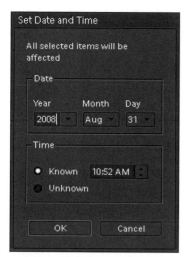

Figure 2.14 The Set Date and Time dialog.

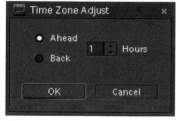

Figure 2.15 Use the Time Zone Adjust dialog to set the time of your images backward or forward in one-hour intervals.

▲ **Change to a specified date and time** opens the Set Date and Time dialog where you can set a specific year, month, day, and time (**Figure 2.14**).

▲ **Change to match file's date and time** reverts the date and time information to what is embedded in the original image file.

Remember, date and time changes you enter here are only for sorting and organizing your images within the Photo Organizer.

▲ **Shift to new starting date and time** allows you to set a new date and time for the earliest (oldest) photo in a selected group, and then changes the date and time of the other photos in the group, in relation to that earliest photo. In other words, if the date of the earliest photo is set back one month from its original date, all the photos in the selected group will be shifted back one month from *their* original dates.

▲ **Shift by set number of hours (time zone adjust)** adjusts the time of selected images forward or backward by the number of hours that you specify (**Figure 2.15**).

✔ Tips

■ You can set a preference so that you can open the Adjust Date and Time dialog by simply clicking on the date in the Photo Browser. From the Edit menu, choose Preferences > General, and then select the Adjust Date and Time by clicking the Thumbnail Dates option.

■ You can view file names in addition to dates. From the View menu, choose Show File Names.

To rate a photo:

1. In the Photo Browser, position your mouse pointer over the gray star icons; they change to yellow depending on the pointer's location (**Figure 2.16**).

2. Click to select the rating you wish to apply: One star typically denotes a low-quality photo, while five stars is excellent. (You can choose your own values, of course; this feature provides an easy way to separate good from bad photos, as you'll see later in "Using Smart Albums.")

To add a caption to a photo:

1. Click to select an image thumbnail.

2. From the Edit menu, choose Add Caption, or press Ctrl+Shift+T.

3. In the Add Caption dialog, enter a caption for your image, and then click OK (**Figure 2.17**). Although captions don't display with images in the Photo Browser window, they will appear along with your photos when you create projects such as Web Photo Galleries and Photo Album Pages.

✔ Tips

■ Captions do appear along with images in Single Photo View, where you can also add and edit captions. In Single Photo View, click the *Click here to add caption* text. The text changes to a text box where you can type a new caption. If you've previously entered a caption, click on the caption text to edit or delete it.

■ You can add the same caption to multiple images at the same time. Select a group of images in the Photo Browser, and then from the Edit menu choose Add Caption to Selected Items. The caption you enter in the Add Caption to Selected Items dialog is applied to the selected images.

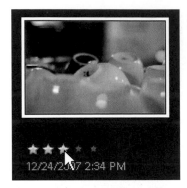

Figure 2.16 Apply a rating to quickly identify your higher-quality photos.

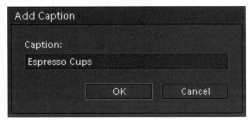

Figure 2.17 The Add Caption dialog.

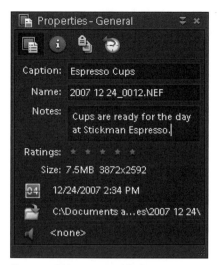

Figure 2.18 Notes entered for Images are accessible only from the Properties pane.

To rename a photo:

1. In the Photo Browser, click to select an image thumbnail.

2. From the Window menu, choose Properties, or press Alt+Enter to open the Properties pane.

3. Enter a new name for your image file in the Name field.

To add a note to a photo:

1. Select an image thumbnail.

2. From the Window menu, choose Properties, or press Alt+Enter to open the Properties pane.

3. In the Notes field, enter the text you want to include with your photo (**Figure 2.18**).

✔ Tip

■ Notes can be viewed only from the Properties pane in the Organizer.

About the Properties Pane

The Properties pane may not look like much at first glance, but it contains a storehouse of information about every image in the Organizer. In the preceding steps you learned how it can be used to enter and record image data like captions, names, and notes—but what are those other icons for?

The icons across the top of the pane actually serve as buttons that allow you to view different property types.

The **General** area displays (and allows you to enter) caption, name, and note information. In addition, three buttons along the lower-left edge give you access to the Adjust Date and Time dialog; provide a jump, via Windows Explorer, directly to the folder containing your images; and (if you have a computer set up with a microphone) allow you to record audio captions.

The **Metadata** area displays all of the detailed camera data (EXIF information) embedded in a digital photo file.

The **Keyword Tags** area displays any tags associated with an image and any albums to which it belongs. I'll discuss tags in the next section.

The **History** area displays date and time information for an image, as well as a general history of where the file has been and what it's been used for. For instance, you can see when the image was printed and if it has been used in creations like Web photo galleries or PDF slide shows.

Creating Keyword Tags

The humble little tag serves as the foundation for the Organizer's sorting and filing system. You can create a tag from scratch or create one based on a set of photos grouped within a folder. Use names that are descriptive, but not so specific that they apply only to a limited number of photos.

To create a new keyword tag:

1. Click the New button (the plus sign) at the top of the Keyword Tags pane.

2. From the drop-down menu, choose New Keyword Tag or press Ctrl+N (**Figure 2.19**). The Create Keyword Tag dialog appears.

3. From the Category menu, choose the category or subcategory in which you want to place your new tag (**Figure 2.20**).

4. In the Name text box, enter a name for your tag.

5. In the Note text box, enter information relevant to the photos that will have the tag applied.

6. Click OK to close the dialog.

   Your new tag appears in the Keyword Tags pane within the category you chose (**Figure 2.21**).

✔ Tips

- The first photo to which you attach a new tag automatically becomes the icon for that tag. This is an easy and convenient way to assign tag icons, so I'll ignore the Edit Icon button for now.

- You can associate a location with a tag (whether or not it's categorized as Places) by clicking the Place on Map button. See "Using the Map," later in this chapter.

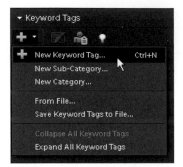

Figure 2.19 Click the New button at the top of the Keyword Tags pane to create a new tag.

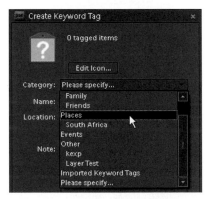

Figure 2.20 All tags reside in categories. You define a category for your new tag in the Create Keyword Tag dialog.

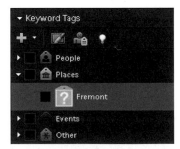

Figure 2.21 Tags appear nested below their categories in the pane.

CREATING KEYWORD TAGS

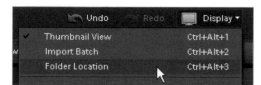

Figure 2.22 The Folder Location option displays photos grouped in folders.

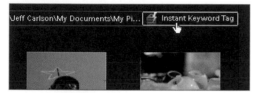

Figure 2.23 Every folder group in the Photo Browser has its own Instant Tag button.

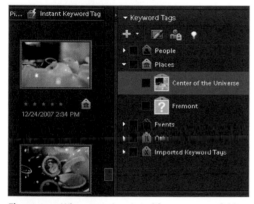

Figure 2.24 When a tag is created from a source folder, all photos in that folder are automatically tagged.

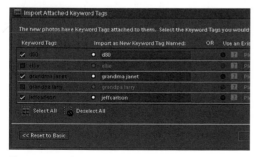

Figure 2.25 When you import photos that already contain keyword tags, you can opt to add them to the list in the Keyword Tags pane.

To create a tag from a folder:

1. Click the Display button and choose Folder Location to display your photos in folder groups (**Figure 2.22**).

2. Identify the folder group that you want to tag and click the Instant Keyword Tag button (**Figure 2.23**).

3. From the Category menu in the Create and Apply New Tag dialog, choose the category or subcategory in which you want to place your new tag.

4. The Name text box is automatically filled with the name of the folder you selected. You can use the folder name for your tag or enter a new name.

5. In the Note text box, enter information relevant to the photos for which you're creating the tag.

6. Click OK. The new tag appears in the Keyword Tags pane within the category you chose, and all of the photos within the folder are automatically selected and tagged (**Figure 2.24**).

   The tag's icon is selected from the first photo in the folder.

To import tags from other images:

1. Using the steps outlined in Chapter 1, import photos from your hard disk that may already contain keywords (for example, if someone sent you the images or you used another program to assign tags).

2. In the Import Attached Keyword Tags dialog, choose which tags you want to add to your list. Click OK. The tags can be applied to any photos in your library.

✔ Tip

■ Click the Advanced button to access more options such as renaming the tags before they're imported (**Figure 2.25**).

To change a tag's properties:

◆ In the Keyword Tags pane, select the tag you want to edit and click the Edit button (the pencil icon).

Or

1. In the Keyword Tags pane, right-click the tag whose properties you would like to change.

2. From the tag contextual menu, choose Edit (*name of tag*) keyword tag (**Figure 2.26**).

3. In the Edit Keyword Tag dialog, make the desired changes and click OK.

To delete a tag:

◆ In the Keyword Tags pane, select the tag you want to delete and click the Delete button (the trash can icon).

Or

1. In the Keyword Tags pane, right-click on the tag you would like to delete.

2. From the tag contextual menu, choose Delete (*name of tag*) keyword tag.

3. In the Confirm Keyword Tag Deletion warning box, click OK (**Figure 2.27**).

The tag is removed from the Keyword Tags pane and from any photos tagged in the Photo Browser.

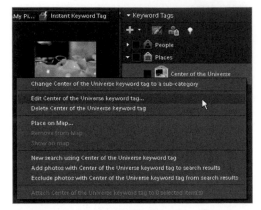

Figure 2.26 Open the Edit Tag dialog from the tag contextual menu.

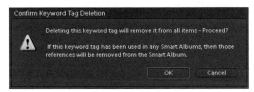

Figure 2.27 The Confirm Tag Deletion warning box reminds you that when a tag is deleted from the Keyword Tags pane, the tags are also removed from the thumbnails in the Photo Browser.

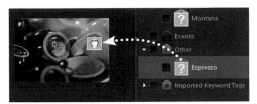

Figure 2.28 To attach a tag to a photo, simply drag it from the Keyword Tags pane to a thumbnail image in the Photo Browser.

Keyword Tag applied   *Tag icon set*

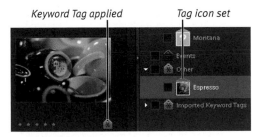

Figure 2.29 When you use a tag for the first time, the photo you attach it to is used for the tag's icon.

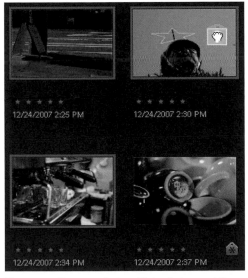

Figure 2.30 You can select multiple photos, and then tag them all by dragging a tag icon over just one.

Using Keyword Tags to Sort and Identify Photos

Tags operate independent of where photos are located on your computer, which means you can attach a tag to photos in different folders—even on different hard drives—and then use that tag to quickly find and view those photos all at once. And since you can attach more than one tag to a photo, tags serve as great cross-referencing tools. For instance, if your daughter plays softball for the college she attends, a photo of her pitching on her home field might include tags called "Emily", "Softball", and "UCSD".

To attach a tag to a single photo:

◆ Drag a tag from the Keyword Tags pane onto any photo in the Photo Browser (**Figure 2.28**).

A category icon appears below the photo in the Browser window to indicate that it has been tagged; in the Keyword Tags pane, the tag assumes that photo for its tag icon (**Figure 2.29**).

To attach a tag to multiple photos:

1. In the Photo Browser, Ctrl+click to select any number of photos.

2. From the Keyword Tags pane, drag a tag onto any one of the selected photos (**Figure 2.30**).

A category icon appears below all of the selected photos in the Browser window to indicate that they have been tagged.

✔ Tips

■ You can also drag a thumbnail to a tag in the Keyword Tags pane to attach it.

■ If you want to reduce the amount of dragging involved, right-click a photo (or selection of photos) and choose a tag from the Attach Tag submenu.

To attach a tag to an import batch or folder:

1. From the Display drop-down menu, choose either Import Batch or Folder Location.

2. Identify the import batch or folder group you want to tag, and then click on either the import batch or folder icon for that group (**Figure 2.31**).

   All of the photos in the group are automatically selected.

3. From the Keyword Tags pane, drag a tag onto any one of the selected photos.

   A category icon appears below all of the selected photos in the Browser window to indicate that they have been tagged.

To view a set of tagged photos:

In the Keyword Tags pane, *do one of the following*:

◆ Double-click a tag.

◆ Click the blank box to the left of a tag.

   A small binoculars icon will appear in the box, and the Photo Browser will change to display just the photo or photos that carry the attached tag (**Figure 2.32**).

   To return to the main Photo Browser window, click the All Photos button, or click the binoculars icon in the Keyword Tags pane.

To remove a tag from a photo:

Select a photo thumbnail in the Photo Browser, and then *do one of the following*:

◆ Right-click a photo thumbnail; then, from the thumbnail contextual menu, choose Remove Keyword Tag > (*name of tag*).

◆ Right-click on the category icon below the photo thumbnail and select Remove (*name of tag*) keyword tag from the small contextual menu (**Figure 2.33**).

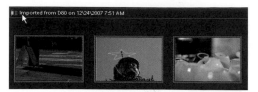

Figure 2.31 When you click on an import batch or folder icon, all of the photos in that batch or folder are selected at once.

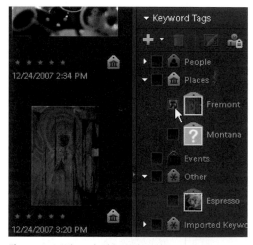

Figure 2.32 When the binoculars icon is visible next to a tag in the Keyword Tags pane, only that tag's photos will appear in the Photo Browser.

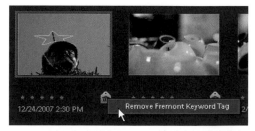

Figure 2.33 Remove a tag from a photo with a single click on the category icon below the thumbnail in the Photo Browser.

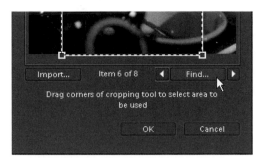

Figure 2.34 Click the Find button in the Edit Tag Icon dialog to browse for a new photo to use as the source for your tag icon.

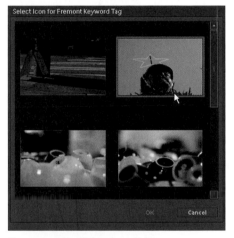

Figure 2.35 The Select Icon dialog.

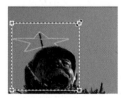

Figure 2.36 Resize the selection rectangle in the Edit Tag Icon dialog to choose the visible area of the icon.

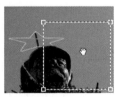

Figure 2.37 Drag the selection rectangle to choose a different area of a photo to use for the tag icon.

To change a tag's icon:

1. In the Keyword Tags pane, right-click on the tag you would like to change.

2. From the tag drop-down menu, choose Edit (*name of tag*) keyword tag.

3. In the Edit Keyword Tag dialog, click the Edit Icon button.

   To assign a new icon image in the Edit Tag Icon dialog, you can select from any of the photos that the tag has been applied to, or you can import a completely new photo.

4. To select a different tagged photo, click the Find button (**Figure 2.34**).

5. In the Select Icon for (*name of tag*) Keyword Tag dialog, click to select a photo thumbnail and click OK (**Figure 2.35**).

   The new image appears in the preview window of the Edit Tag Icon dialog.

6. To crop the area of the photo that will appear on the tag icon, click and drag any of the four cropping handles in the image preview (**Figure 2.36**).

7. To select a different cropped area of the photo to appear on the tag icon, click inside the crop box and drag it in the preview window (**Figure 2.37**).

8. When you're satisfied with the look of your icon, click OK to close the Edit Tag Icon dialog, and then click OK again to close the Edit Keyword Tag dialog. The new icon appears on the tag in the Keyword Tags pane.

✔ Tip

- If you'd like to use an image for your icon different than any of the photos you've tagged, click the Import button in the Edit Tag Icon dialog to browse your computer and select an image.

USING TAGS TO SORT AND IDENTIFY PHOTOS

Marking Photos as Hidden

In addition to marking your photos with keyword tags, you can assign another attribute: Hidden. If you have some photos you feel are cluttering up the Photo Browser, use the Hidden attribute to keep them out of sight until you need them.

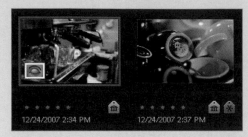

Select a photo and choose Edit > Visibility > Mark as Hidden (or press Alt+F2) to make the image disappear from view.

Figure 2.38 Photos marked as Hidden display a closed eye icon when you've chosen to view hidden files.

To view hidden photos, choose View > Hidden Files and choose either Show All Files or Show Only Hidden Files. A closed eye icon appears on the face of each photo thumbnail (**Figure 2.38**). You can hide them again by choosing View > Hidden Files > Hide Hidden Files. (Those commands can also be found on the Edit > Visibility submenu.)

To make a photo permanently visible, choose Edit > Visibility > Mark as Visible, which removes the Hidden attribute.

Using Face Recognition to Apply Tags to Photos

The Find Faces for Tagging feature offers an easy way to sort, identify, and tag photos based on the people pictured in your photos. Simply click the Find Faces for Tagging button at the top of the Keyword Tags pane to open the Face Tagging window, whose unique browser fills with faces cropped from your Organizer photos (**Figure 2.39**).

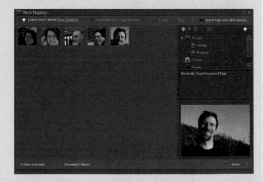

The Face Tagging window has its own Keyword Tags pane from which you can create tags for all of the people represented in its browser. As you assign tags to faces,

Figure 2.39 The Face Tagging window.

they vanish from the Face Tagging browser, so you can't mistakenly tag the same face twice. Once you've finished with your tagging, click the Done button to return to the main Photo Browser. There you'll find that all of the photos containing the tagged faces have been tagged, and the new tags you created appear in their proper place in the Keyword Tags pane.

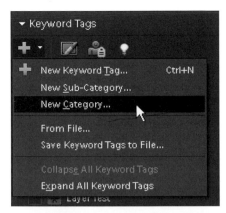

Figure 2.40 Use the New menu in the Keyword Tags pane to open the Create Category dialog.

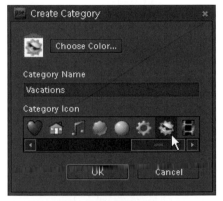

Figure 2.41 The Create Category dialog includes a variety of icons you can use to represent your new category.

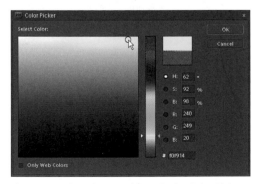

Figure 2.42 The color you choose in the Color Picker appears on the icons for tags in your new category.

Using Categories to Organize Tagged Photos

All tags must reside in either a category or subcategory. The Organizer starts you off with four ready-made categories, but you can create as many new categories and subcategories as you want. Tags can be easily moved from one category to another and also converted to a subcategory that contains its own set of tags.

To create a new category:

1. Click the New button at the top of the Keyword Tags pane.

2. From the New drop-down menu, choose New Category to open the Create Category dialog (**Figure 2.40**).

3. In the Create Category dialog, enter a name in the Category Name text box.

4. In the Category Icon area of the dialog, use the scroll bar or arrows to search for an icon you would like to use to identify your new category (**Figure 2.41**).

5. Click to select a category icon. The icon appears in the category preview at the top of the dialog.

6. At the top of the dialog, click the Choose Color button to open the Color Picker.

7. Select the color that you would like to appear on all the subcategory and tag icons within your new main category and click OK (**Figure 2.42**).

8. If you're satisfied with your other category settings, click OK to close the Create Category dialog.

    Your new category appears at the bottom of the Keyword Tags pane.

To create a new subcategory:

1. Click the New button at the top of the Keyword Tags pane.

2. From the New drop-down menu, choose New Sub-Category to open the Create Sub-Category dialog.

3. In the Create Sub-Category dialog, enter a name in the Sub-Category Name text box.

4. From the Parent Category or Sub-Category drop-down menu, choose a location in which to place your new subcategory (**Figure 2.43**).

5. Click OK to close the Create Sub-Category dialog.

6. Your new subcategory appears in the Keyword Tags pane, within the category or subcategory you selected.

To convert a tag to a subcategory:

1. In the Keyword Tags pane, right-click on the tag you want to convert.

2. From the tag contextual menu, choose Change (*name of tag*) keyword tag to a sub-category (**Figure 2.44**). The tag icon changes to a subcategory icon.

✔ Tips

- An easy way to convert a tag to a subcategory is to drag the tag's icon to a category name.

- If you decide you'd like to convert a subcategory (that was formerly a tag) back to a tag, go to the Sub-Category contextual menu and choose the Change sub-category to a tag option. All of the tag's properties, including its icon, are retained.

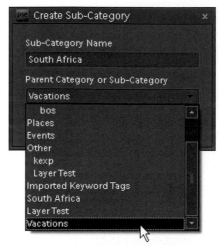

Figure 2.43 Subcategories can be nested within categories or other subcategories.

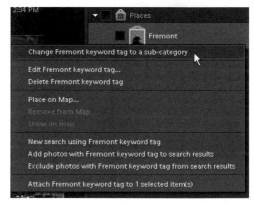

Figure 2.44 Convert a tag to a subcategory from the tag contextual menu in the Keyword Tags pane.

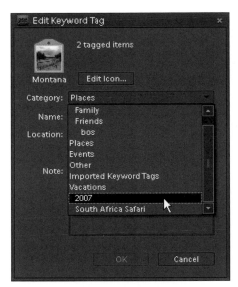

Figure 2.45 You can easily move a tag from one category to another using the Edit Keyword Tag dialog.

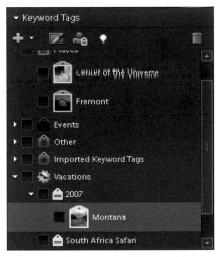

Figure 2.46 Changes you make to a tag's placement in the Edit Keyword Tag dialog appear instantly in the Keyword Tags pane.

To assign a tag to a new category or subcategory:

1. In the Keyword Tags pane, right-click the tag you want to place.

2. From the tag contextual menu, choose Edit (*name of tag*) keyword tag.

3. From the Category menu in the Edit Keyword Tag dialog, choose the category or subcategory in which you want to place the tag (**Figure 2.45**).

4. Click OK to close the Edit Keyword Tag dialog. In the Keyword Tags pane, the tag appears within the category and subcategory you defined (**Figure 2.46**).

   If you've already applied the tag to a photo or photos in the Photo Browser, the category icons below the photo thumbnails will automatically update to display the icon of the new category.

✔ Tip

- You can also move tags into new categories or subcategories right in the Keyword Tags pane. With both the tag and the category or subcategory visible, simply click to select a tag and then drag it onto a category or subcategory icon. The tag will nest beneath the category or subcategory you choose. The disadvantage of this method (as compared to the one outlined in the procedure) is that you must be able to see the tag and category or subcategory in the Keyword Tags pane. Since the Keyword Tags pane can get filled with categories quickly, it may require that you do quite a bit of scrolling and searching, whereas the Category menu in the Edit Keyword Tag dialog gives you a list of every category and subcategory in one convenient place.

To view photos belonging to a category or subcategory:

In the Keyword Tags pane, *do one of the following*:

◆ Double-click a category or subcategory.

◆ Click the blank box to the left of a category or subcategory.

A small binoculars icon appears in the box, and the Photo Browser changes to display just the photos in that category or subcategory set.

To return to the main Photo Browser window, click the All Photos button, or click the binoculars icon in the Keyword Tags pane.

To delete a category or subcategory:

In the Keyword Tags pane, click a category or subcategory, and then *do one of the following*:

◆ Right-click to display the category contextual menu, and then select Delete (*category name*) category.

◆ Click the Delete icon at the top of the Keyword Tags pane (**Figure 2.47**).

✔ Tips

■ Before you delete a category or subcategory, bear in mind that you will also delete all related subcategories and tags and will remove those tags from all tagged photos. In some circumstances, a better alternative may be to change a category or subcategory's properties to better match the content or theme of related tagged photos.

■ Deleting a category does not delete the photos that belong to the category.

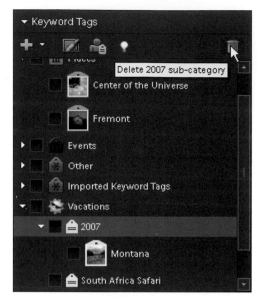

Figure 2.47 Delete a category or tag from the Keyword Tags pane by clicking the Delete button.

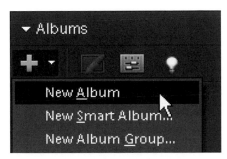

Figure 2.48 Use the New menu in the Albums pane to open the Create Album dialog.

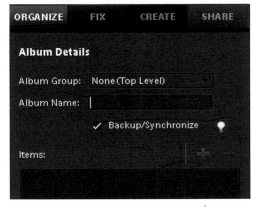

Figure 2.49 The Album Details dialog uses the entire Organize pane while you're creating an album.

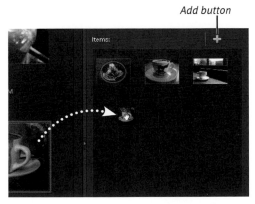

Add button

Figure 2.50 Populate the album by dragging photos to it or by selecting them and clicking the Add button.

Using Albums to Arrange and Group Photos

Photos have gone digital, but we don't have to discard our analog thinking. Just as you store your Polaroids and prints in a photo album, you can collect your digital photos in Elements albums.

An album can be composed of photos from several different tags or categories. Plus, the photos within albums can be sorted and reordered, independent of their date or folder structure—particularly useful when you're creating a project such as a PDF slide show or Web photo gallery.

To create a new album:

1. Click the New button at the top of the Albums pane.

2. From the New drop-down menu, choose New Album (**Figure 2.48**). The Organize pane fills with the Album Details dialog (**Figure 2.49**).

3. Leave the Group menu set to None (Top Level). You'll learn more about album groups later in this section.

4. In the Album Name text box, enter a name for your album.

5. If you want to automatically back up the album, leave the Backup/Synchronize check box enabled (see "Backing Up Photos Online," later in this chapter).

6. Drag the photos you want to add to the album to the Items field (**Figure 2.50**). Or, select one or more photos and click the Add (+) button.

7. Click Done to close the Album Details dialog. Your new album appears in the Albums pane. By default, albums are sorted in alphabetical order.

To view a photo album:

◆ Click an album name in the Albums pane. The Photo Browser displays only the photos in that album (**Figure 2.51**).

To view your entire catalog, click the All Photos button, or click the binoculars icon (making it disappear).

To add photos to an album:

Do one of the following:

◆ From the Photo Browser, drag a photo onto the appropriate album in the Albums pane.

◆ From the Albums pane, drag an album onto a photo thumbnail in the Photo Browser (**Figure 2.52**). An album icon appears below the photo in the Browser window to indicate it is part of an album.

Or

1. In the Albums pane, select an album and click the Edit icon.

2. Drag photos to the Items field; or, make selections in the Photo Browser and click the Add (+) button.

To arrange photos within an album:

1. In the Albums pane, click an album name.

2. In the Photo Browser, click to select a photo, and then drag it to a new location (**Figure 2.53**).

Or

1. In the Albums pane, select an album and click the Edit icon.

2. Drag to rearrange the photos in the Items field.

✔ Tip

■ You can also right-click an album name and choose Sort the Album by Date (Oldest First) from the contextual menu.

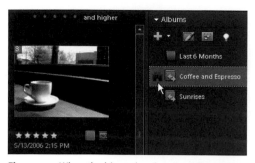

Figure 2.51 When the binoculars icon is visible next to an album's name, only that album's photos will appear in the Photo Browser.

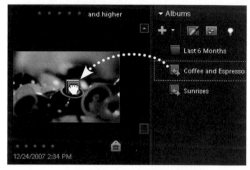

Figure 2.52 One way to populate an album is to drag its icon from the Albums pane to one or more photos.

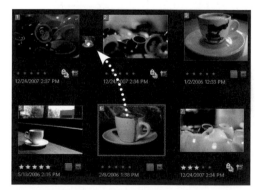

Figure 2.53 To reorder photos within an album, drag a thumbnail to a new location in the Photo Browser. The numbers on the thumbnails indicate their order.

USING ALBUMS TO ORGANIZE PHOTOS

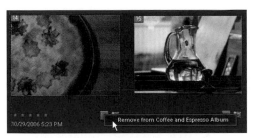

Figure 2.54 Right-click a photo's album icon to remove it from the album.

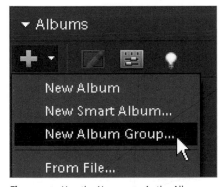

Figure 2.55 Use the New menu in the Albums pane to open the Create Album Group dialog.

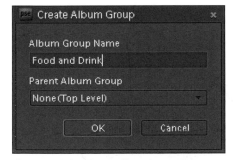

Figure 2.56 The Create Album Group dialog.

To rename an album:

1. In the Albums pane, select an album and click the Edit icon.

2. Change the Album Name field and click Done.

To remove photos from an album:

With an album displayed in the Photo Browser, select a photo thumbnail and then *do one of the following:*

◆ Right-click on the album icon below the photo thumbnail and select Remove from (*name of album*) Album from the contextual menu (**Figure 2.54**).

◆ Right-click inside a photo thumbnail, and then from the contextual menu choose Remove from Album > (*name of album*).

Or

1. In the Albums pane, select an album and click the Edit icon.

2. Select one or more photos and click the Remove (−) button

To create an album group:

1. Click the New button at the top of the Albums pane.

2. From the New drop-down menu, choose New Album Group to open the Create Album Group dialog (**Figure 2.55**).

3. In the Album Group Name text box, enter a name for your group (**Figure 2.56**).

4. Leave the Parent Album Group option set to None (Top Level).

5. Click OK to close the Create Album Group dialog.

   Your new album group appears at the bottom of the list in the Albums pane.

To add an album to an album group:

◆ In the Albums pane, drag an album icon onto the name of the album group (**Figure 2.57**).

Or

1. In the Albums pane, right-click the album you want to include in the album group.

2. From the album contextual menu, choose Edit (*name of album*) album.

3. From the Group menu in the Edit Album dialog, choose the group in which you want to place the album.

4. Click OK to close the Edit Album dialog. In the Albums pane, the album appears within the album group you defined (**Figure 2.58**).

To delete an album:

◆ In the Albums pane, select an album and click the Delete icon.

Or

1. In the Albums pane, right-click the album you would like to delete.

2. From the album contextual menu, choose Delete (*name of album*) album.

3. In the Confirm Album Deletion warning box, click OK. The album is removed from the Albums pane, and the links to any images in the Photo Browser are broken.

✔ Tips

■ It's possible to group one album group within another when creating a group. If you've already created an album group, its name appears in the Parent Album Group menu of the Create Album Group dialog. You then have the option of nesting your new album group within the existing one.

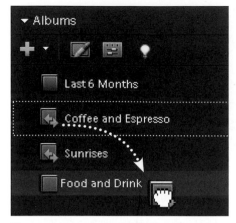

Figure 2.57 Once you've created an album group, you can add albums to it from the Albums pane.

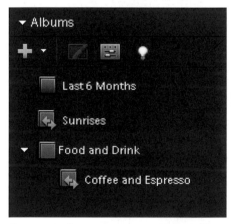

Figure 2.58 Albums appear nested in their album groups in the Albums pane.

■ Deleting a shared album also removes it from public view at Photoshop.com, although the photos remain online.

■ You can't drag an album out of an album group to take it back to the top level. Instead, click the Edit Album button, and then choose None (Top Level) from the Album Group drop-down menu.

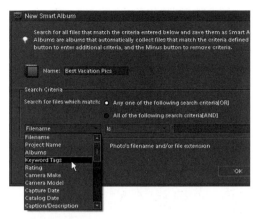

Figure 2.59 Choose from several attributes to start building the smart album.

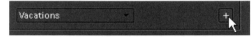

Figure 2.60 Click here to add additional criteria.

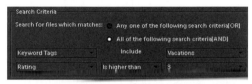

Figure 2.61 This smart album will display only photos marked with the Vacations keyword tag and having a rating of 4 or 5 stars.

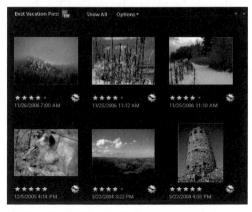

Figure 2.62 After the smart album is created, the pictures that match its criteria are displayed.

Using Smart Albums

One of my grandmother's cupboards was filled with photo albums, organized roughly chronologically, along with a bunch of envelopes and stacks of free-floating pictures that weren't in any order. The problem with lots of photos is that there's only so much time you can spend sorting them.

But what if you had an assistant who could do the organizing for you? Not just once, but ongoing, changing the albums based on new photos or keyword tags or other criteria? Smart albums operate just like that (and they don't mind the workload).

To create a smart album:

1. Click the New button at the top of the Albums pane.

2. From the New drop-down menu, choose New Smart Album to open the New Smart Album dialog.

3. Type a descriptive title in the Name field.

4. In the Search Criteria area, choose an attribute from the first drop-down menu (**Figure 2.59**).

   The other drop-down menu and field change depending on the criteria. For example, choosing Keyword Tags presents a list of tags.

5. To add more criteria, click the plus button (**Figure 2.60**) and specify the attributes.

6. By default, the album picks up photos containing any of the criteria you specify. To view only photos that match every attribute, choose the radio button labeled All of the following search criteria [AND] (**Figure 2.61**).

7. Click OK. Only the images matching the criteria are displayed (**Figure 2.62**).

To modify a smart album:

1. Select a smart album in the Albums pane to view its contents.

2. From the Options drop-down menu at the top of the Photo Browser, choose Modify Search Criteria (**Figure 2.63**).

3. In the Find by Details (Metadata) dialog that appears, edit the attributes you set up originally.

4. To keep the new criteria, mark the check box labeled Save this Search Criteria as Smart Album (**Figure 2.64**).

5. Enter a name for the album (see the tip below).

6. Click Search to save the settings. The images in the Photo Browser reflect the new criteria.

To turn an album into a smart album:

1. Select a regular album in the Albums pane.

2. From the Options drop-down menu, choose Save Search Criteria As Smart Album.

3. In the Create Smart Album dialog, give the smart album a name and click OK (**Figure 2.65**).

✔ Tips

- If you give a modified smart album the same title as the original album you're editing, Elements creates a brand new album instead of replacing the old one.

- To easily view all photos *except* those in the smart album, go to the Options drop-down menu and choose Show results that do not match.

- When you create a smart album from a regular album, you lose the capability to modify the smart album's criteria.

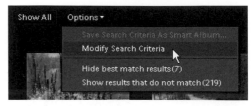

Figure 2.63 Choose Modify Search Criteria when you're viewing the contents of a smart album.

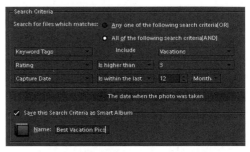

Figure 2.64 Make sure you mark the criteria as a smart album, or else Elements modifies the search for that instance only.

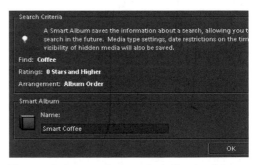

Figure 2.65 A smart album can be built using the criteria of a regular album.

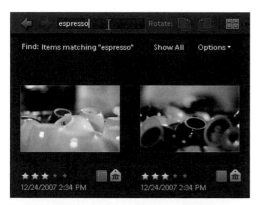

Figure 2.66 Type a word in the Search field to view photos that include that term.

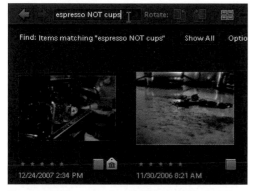

Figure 2.67 You can omit terms by specifying NOT in the Search field.

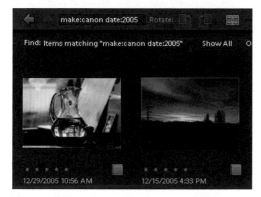

Figure 2.68 Here I've used two terms to define a more specific search (photos shot with a Canon camera sometime in 2005).

Finding Photos

In addition to locating photos using the Keyword Tags and Albums panes, the Organizer offers a host of other options for searching, finding, and viewing photos in your catalog. I'll touch on just a couple of the more popular methods here for locating photos by their embedded date information. For example, the new text search capability takes advantage of the keyword tags you applied earlier (and that's just the start).

To find photos using a text search:

◆ Type a term into the Search field in the Options bar. The Photo Browser searches the photos' metadata and displays matches as you type (**Figure 2.66**).

◆ The Organizer is smart enough to understand the operators AND, OR, and NOT, which allow you to quickly narrow your search (**Figure 2.67**).

◆ For more specific searching, enter any of the following search tags into the field. For example, typing model:d80 (note the lack of a space after the colon) finds all photos in my library shot using a Nikon D80 camera. You can also group tags to narrow the results (**Figure 2.68**).

▲ tag:

▲ filename:

▲ caption:

▲ make:

▲ model:

▲ author:

▲ notes:

▲ date: ##/## (month/day, depending on date preferences in Organizer)

▲ date: #### (year)

▲ date: (today, yesterday, lastweek, thisyear, or lastyear)

To find photos using the timeline:

1. If the timeline isn't visible, choose Window > Timeline (Ctrl+L).

2. In the timeline, click on a bar corresponding to a specific month and year (**Figure 2.69**). The Photo Browser automatically scrolls to display the photos for the month you selected.

To display photos within a date range:

1. From the Find menu, choose Set Date Range, or press Ctrl+Alt+F.

2. In the Set Date Range dialog, use the text boxes and drop-down menus to enter your dates.

3. The timeline highlights just the range of dates that you selected (**Figure 2.70**).

To quickly search by attributes:

◆ Drag keyword tags, albums, or other criteria to the Find bar at the top of the Photo Browser (**Figure 2.71**).

✔ Tips

■ You can also simply move the date range markers on the timeline to view photos within that range.

■ When you drag photos to the Find bar, Elements displays images with similar qualities such as color.

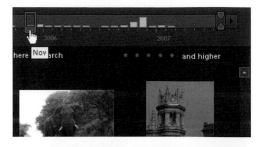

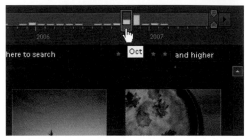

Figure 2.69 Bars (month markers) in the timeline represent sets of images shot or acquired in specific months. Click a timeline marker to view its photos.

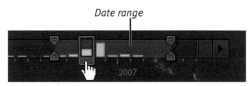

Figure 2.70 After you set a date range, only those photos that fall within the specified range are visible.

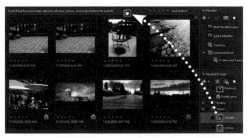

Figure 2.71 Dragging the "clouds" keyword tag to the search bar above the Photo Browser narrows the number of displayed photos.

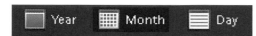

Figure 2.72 The date view offers three calendar layouts for viewing photos.

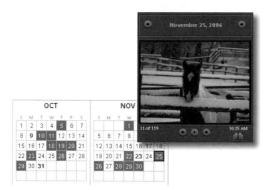

Figure 2.73 Click a shaded date in Year view to see the photos associated with that day.

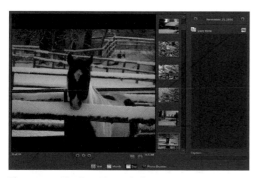

Figure 2.74 The Day View window.

To find photos in the date view:

1. From the Display drop-down menu, choose Date View (Ctrl+Alt+D).

2. At the bottom of the Date View window, click to select a view option (**Figure 2.72**).

3. Use the navigation buttons in calendar view to move from one year, month, or day to another.

   In Year view, dates shaded in blue indicate the days those photos were taken. A preview window to the right contains a thumbnail of the first photo in the set, plus navigation buttons to view the remaining photos in the set (**Figure 2.73**). In Month view, thumbnails appear on the dates the photos were taken.

4. To view the complete set of photos for any given day, *do one of the following:*

   ▲ Double-click either a shaded day in Year view or a day thumbnail in Month view.

   ▲ Click to select a day in either Year or Month view, and then click the Day button at the bottom of the Date View window.

   In the Day View window you can see large, single-image views of your photos (**Figure 2.74**). You can also add notes for a complete day's set of photos and enter a caption for individual photos.

✔ Tip

■ From the Find menu, you can search for photos to view by a number of different criteria. Some that you'll probably use most often are by caption or note; by filename; by history (imported on date, and printed on date, among others); and by media type (photos, video, audio, and creations). Just choose an option and then fill in its dialog (when applicable) to refine your search.

Using Stacks to Organize Similar Photos

You've spent a day on the valley floor of Yosemite shooting picture after picture, and when you return home in the evening and download all of those photos to your Photo Browser, you realize you have about a dozen shots of the same waterfall: some lit a little differently than others; some with different zoom settings; but all very similar just the same.

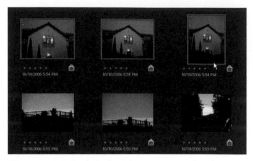

Figure 2.75 Select similar photos to organize them into a stack.

Stacks serve as a convenient way to group those related photos together. They not only save valuable space in the Photo Browser, they also make assigning tags much faster, because tagging a stack automatically tags every photo in the stack. When you're ready to take a careful look at all of those waterfalls and weed out the greats from the not-so-greats, you simply expand the stack to view all of the stacked photos at once.

To create a stack:

1. In the Photo Browser, Ctrl+click to select the photos you want to include in a stack (**Figure 2.75**).

2. Right-click inside any of the selected photo thumbnails; then from the thumbnail contextual menu choose Stack > Stack Selected Photos, or press Ctrl+Alt+S.

   The photos are stacked together, indicated by a Stack icon in the upper-right corner of the top photo in the stack (**Figure 2.76**).

Stack icon

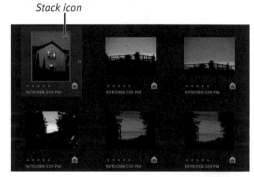

Figure 2.76 When stacked, the photos occupy just one thumbnail, and are indicated by the Stack icon.

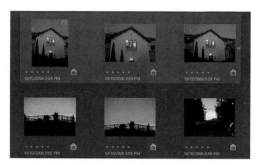

Figure 2.77 An expanded stack reveals the photos that have been grouped together.

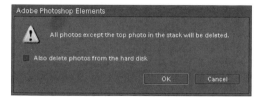

Figure 2.78 A warning box reminds you that you are about to delete all but the top photo in your stack.

To view all photos in a stack:

◆ In the Photo Browser, click the arrow icon at the right of the stack. Or, right-click on a stack thumbnail, and choose Stack > Expand Photos in Stack; or press Ctrl+Alt+R. The photos in the stack appear (**Figure 2.77**).

   To return to the main Photo Browser window, click the All Photos button.

To flatten a stack:

1. If you're certain you don't want any photo in a stack except for the top one, you can "flatten" the stack and delete the others. In the Photo Browser, right-click on a stack thumbnail; then from the thumbnail contextual menu choose Stack > Flatten Stack.

2. In the warning dialog that appears, click OK to delete all of the photos except for the top photo in the stack (**Figure 2.78**).

   You can also choose to delete the associated image files from your hard disk.

To unstack photos in a stack:

◆ In the Photo Browser, right-click on a stack thumbnail; then from the thumbnail contextual menu choose Stack > Unstack Photos.

   The stacked photos return to their original locations in the Photo Browser window.

✔ Tip

■ While you're viewing the expanded stack, you can also remove specific photos from a stack, or designate a new photo to be the top photo (the photo that appears at the top of the stack in the Photo Browser). Just right-click on any stacked photo and then, from the thumbnail contextual menu, select an option from the Stack submenu.

USING STACKS TO ORGANIZE SIMILAR PHOTOS

Using the Map

Sometimes where you took a photo is as important as what's in the image. The Map feature lets you associate locations with your photos, using support from Yahoo! Maps (**Figure 2.79**).

To place a photo on the map:

1. Right-click one or more photos and choose Place on Map from the contextual menu.

2. In the Photo Location on Map dialog, type an address (**Figure 2.80**).

3. Elements checks online for a match and displays the results; select the one closest to the location you're looking for and click OK.

    A red pushpin icon appears in the Map pane at the location you specified. Clicking the icon displays the photo (**Figure 2.81**).

4. Use the Zoom, Hand, and Move tools to navigate the map.

✔ Tips

■ You can also choose Show Map from the Display drop-down menu to view the Map pane and then simply drag photos to a location on the map to place them. However, the steps above make it easier to find specific locations, versus dropping a bunch of pictures onto "North America" and calling it good.

■ When creating tags, click the Place on Map button to specify a location in the Map pane. Any photo assigned that tag automatically appears on the map.

■ The pop-up menu at the lower-right corner of the Map pane lets you display a traditional map, a satellite image, or a hybrid version (satellite with street names superimposed over it).

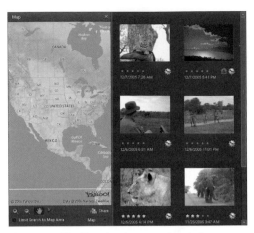

Figure 2.79 The Map view lets you plot photos anywhere on the globe.

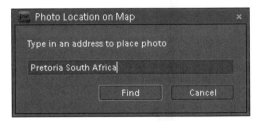

Figure 2.80 Enter an address, city, state, or country (or any of the above) to find the location.

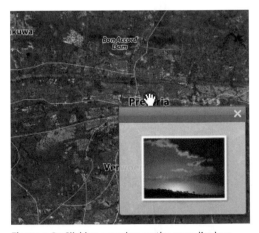

Figure 2.81 Clicking a marker on the map displays a window containing thumbnails of the photos associated with that location.

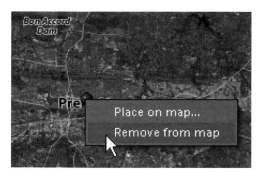

Figure 2.82 Right-click a pushpin icon on the map to remove the photos from the map.

To move a location on the map:

◆ Right-click a pushpin icon and choose Place on Map; follow the directions on the previous page.

Or

1. Click the Move tool in the Map pane.

2. Drag a pushpin icon to another location. All photos associated with that location are marked with the new location.

To remove a photo from the map:

◆ In the Map pane, right-click a pushpin icon and choose Remove from Map (**Figure 2.82**).

✔ Tip

■ Placing images on the map can also be a convenient way for others to view your photos.

Using Catalogs to Store Your Photos

Catalogs are the behind-the-scenes backbone of the Organizer workspace, where all the information for tags and categories and albums are stored. When you install Elements, a default catalog (called My Catalog) is automatically set up for you. That might be enough to work with, but you can also create additional catalogs—for example, if more than one person is sharing and downloading images to the same computer. You may want discrete catalogs for each person's photos: Bob's Catalog, Sara's Catalog, and so on.

To create a new catalog:

1. From the File menu choose Catalog, or press Ctrl+Shift+C (**Figure 2.83**).

2. In the Catalog Manager dialog, click a radio button to specify whether the catalog is available to all user accounts on the computer, just the current user, or saved to a custom location (**Figure 2.84**).

3. Click New.

   If online backups are enabled for your existing catalog, a warning dialog appears stating you'll need to set the new catalog to be backed up in the Backup/Synchronize preferences (see the next section). Click OK to continue.

4. In the File name text box, enter a name for your new catalog (**Figure 2.85**).

   At the bottom of the naming dialog is the Import free music into this catalog check box. Leave this option selected so the music files you received with Elements (to use as background tracks for PDF slide shows and other creations) will be available in the new catalog.

5. Click OK to create your new catalog.

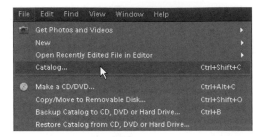

Figure 2.83 Choose Catalog from the File menu to open the Catalog Manager dialog.

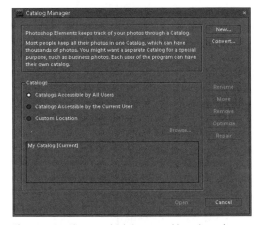

Figure 2.84 Choose which users and locations the catalog belongs to.

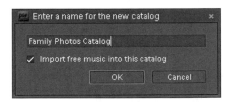

Figure 2.85 Make sure to name your new catalog differently than any existing catalogs.

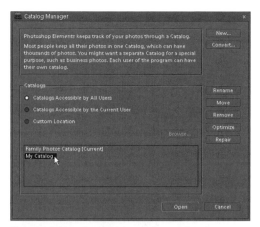

Figure 2.86 Juggle multiple catalogs using the Catalog Manager dialog.

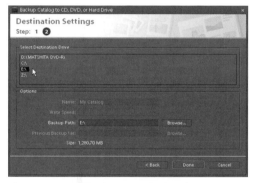

Figure 2.87 Specify where your backup files are to be located; in this case, they're on external hard drive E.

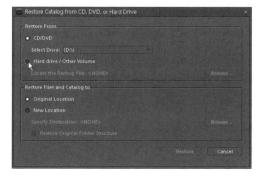

Figure 2.88 If you need to reconstruct a catalog from your backup, use the Restore Catalog command.

To access saved catalogs:

1. From the File menu choose Catalog, or press Ctrl+Shift+C.

2. Select the name of the saved catalog you want to open (**Figure 2.86**).

3. Click the Open button.

To make a backup of a catalog:

1. Since you obviously don't want to lose your photos, choose File > Backup Catalog to CD, DVD, or Hard Drive.

2. In the Backup dialog, choose Full Backup to make a complete copy of the catalog. On subsequent backups, you can choose Incremental Backup to copy only new and changed image files to the backup.

3. Click Next.

4. Select a destination drive from the list (such as an external hard drive), and specify a location by clicking the Browse button for Backup Path (**Figure 2.87**).

5. Click Done when you're ready. Elements copies the image files and catalog information to the drive.

To restore a catalog from backup:

1. In the event that your catalog becomes unreadable, choose Restore Catalog from the File menu.

2. In the Restore dialog, choose the media on which the backup is stored (**Figure 2.88**); if you choose Hard drive/Other Volume, click the Browse button to locate the .tly file that accompanies the backup.

3. Choose where to copy the restored files: the catalog's original location or another location.

4. Click Restore. The images and catalog information are copied to the destination.

Backing Up Photos Online

The capability to back up your catalog to an external hard disk or removable media has one limitation: You need to actually do it. And speaking from experience, that's something easily forgotten or put off for another day. But hard drives don't fail on a schedule, and thieves don't wait to pilfer your laptop until it's most convenient for you.

I covered the basics of the integration between Elements and Photoshop.com in Chapter 1. With an account set up, you can direct Elements to back up your photos over the Internet in the background. Even if your computer perishes in a natural disaster, your photos are safe on Adobe's servers.

Elements also *synchronizes* your backup. If you make a change to a photo in your library or online, the change is reflected in both locations.

To set up Photoshop.com backups:

1. Sign in to your Photoshop.com account if you haven't already.

2. On the Welcome screen, click the Backup Settings button. Or, in the Organizer, choose Edit > Preferences > Backup/ Synchronization.

   You can also click the synchronization status icon at the bottom of the Organizer screen and choose Open Backup/Synchronization preferences from the pop-up menu that appears (**Figure 2.89**).

3. Enable the Backup/Sync is On check box if it's not already active (**Figure 2.90**), and click OK.

✔ Tip

■ You can also click the Backup/Synchronization Preferences icon in the Albums pane to display the preferences.

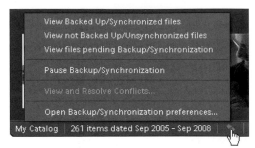

Figure 2.89 Access the Photoshop.com backup settings from the synchronization status icon.

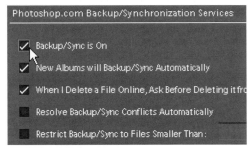

Figure 2.90 The master switch for enabling backups is in the Backup/Synchronization preferences.

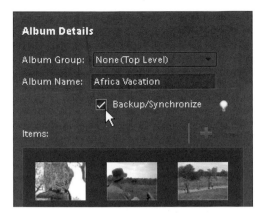

Figure 2.91 Enable the Backup/Synchronize check box to copy the contents of an album to Photoshop.com.

Backup/Synchronization   Backup
Pending icon   enabled

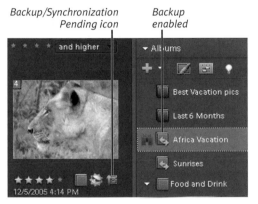

Figure 2.92 You can tell at a glance which photos and albums are getting backed up.

Backing up albums

Elements organizes online backups by album. This approach cuts the amount of data transferred (since image files tend to be quite large) and lets you decide which photos are backed up.

To enable an album for online backup:

1. Create a new album, or select an existing album and edit it (see "Using Albums to Arrange and Group Photos," earlier in this chapter). The Album Details dialog fills the Organize pane.

2. Enable the Backup/Synchronize check box (**Figure 2.91**).

3. Click Done. The album icon displays a pair of icons indicating that it gets synchronized, and each photo in the album gains a pending synchronization icon (**Figure 2.92**).

   Elements copies the images to the Photoshop.com servers in the background while you perform other tasks.

To view the backup status:

◆ Click the synchronization status icon and choose one of the first three items in the menu to display: files that have been backed up; files that are not set for backup; or files that are due to be backed up. The photos appear in the Photo Browser.

✔ Tips

■ New albums are automatically set to be backed up. To turn off this behavior, disable the New Albums Will Backup/Sync Automatically check box in the preferences.

■ If you've paid for more storage space at Photoshop.com and want to back up your entire library—warts and all—create a new album and add every photo to it.

To control when backups occur:

◆ Click the synchronization status icon and choose Pause Backup/Synchronization from the pop-up menu to temporarily halt copying. Use this command when you want to maximize your Internet bandwidth for other tasks.

◆ In the Windows system tray, right-click the Photoshop.com Backup/Synchronization Agent and choose one of the following options (**Figure 2.93**):

▲ **Backup/Sync only when idle**: Elements copies files only when you're not using the computer.

▲ **Pause Backup/Synchronization**: Temporarily halts copying.

▲ **Stop Backup/Synchronization**: Disables the Backup/Sync is On setting in the Elements preferences and ends the agent. You must go back to the preferences to restart the service.

To stop backing up an album:

1. Select an existing album and edit it.

2. In the Album Details dialog, disable the Backup/Synchronize check box.

3. Click Done.

   When you turn off backup/synchronization, Elements no longer communicates with Photoshop.com about the photos in that album. However, the images still remain online; if you want to delete them from Photoshop.com, you need to do so there.

✔ Tip

■ Unfortunately, there's no status indicator to tell you what's currently being copied. You have to wait for the images to appear at Photoshop.com.

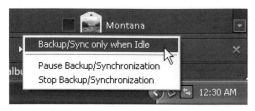

Figure 2.93 The Photoshop.com Backup/Synchronization Agent controls when images are copied.

Keep a Backup Backup

The best approach, of course, is to have multiple backups of your precious photos. The advantage of an online backup is that it's performed automatically and the data is stored in a physically separate location. But that also means the backup is out of your hands—if Adobe's servers go down or become corrupted, your backup is gone. It's unlikely, but still possible. So make a point of keeping multiple backups: online, on external hard disks, on CD or DVD media, or whatever combination works best for you.

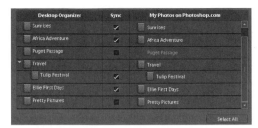

Figure 2.94 In the Backup/Synchronization preferences, click the Sync check box for the albums you wish to sync.

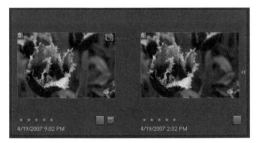

Figure 2.95 The left image, which was edited at Photoshop.com, appears in Elements as a new version.

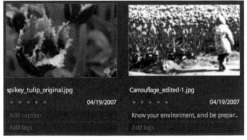

Figure 2.96 At Photoshop.com, the original version of the image at right was replaced by this version that was edited in Elements.

Synchronizing Photos with Photoshop.com

Communication between Elements and Photoshop.com goes both ways. When you edit a photo in Elements, the changes are automatically uploaded to your library at Photoshop.com and vice-versa. You can specify which albums are synchronized in the Backup/Synchronization preferences (**Figure 2.94**).

Here's how synchronization works:

◆ Elements copies all files in an album to Photoshop.com. However, the online service only works with JPEG images, so if you want to edit a raw file, for example, Photoshop.com first converts the image.

◆ When you edit a file at Photoshop.com, the edited version is added to your Elements library as a new version; the original is still available (**Figure 2.95**).

◆ If you edit an image in Elements, only the most recent version of the file is uploaded to Photoshop.com (**Figure 2.96**). The original version exists only in your Elements library.

◆ If your Elements album contains a version set, only the "top" version (the latest) is uploaded to Photoshop.com, not all versions in the set.

◆ Removing a photo from an album in either Elements or Photoshop.com does not delete the file; it's still available in the libraries at both locations.

◆ If you delete an album in Elements that you've shared (made public), the photos still reside at Photoshop.com but are no longer publicly available.

continues on next page

◆ If you delete a synchronized photo from Photoshop.com, Elements alerts you that a synchronization problem exists (see below). You can remove this confirmation step by disabling the preference labeled When I Delete a File Online, Ask Before Deleting It from My Computer.

◆ If you edit several different aspects of a photo—for example, adding a caption at Photoshop.com and applying keywords in Elements—those changes are merged so that each version is the same.

Resolving synchronization issues

Sometimes synchronization isn't straightforward. What happens when you add a caption to a photo in Elements and then accidentally add a different caption for the same photo at Photoshop.com? The synchronization status icon turns yellow to indicate a conflict.

To resolve synchronization issues:

1. Click the synchronization status icon and choose View and Resolve Conflicts from the pop-up menu (**Figure 2.97**).

2. In the Backup/Synchronization Resolution dialog, review the conflicts and choose the version you wish to keep (**Figure 2.98**).

   If you've deleted a file from the library (not just removed it from an album), as I mentioned above, the Deletions tab lets you confirm or reject the deletion.

3. Click the Apply Changes and Quit button to resolve the conflicts.

✔ Tip

■ Photoshop.com doesn't auotmatically update its library when you're viewing an album online. If you're expecting synchronized files to appear, click the Refresh button to update the library (**Figure 2.99**).

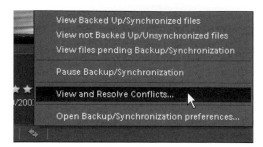
Figure 2.97 The yellow synchronization status icon indicates you need to resolve a conflict.

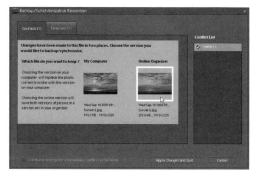
Figure 2.98 Elements details the sync conflicts and lets you choose which version to keep.

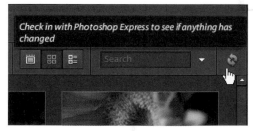
Figure 2.99 Click the Refresh button to update the library.

CREATING AND MANAGING IMAGES

So far, I've introduced Photoshop Elements and worked mostly in the Organizer, importing and arranging photos for manipulation later. But Elements isn't just a photo album (in fact, its organizing features are relatively new). It's built on the code from Photoshop, the industrial-strength image editor used by the pros. As such, it's important to build a foundation of knowledge about digital images in preparation for editing them later.

This chapter offers some basic guidelines on adjusting image size and resolution. If you want to e-mail a photo to a friend, you'll need a small file size for easy delivery—so you'll want to create a low-resolution image, which means it contains a smaller number of pixels. If you're planning to print high-quality images on your ink-jet printer, you'll want to maintain as high a resolution as your printer can handle (meaning a greater density of pixels) to ensure a crisp, clear print.

I also cover creating images from scratch (which is what some people use Elements for, ignoring the Organizer entirely). You'll also learn the different methods for viewing additional information about your images.

Understanding Resolution and Image Size

Resolution and image size are frequently used and often misunderstood terms.

Resolution simply refers to the number of *pixels*, or picture elements—tiny, square, building blocks—that are packed into a digital image. Today's computer monitors and LCD displays pack millions of pixels into the screen you're viewing; the more pixels, the higher the resolution, and in general the more detail you're able to see.

Image size refers to both the print size and resolution of an image. Depending on whether you want to print a photograph, post it on a Web page, or e-mail it to a friend, you'll need to adjust its image size and resolution accordingly.

Pixel basics

Everything you do in Photoshop Elements involves controlling and changing pixels. Pixels make up your entire image and are typically not visible as individual elements until you zoom in on your picture (**Figure 3.1**).

Images are often described using pixels as the unit of measure. For example, a digital camera may shoot images at 1600 x 1200 pixels (the *x* is pronounced "by," just as in "3 x 5 photo"). Multiplying 1600 times 1200 gives you the total number of pixels in the image, which in this case is 1.92 million pixels.

Digital cameras often include preset resolution modes. These settings determine both the physical dimensions and file size of the image (**Figure 3.2**).

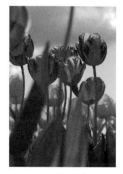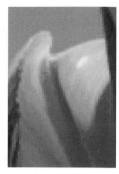

Figure 3.1 Pixels become more visible as you increase the magnification of your image.

3872 x 2592 pixels, 16.9 MB

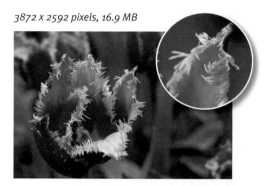

640 x 480 pixels, 1.4 MB

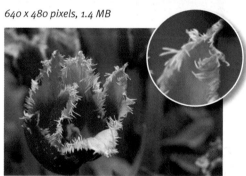

Figure 3.2 Examples of common digital camera resolutions and associated file sizes, all viewed at 100% (also referred to as actual pixels). Higher-resolution images, like the photo on top, provide a sharp, clear picture that's excellent for printing. Lower-resolution images, like the bottom photo, lack sufficient pixel information for printing purposes, but work fine for e-mailing or posting on the Web.

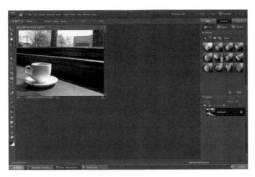

Figure 3.3 The display of an onscreen image is based on the resolution of the image, the size of the monitor, and the monitor resolution.

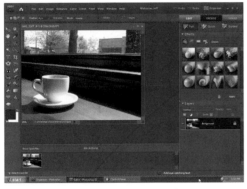

Figure 3.4 A monitor set to 1024 x 768 is a more common setting, and allows program menus to be seen more easily.

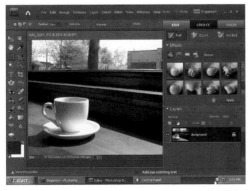

Figure 3.5 The same monitor set to 800 x 600 displays fewer pixels per inch, so less of the image is visible.

Displaying and printing images

Any discussion of resolution and output can be confusing, so you need to keep a few basic details in mind. Image resolution is described in *pixels per inch*, or *ppi*.

The ideal amount of detail and level of resolution depend on how you intend to use an image. If you're going to display your photos on the Web, keep in mind that large files take forever to download and view, so you'll want to choose a lower resolution like 72 ppi (72 ppi is the most common image resolution for monitor displays).

Three factors affect the way an image is displayed on a computer monitor: the number of pixels in the image, the screen resolution, and the screen size (**Figure 3.3**). The size of each pixel is determined by the resolution and size of the monitor. For example, a 17-inch monitor set to a resolution of 1024 x 768 pixels would have 82 pixels per inch (**Figure 3.4**). The same monitor set to a resolution of 800 x 600 would have fewer pixels per inch, so each pixel takes up more screen space (**Figure 3.5**). If you change your monitor resolution to a lower resolution setting, the images and icons appear larger on your screen. It takes fewer pixels to fill the monitor, so the size of each pixel appears larger.

Print resolution is usually described by the number of *dots per inch*, or *dpi*, a printer is capable of printing. If you want to print a high-quality flyer or photo, you may want to use an image resolution as high as 300 pixels per inch, so that a maximum amount of image information is sent to the printer. Fortunately, a wide range of image resolutions are available that work well for different types of situations, and Photoshop Elements includes some automatic functions (such as the Save for Web command) that take the guesswork out of the process.

UNDERSTANDING RESOLUTION AND IMAGE SIZE

Creating a New Image

If you want to start with a blank canvas, use the New dialog to set up the basic dimensions, image resolution, and color mode. You can create your own work of art using Photoshop Elements' many painting and drawing tools, or you can assemble a collage of multiple images. But for now, I'll stick with the basics.

To create a new image:

1. To create a new image in either the Organizer or the Editor, go to the File menu and choose New > Blank File, or press Ctrl+N.

2. In the New dialog, enter a filename; then enter dimensions for the width and height (**Figure 3.6**). The default size is 6 x 4 inches, which works fine as a starting point. You can always change it later.

3. Set the resolution and color mode. For more information, see Chapter 7, "Changing and Adjusting Colors."

4. From the Background Contents drop-down menu, choose an option for the background layer of the image.

   ▲ **White** is the default background option and creates a pure white background layer for the image. This option is just fine for most purposes.

   ▲ **Background Color** fills the background with the current background color—useful if you want a Web graphic that matches the background color of your Web page.

   ▲ **Transparent** makes the first layer transparent and results in an image with no background at all—a good choice if you're creating an image for the Web and want it to appear transparent on the page.

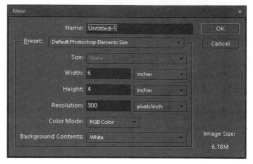

Figure 3.6 The New dialog lets you name your new image and set its dimensions, resolution, and color mode.

Don't Panic

Don't be intimidated by the sheer number of size, resolution, and transparency settings available when you first create a new image. All of these settings will be covered in more detail as you progress through the book. If you're brand new to Photoshop Elements, creating a new image can be as simple as pressing Ctrl+N and accepting the default settings.

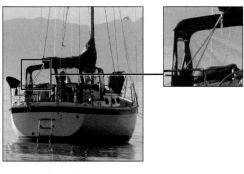

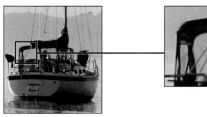

Figure 3.7 This image was duplicated (top) then reduced 50% (bottom). Notice in the zoom views that the reduced image isn't as detailed as the original. That's because, even though both have the same number of pixels per inch, the reduced image contains fewer pixels overall.

Changing Image Size and Resolution

Pixel dimensions, image dimensions, and resolution are all adjusted using the Image Size dialog. You will often capture one image and then use it for different purposes, so it's important to understand how these adjustments affect your image file.

For the Web and other onscreen viewing, it's common to adjust the pixel dimensions, or number of pixels, to control the resolution and/or file size of the image. This is known as *resampling*. The Resample Image check box is probably the most important feature to understand. When this box is checked, the pixel dimensions change—that is, the pixels will increase or decrease in number as the image is resampled (**Figure 3.7**). When the box is *not* checked, the pixel dimensions are locked in, and no resampling can occur. You can change the *document* size (the size the image will print), but the number of pixels in the image and the size that the image displays onscreen will stay the same.

Recommended Resolutions

There are no absolute rules for the best resolution to use when working with images for the Web or for printing. The best approach is to try a couple of settings, using the following guidelines, and see what works well for your specific situation. Here are some typical situations and recommended resolution ranges:

◆ For onscreen viewing of Web images, 72 ppi is a standard and safe resolution.

◆ For color images printed on color ink-jet printers, a range of up to 150 ppi is often ideal. The exact resolution will depend on your printer and the type of paper on which you are printing.

◆ For color or high-resolution black and white images printed on photo printers, you'll want a resolution between 150 and 300 ppi.

If you want to create higher-quality professional projects, such as magazine or print design work, be aware that Photoshop Elements is not capable of producing CMYK files (the color-separated files used for high-end printing). If you need an image-editing program that can handle these kinds of jobs, you should consider buying the full version of Adobe Photoshop.

To resize an image for screen viewing:

1. From the Image menu, choose Resize > Image Size to open the Image Size dialog.

2. Make sure the Resample Image box is checked (**Figure 3.8**), and click the Resample Image drop-down menu.

   When you resample an image, its pixels are transformed using a process known as an *interpolation*. Interpolation is a computer calculation used to estimate unknown values based on existing known values—in this case, pixel color values. So, when you resample an image in Elements, its existing pixels are changed using one of five primary interpolation methods (**Figure 3.9**):

   ▲ **Bicubic** is the default option and generally produces the best results and smoothest gradations.

   ▲ **Bilinear** produces medium-quality results.

   ▲ **Nearest Neighbor** is the fastest method, but may produce jagged effects.

   ▲ **Bicubic Smoother** can be used when you're increasing the size of an image, or *upsampling*. Typically, I strongly advise against upsampling, because there is usually a noticeable loss of image quality and sharpness. But I've seen acceptable results with Bicubic Smoother, as long as I don't resize much above 120 percent.

   ▲ **Bicubic Sharper** can be used when you're reducing the size of an image, or *downsampling*. Its purpose is to help to retain sharpness and detail. My success with this option has been mixed.

3. To maintain the current width-to-height ratio, make sure Constrain Proportions is checked.

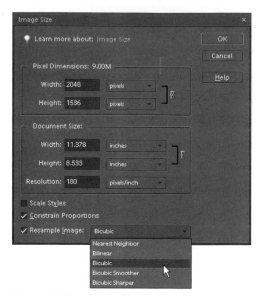

Figure 3.8 The Resample Image drop-down menu includes five options for specifying how the resampling occurs.

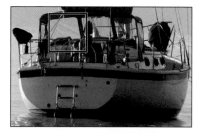

Figure 3.9 You can resample an image using one of three calculation methods: Bicubic (left), Bilinear (center), or Nearest Neighbor (right). Bicubic does the best job at retaining detail and anti-aliasing, whereas Nearest Neighbor creates images with a rougher quality.

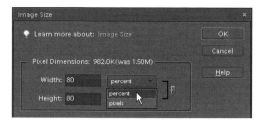

Figure 3.10 Pixel dimensions can be entered as pixels or as a percentage.

4. Enter new values in the Pixel Dimensions fields. You can enter values in pixels or as percentages (**Figure 3.10**).

   If you choose percent, you can enter a percentage amount in either the Height or Width box to automatically scale the image to that percentage. The new file size for the image is displayed at the top of the dialog (along with the old file size in parentheses).

5. Click OK to complete the change. The image is resized larger or smaller, depending on the pixel dimensions or percentage you entered.

✔ Tip

■ When you change an image's size by changing its pixel dimensions, you also change its print size (you'll see the change in the width and height dimensions in the Document Size fields of the Image Size dialog). Although these images are acceptable for onscreen viewing or as quick test prints, you may be disappointed with their printed quality. That's because you discard image information by resampling, and so lose some sharpness and detail.

Downsampling vs. Upsampling

Downsampling, which is the term for decreasing resolution by *removing* pixels from your photo, is one of the easiest and most common ways to make your files smaller. If you take an 8 x 10 photograph of your grandmother and shrink it to a 4 x 5 image by reducing its pixel count, you've just downsampled it. Elements "throws away" unneeded pixels intelligently, with little visible impact on the quality of your image.

But *upsampling*, which is the term for increasing resolution by *adding* new pixels to your photo, should be avoided whenever possible. If you take a 4 x 5 photograph and try to enlarge it to 8 x 10, Elements must manufacture those pixels out of thin air. They tend to add a ghosted, fuzzy appearance to any hard edge—the overall effect is that your image can look out of focus.

Because downsampling rarely detracts from the quality of your images, you should capture all your original files at the highest resolution possible, whether you're scanning an image or snapping a digital photo.

CHANGING IMAGE SIZE AND RESOLUTION

To resize an image for printing:

1. From the Image menu, choose Resize > Image Size.

2. To maintain the current width-to-height ratio, check that the Constrain Proportions option is selected.

3. Uncheck the Resample Image box.

4. Choose a unit of measure (or a percentage) and then enter new values for the width or height in the Document Size portion of the dialog (**Figure 3.11**).

    In the Document Size portion of the dialog, the resolution value changes accordingly. For instance, if you enter width and height values of half the original image size, the resolution value will double, and the image will print clearer and sharper. That's because you're compressing the same number of pixels into a smaller space. So, when scaled at 50 percent, an image 4 inches wide with a resolution of 150 pixels per inch (ppi) will print at 2 inches wide and at a resolution of 300 ppi.

5. Click OK to complete the change.

    The image's print size will be changed, but since it still contains the same number of pixels, it will appear to be unchanged on your screen. You can, however, view a preview of the final print size onscreen:

    ▲ From the View menu, choose Print Size. The image is resized on your screen to approximate its final, printed size (**Figure 3.12**).

    ▲ From the View menu, choose Actual Pixels, or press Alt+Ctrl+0 to return the display size on your screen to 100 percent.

✔ Tip

■ To return the dialog to its original settings, press Alt to change the Cancel button to Reset, then click Reset.

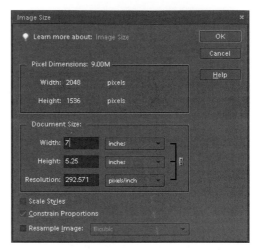

Figure 3.11 Enter new width and height values to change an image's print size.

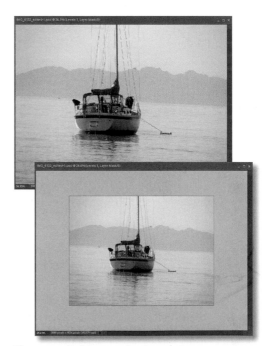

Figure 3.12 An image can be viewed at an approximation of its final print size, even when its resolution differs from the computer's display.

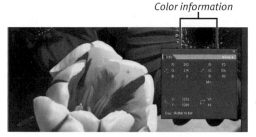

Color information

Figure 3.13 Any two sets of color information (RGB, HSB, Web Color, or Grayscale) can be viewed at once.

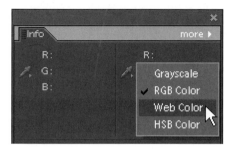

Figure 3.14 Color modes (and other settings) can be changed from pop-up lists in the palette.

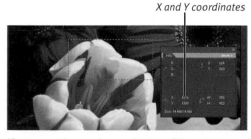

X and Y coordinates

Figure 3.15 The x and y coordinates of the pointer are shown in the Info palette.

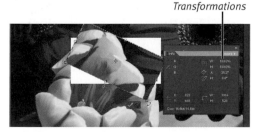

Transformations

Figure 3.16 Any change in the scale or transformation of a selection or layer is visible in the Info palette.

Getting Information about Your Image

The Info palette displays measurement and color information as you move a tool over an image. In addition, you can customize the status bar at the bottom of the Info palette to display different file and image information.

To use the Info palette:

1. From the Window menu, choose Info to open the Info palette.

   If you like, you can drag the Info palette into the Palette Bin.

2. Select the desired tool and then move the pointer over the image. Depending on the tool you are using, the following types of information appear:

   ▲ The numeric values for the color beneath the pointer. You can view any two sets of color modes at the same time (**Figure 3.13**). Information for different color modes can be displayed at any time by clicking either of the eyedropper cursor buttons in the Info palette (**Figure 3.14**).

   ▲ The x and y coordinates of the pointer, and the starting x and y coordinates of a selection or layer, along with the change in distance as you move the pointer over your image (**Figure 3.15**).

   ▲ The width and height of a selection or shape and the values relating to transformations, such as the percentage of scale, angle of rotation, and skew (which distorts a selection along the horizontal or vertical axis) (**Figure 3.16**).

✔ Tip

■ It's usually quicker to change units of measure using the Info palette rather than by using the Preferences menu.

To display different Info palette options:

1. Click the More button on the Info palette to open the palette menu, and then choose Palette Options (**Figure 3.17**).

2. Use the drop-down menus in the top three areas of the dialog to change the color and unit options you would like the palette to display (**Figure 3.18**).

3. In the Status Information area of the dialog, click the check box next to the options you would like the palette to display (**Figure 3.19**).

    Here are descriptions of some of the most useful options:

    ▲ **Document Sizes** displays information relating to the file's size. The first number represents the approximate size of the file if flattened (all layers combined into one) and saved. The second number represents the current file size, with layers.

    ▲ **Document Profile** displays the color mode of the image.

    ▲ **Document Dimensions** displays the width and height of the image.

    ▲ **Scratch Sizes** displays the amount of memory needed to process the image. The first number represents the memory currently used to display all open images. The second number represents the total available RAM. If you think you're running into memory problems and need to add more RAM to your computer, viewing this information will help you evaluate the problem.

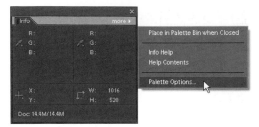

Figure 3.17 Access Palette Options from the Info palette's More menu.

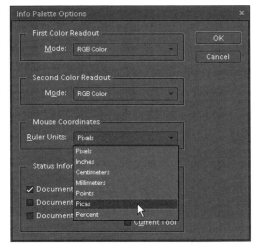

Figure 3.18 You can control what type of information will be displayed for color modes and for units of measurement.

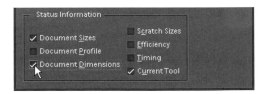

Figure 3.19 The Info palette can display the status for up to seven different types of information, all at the same time.

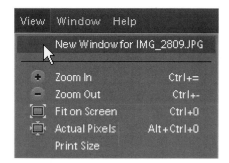

Figure 3.20 You can open multiple windows of the same image from the View menu.

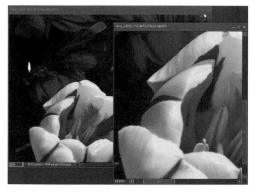

Figure 3.21 Multiple image views let you work on a detailed area while at the same time allowing you to see how the changes affect the overall image.

Opening and Arranging Multiple Views

You can open multiple windows with different images, or, if you prefer, you can open multiple views of the same image. This is a handy way to work on a detailed area of your image while viewing the full-sized version of the image at the same time. It's especially useful when you're doing touch-up work, such as correcting red eye or erasing a blemish in a photo.

To open multiple views of an image:

1. From the View menu, choose New Window for *the name of current file* (**Figure 3.20**).

2. Drag the title bar to move the additional window(s) as necessary to view them simultaneously.

   You can set different levels of magnification for each window to see both details and the big picture at the same time (**Figure 3.21**).

To arrange multiple views:

Do one of the following:

◆ To create cascading, overlapping windows from the upper left to the lower right of your screen, from the Window menu, choose Images > Cascade (**Figure 3.22**).

◆ To display windows stacked, from the Window menu, choose Images > Tile (**Figure 3.23**).

To close multiple view windows:

Do one of the following:

◆ To close a single window, click the close button on that window's title bar.

◆ To close all document windows, from the File menu, choose Close All or press Alt+Ctrl+W.

✔ Tips

■ To quickly switch from one open window to another, press Ctrl+Tab.

■ When you're working on a zoomed-in image, it's easy to get lost. From the Window menu, choose Images > Match Zoom to set all open windows to the same zoom level. Or, choose Images > Match Location to make the same visible pixels appear in all windows. That's a quicker option than scrolling around looking for a match, or using the Navigator palette.

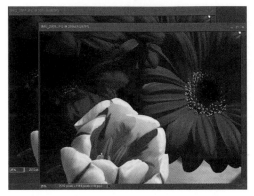

Figure 3.22 Cascading windows overlap from the upper left to the lower right. They allow you to keep multiple windows open at once, without cluttering the work space.

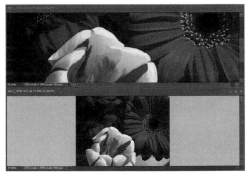

Figure 3.23 Tiled windows are arranged in a stack, from top to bottom.

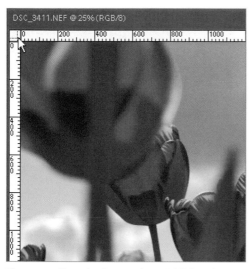

Figure 3.24 The rulers' zero point establishes the origin of the rulers.

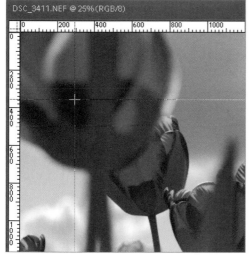

Figure 3.25 Drag the zero point to a new location anywhere in the document window.

Using Rulers

Customizable rulers, along the top and left sides of the document window, can help you scale and position graphics and selections. The rulers are helpful if you are combining photos with text (in a greeting card, for example) and want to be precise in placing and aligning the various elements. Interactive tick marks in both rulers provide constant feedback, displaying the position of any tool or pointer as you move it through the window. You can also change the ruler origin, also known as the *zero point*, to measure different parts of your image.

To show or hide the rulers:

◆ From the View menu, choose Rulers to turn the rulers on and off, or press Shift+Ctrl+R.

To change the zero point:

1. Place the pointer over the zero point crosshairs in the upper-left corner of the document window (**Figure 3.24**).

2. Drag the zero point to a new position in the document window.

   As you drag, a set of crosshairs appears, indicating the new position of the zero point (**Figure 3.25**).

3. Release the mouse button to set the new zero point.

To change the units of measure:

◆ Right-click on either ruler. A contextual menu appears, from which you can choose a new measurement unit.

✔ Tip

■ To reset the zero point to its original location, double-click the zero point crosshairs in the upper-left corner of the document window.

USING RULERS

Setting Up the Grid

The nonprinting, customizable grid appears as an overlay across the entire document window. As with the rulers, it can be used for scaling and positioning, but it can be especially helpful for maintaining symmetry in your layout and design, or for occasions when you'd like objects to snap to specific points in the window.

To show or hide the grid:

◆ From the View menu, choose Grid to turn the grid on and off (**Figure 3.26**).

To change the grid settings:

1. From the Edit menu, choose Preferences > Grid to open the Grid Preferences dialog.

2. From the Color drop-down menu, choose a preset grid color, or choose Custom (**Figure 3.27**).

   Choosing Custom displays the Color Picker, where you can select a custom grid color.

3. From the Style drop-down menu, choose a line style for the major grid lines (**Figure 3.28**).

4. In the Gridline every drop-down menu, choose a unit of measure; then enter a number in the accompanying field to define the spacing of the major grid lines.

5. In the Subdivisions field, enter a number to define the frequency of minor grid lines (**Figure 3.29**).

6. Click OK.

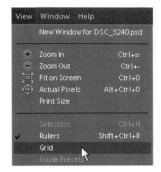

Figure 3.26 Activate the document grid by choosing Grid from the View menu.

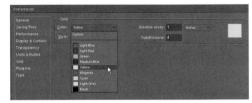

Figure 3.27 Choose a grid color from the list of preset colors or create a custom color.

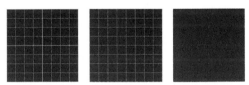

Figure 3.28 Examples of grid line styles.

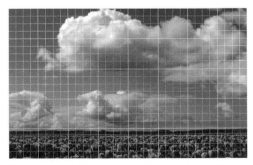

Figure 3.29 This figure shows a document grid with major grid lines set every inch, subdivided by four minor grid lines.

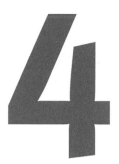

QUICK FIX EDITS

As you'll discover in the rest of the book, Photoshop Elements is a sophisticated image editor, enabling anyone to make photo corrections that would have been absurdly difficult years ago. But sometimes you don't want to be an image expert. Let the computer do the work for you, analyzing photos and correcting them automatically.

Elements offers a couple ways to get started. In the Organizer, the Fix pane provides one-click automatic fixes, which may be all you need. In the Editor, the Quick pane offers sliders for making common adjustments.

When you don't want to mess with the particulars, or when you know that a photo needs just a bit of tweaking but you want a bit more control over the adjustments, turn to the Quick Fix features. You can experiment on your photo—ranging from slight tonal changes to radical tints and lighting adjustments—and then undo those changes if they seemed better in your mind's eye than on the screen.

The concepts behind the tools in Quick Fix, such as adjusting levels and sharpening, are dealt with later in the book. Use this chapter as a jumping-off point.

Making Quick Fix Edits

When you want Elements to take over and make corrections according to its analysis of a photo, the speediest method is directly in the Organizer.

To edit photos in the Fix pane:

1. In the Organizer, select a photo to edit.

2. Click the Fix tab to view the Fix pane (**Figure 4.1**).

3. Click a button to apply an automatic fix. For example, if the color of your photo seems off, clicking the Auto Color button makes Elements examine the color values and change them without any additional input from you.

   If you're working on a RAW image file, Elements asks you to choose a file format that the program can edit directly; the changes are then applied to a copy of the original.

Using the Quick Fix editor

Quick Fix is a component of the Editor workspace and gives you a bit more control than the buttons in the Fix pane. The interface is simple and straightforward, with a few options to preview your changes easily.

To edit photos in Quick Fix:

1. In the Organizer, select one or more photo thumbnails.

2. From the Editor drop-down menu above the Organize bin, choose Quick Fix. Or, right-click a photo and choose Quick Fix from the contextual menu. You can also click the Quick Fix button at the bottom of the Fix pane. (Clearly, Adobe wants to make sure you can get to the Quick Fix editor!) The Quick Fix workspace opens (**Figure 4.2**).

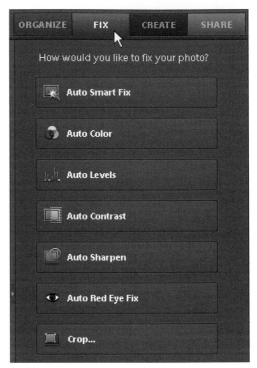

Figure 4.1 The Fix pane includes automatic tools for correcting common aspects of photos.

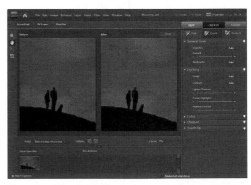

Figure 4.2 The Quick Fix workspace includes your image and a set of common photo manipulations.

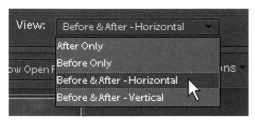

Figure 4.3 The Before and After options offer split-screen views of how fixes are affecting the photo.

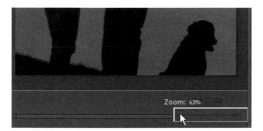

Figure 4.4 Use the Zoom field or slider to view the photo close-up.

To set view options:

◆ From the View menu located below the photo, choose whether you want to see the end result (After Only), the original (Before Only), or a comparison layout (the two Before and After options) (**Figure 4.3**).

◆ Use the Zoom field and slider to specify how zoomed-in you want to be (**Figure 4.4**). In the Before and After views, the zoom level applies to both versions.

When the Zoom or Hand tool is active, you can also click the Actual Pixels, Fit Screen, or Print Size buttons to switch to those zoom levels.

◆ If Elements did not rotate your image correctly during import (or if you just prefer a skewed worldview), click the Rotate buttons to turn it clockwise or counter-clockwise in 90-degree increments.

Walk Through Adjustments with Guided Edit Mode

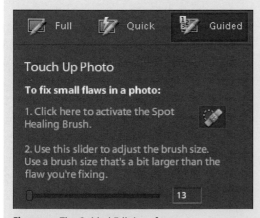

Figure 4.5 The Guided Edit interface.

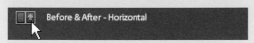

Figure 4.6 Set an editing layout with one click.

If you want to start with a little more hand-holding than what's offered by Quick Fix, try the Guided Edit mode; access it by clicking the Guided button in the Edit pane. Geared toward new users, this mode gives you step-by-step instruction on performing common editing tasks (**Figure 4.5**).

Click the View icon (**Figure 4.6**) to display comparative layouts.

When you've accomplished each step, click the Done button to apply the changes, or click Cancel to discard them. You can also click the Reset button that appears in each category to go back to the state before you applied those particular edits if you want to try a different setting.

The Guide for Editing a Photo (under the Guided Activities heading) walks you through all of the edit steps.

MAKING QUICK FIX EDITS

Applying Quick Fixes

The following tools perform common image correction tasks, but we want to start with the most important command first: Reset.

To reset and undo changes:

◆ After making an adjustment using the tools described in this chapter, click the Cancel button that appears in the tool's title bar (**Figure 4.7**).

◆ Choose Undo from the Edit menu to undo the previous command.

◆ If you've made several edits and want to revert to the original image, click the Reset button (**Figure 4.8**). This removes any Quick Fix adjustments.

To crop the image:

1. Select the Crop tool from the toolbar.

2. In the image's After version, drag to select the area you wish to keep (**Figure 4.9**).

3. Click the Commit button (the check mark) that appears outside the selection to apply the crop.

To remove red eye:

◆ In the General Fixes area, click the Auto button next to Red Eye Fix.

Or

1. Select the Red Eye Removal tool from the toolbar.

2. In the After version, drag a selection around the red-eye area. The fix applies when you release the mouse button.

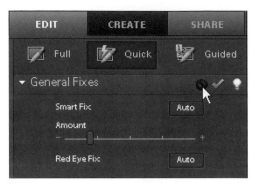

Figure 4.7 Clicking the Cancel button restores the image to the state before you made the adjustment(s).

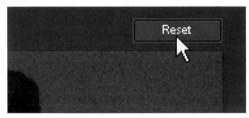

Figure 4.8 The Reset button removes all fixes made since you opened or saved the image.

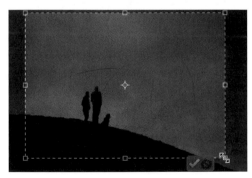

Figure 4.9 Drag a selection using the Crop tool to keep only that area and discard the rest of the image.

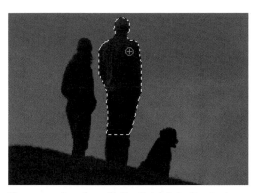

Figure 4.10 Drawing with the Quick Selection tool creates a selection based on that area.

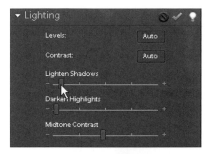

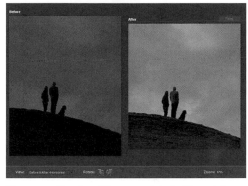

Figure 4.11 Use the sliders associated with each type of fix to adjust the After image.

To select areas for applying edits:

1. Select the Quick Selection tool from the toolbar.

2. Draw within an area that you want to select. Elements makes a selection based on the colors of the pixels you drew upon (**Figure 4.10**).

To apply lighting, color, and sharpening fixes:

1. To apply fixes to a specific area of the image, use the Quick Selection tool to select an active area. Otherwise, skip to step 2.

2. Click the Auto button for one or more fixes in the General Fixes, Lighting, Color, or Sharpen panes.

3. Drag the sliders for specific adjustments (such as Lighten Shadows) to fine-tune the settings (**Figure 4.11**).

4. Click the Commit button (the check mark) to apply the fixes.

To apply all edits and return to the Organizer:

1. Choose File > Close, or click the close box in the upper-right corner of the workspace.

2. When prompted, save your changes.

✔ Tips

- See Chapter 6 for details on the settings offered by each tool.

- It never hurts to see what Elements thinks of your image by playing with the Smart Fix slider in the General Fixes area. Smart Fix adjusts lighting, color, and sharpening based on its algorithms. In some cases, this may be the only edit you need.

Making Touch Up Edits

Elements 7 adds a few new tools to the Quick Fix editor that are designed to easily fix some specific situations. In the Quick pane, expand the Touch Up heading to view four icons: Red Eye Removal Tool, Whiten Teeth, Make Dull Skies Blue, and Black and White–High Contrast (**Figure 4.12**).

Unlike the other Quick Fix edits, which apply their adjustments to the entire image or to an area that you first specify using the Quick Selection tool, these Touch Up tools perform the selection and apply the edit in one step.

To make a Touch Up edit:

1. With a photo active in the Editor, click one of the Touch Up tool icons to select it.

2. Click and drag to define the area to be edited; for example, with the Make Dull Skies Blue tool active, drag in the sky area.

   Elements makes a selection and applies the effect (**Figure 4.13**).

3. Adjust the affected area using the selection tools (**Figure 4.14**).

✔ Tips

- You can apply multiple Touch Up tool edits to the same image. When you click an icon, any adjustment you've already made is highlighted for further editing.

- The Touch Up tools are actually simplified versions of edits that the Smart Brush makes. You can apply one and then edit it further in the Full Edit mode later. See Chapter 6 for more information.

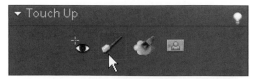

Figure 4.12 New Touch Up tools.

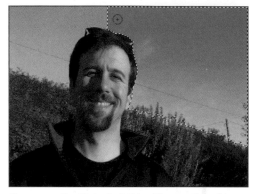

Figure 4.13 The Make Dull Skies Blue applies a blue gradient to the selected area.

New selection   *Add to selection*   *Subtract from selection*

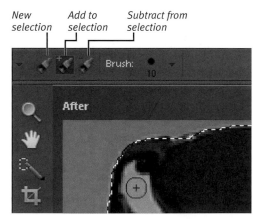

Figure 4.14 Use the selection tools to refine where the effect is applied.

Run Automated Actions with the Guided Edit Action Player

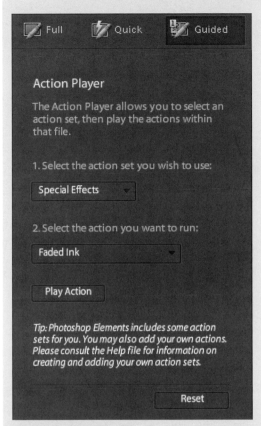

Figure 4.15 The Action Player can run automated combinations of adjustments.

Another new addition to Photoshop Elements 7 is the Action Player, a feature found in the Guided Edit pane for applying preset effects such as creating captions or applying combination edits like changing a photo's colors to sepia and adding grain to the image. In the Guided Edit pane, click Action Player under Automated Actions to reveal a set of automated effects that ship with Elements (**Figure 4.15**). Choose a set, pick a specific action, and then click the Play Action button.

That's not the whole story, though. The Action Player can run any action created in Photoshop CS. So, for example, if a photographer friend of yours uses Photoshop extensively and has created an action that resizes an image and adds a border and photo credit, you could run that action in Elements instead of performing each step. (Elements can currently only *run* actions, not create them.)

Adding a new action isn't straightforward, however. Here's how to do it:

Take a Photoshop action file—it ends in .atn—and place it in the following directory on your hard disk (each backslash represents a folder name; you may need to specify that hidden folders are visible in the Folder Options dialog accessed from the Tools menu in Windows Explorer):

```
\Documents and Settings\All Users\Application Data\Adobe\Photoshop Elements\7.0\
Locale\en_US\Workflow Panels\actions
```

Relaunch Elements, go to the Guided Edit pane of the Editor, and you'll see the action set appear in the first drop-down menu.

MAKING
SELECTIONS

Photoshop Elements offers many sophisticated options for enhancing and retouching your image. Those options include colors, filters, resizing tools, vignettes, and all sorts of special effects. But before you can start tinkering, you need to learn how to make selections. Once you select a specific area of an image, you can change its color, copy and paste it into another image, or change its size and rotation.

You can also use selections to create a protective mask for specific portions of an image. It's easy to select one area of an image, apply a change to the rest, and keep the selected area untouched.

In this chapter, you learn about all of Photoshop Elements' selection tools and when to choose one tool over another. You also learn how to use these tools in tandem to make the quickest and most accurate selections, depending on your specific needs.

About the Selection Tools

Often, you'll want to make changes and adjustments to just a portion of an image. For example, you may want to eliminate a distracting element in your photo, change the color of a specific item in a photograph, or adjust the brightness of the background. Photoshop Elements gives you a wide variety of selection tools from which to choose.

The selection tools are all grouped near each other at the top of the toolbar (**Figure 5.1**). You make rectangular and elliptical selections using the marquee tools. When you select a marquee tool, the selection area is indicated by a row of moving dots, like the sign outside an old-style movie theater—hence the name (**Figure 5.2**).

You select free-form, or irregular, areas using the lasso tools (**Figure 5.3**). These include the regular Lasso tool; the Polygonal Lasso, which is great for selecting areas that include straight sections; and the Magnetic Lasso, which can select the edge of an area based on its color or tonal values.

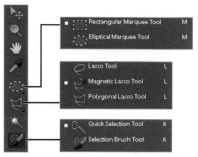

Figure 5.1 Access additional tools by clicking and holding on a menu item or right-clicking the selection tools in the toolbar.

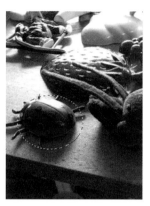

Figure 5.2 A selection border is represented by a row of moving dots, called a marquee.

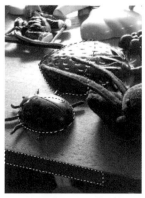

Figure 5.3 Each of the three lasso tools works best in a particular situation.

ABOUT THE SELECTION TOOLS

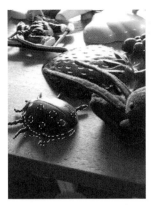

Figure 5.4 The Magic Wand lets you select areas based on color.

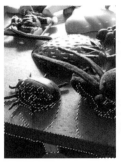 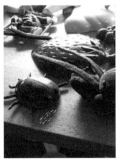

Figure 5.5 The Magic Wand also lets you set the tolerance, or range of colors selected.

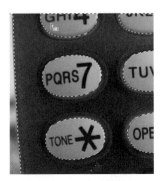

Figure 5.6 Here, the black background was selected with the Magic Wand, and then the selection was inverted to capture the buttons.

The Magic Wand lets you select areas with the same (or similar) color or tonal value. This tool is probably the most difficult to master, but with a little practice it allows you to make selections that would be difficult to make with any of the marquee or lasso tools (**Figure 5.4**). For example, if your photo displays a field of yellow poppies, you can select all of them at once, rather than having to select each flower individually.

The selection tools work well on their own, but often the area you want to edit includes all sorts of angles and edges. In these situations, you can use the tools in combination to expand and change the selection area.

You can also expand or contract a selection area using the same tool with different settings. For example, the Magic Wand allows you to alter the range of your selection by adjusting the tolerance using the options bar before making a selection (**Figure 5.5**).

When a photo includes an object surrounded by a large background area, it's often easier to select the background and then invert the selection to select the object. Once the selection is made, you can copy and paste it into another composition or make any other changes (**Figure 5.6**).

continues on next page

ABOUT THE SELECTION TOOLS

With a selection area made, you can add to or subtract from the selection. Using one tool to make your initial selection and then editing the selection area using another selection tool is often easier than trying to make a perfect selection with a single tool all at once (**Figure 5.7**).

The Selection Brush allows you to make selections simply by dragging across any area or object in an image. Like the lasso tools, it works especially well for selecting irregular areas. Unlike the other selection tools, you actually "paint on" the selection using any of the brush shapes available in Elements' vast collection of brush sets (**Figure 5.8**). This method of selection affords you great control and flexibility, although you need quite a bit of dexterity.

The Quick Selection tool works in much the same way as the Magic Wand tool—selecting areas based on similar color and tonal values. What distinguishes the Quick Selection tool from the other selection tools is the method you use to make the selections. By *painting* a series of scribbles and dots on the image, Photoshop Elements creates a selection area based on the color or tonal values below the painted marks (**Figure 5.9**). Selections are additive: As you paint, the selection grows larger; use other selection tools to shrink the area.

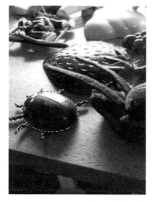

Figure 5.7
Here, the Elliptical Marquee tool was used to select the ladybug's main body, and then the Magic Wand tool was used to add the legs and head.

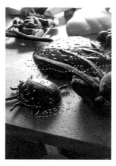 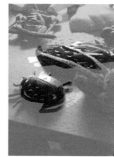

Figure 5.8 The Selection Brush can be used in either Selection or Mask mode, selectable from the Mode menu in the options bar.

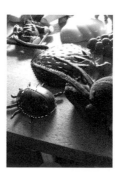 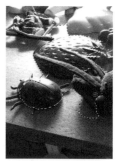

Figure 5.9 When you "paint" through an area with the Quick Selection tool (a small area painted at left, and a larger area at right), any pixels similar in color or tonal value to those you brush over will be selected.

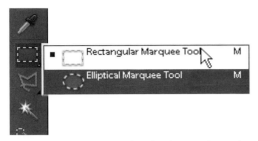

Figure 5.10 Simple geometric selections can be made with the Rectangular or Elliptical Marquee Tool.

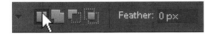

Figure 5.11 The default setting on the options bar creates a new selection.

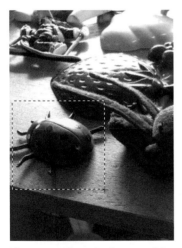

Figure 5.12 After selecting one of the marquee tools, just click and drag to make a selection.

Using the Marquee Tools

The Rectangular and Elliptical Marquee tools are the easiest and most straightforward selection tools to use. With these tools, you can select rectangular or oval (elliptical) areas. You can also select a perfectly square or circular area. You'll often want to move a selection area (or marquee) to align the area perfectly, and Photoshop Elements offers a couple of quick and simple ways to make these kinds of adjustments.

To make a rectangular or elliptical selection:

1. From the toolbar, choose either the Rectangular Marquee tool (or press the M key) or Elliptical Marquee tool (M again) (**Figure 5.10**).

   The default setting on the options bar creates a new selection (**Figure 5.11**). See "Adjusting Selections" later in this chapter for more information on other options when creating selections.

2. Click and drag to choose the selection area (**Figure 5.12**).

   continues on next page

✔ Tips

- You can create a perfect circle or square selection using the marquee tools by holding down the Shift key as you drag (**Figure 5.13**).

- You can draw the marquee from the center outward by holding down the Alt key (**Figure 5.14**).

- To toggle between marquee tools, press the M key. In fact, this works for any tool with hidden tools—simply press the keyboard shortcut key repeatedly to toggle through all of the choices.

- To select all pixels on a layer, press Ctrl+A. This creates a selection around your entire image window, and is useful when you want to make universal color corrections or add special effects to your image.

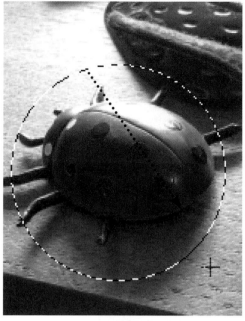

Figure 5.13 To select a perfect square or circle, hold down the Shift key while dragging.

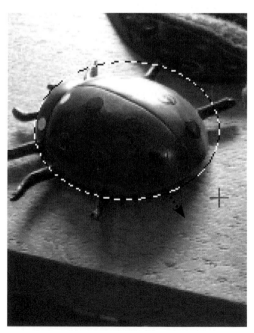

Figure 5.14 To draw a selection from the center outward, hold down the Alt key.

USING THE MARQUEE TOOLS

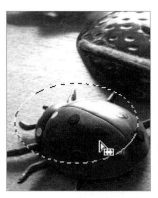

Figure 5.15
To move the selection area, position the pointer within the selection boundary.

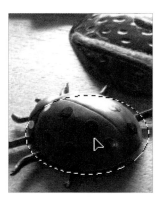

Figure 5.16
Drag the selection border to a new location.

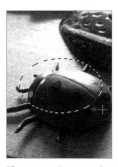
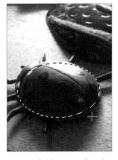

Figure 5.17 To move the marquee during a selection, just press the spacebar while holding down the mouse button and adjust the border's location.

To reposition a selection border:

1. Once you've made a selection, with the New selection icon active, position the pointer anywhere inside the selection area.

   The pointer becomes an arrow with a small selection icon next to it (**Figure 5.15**). Note that if the Add to, Subtract from, or Intersect with icons are active, the pointer indicates that choice and the selection can't be moved.

2. Click and drag to reposition the selection area.

   The pointer arrow changes to solid black as you move the selection (**Figure 5.16**).

To reposition a selection border while making a selection:

1. Click and drag to create the selection area.

2. While keeping the mouse button pressed, press the spacebar. (The pointer arrow shows a set of crosshairs whether or not the spacebar is pressed.)

3. Move the selection area to the desired location and release the spacebar and mouse button (**Figure 5.17**).

✔ Tip

■ You can use the arrow keys on your keyboard to move a selection in 1-pixel increments. Holding the Shift key at the same time moves the selection in 10-pixel increments.

USING THE MARQUEE TOOLS

Selecting Areas Using the Lasso Tools

Use the lasso tools to select areas with irregular shapes. The standard Lasso tool lets you draw or trace around an object or area freehand, much as you would draw with a pencil. This method takes patience, but with practice you can use the Lasso tool to make accurate selections.

The Polygonal Lasso tool is useful for selecting areas that include straight edges; you can toggle between the freehand and straight-edge mode when your object includes both irregular and straight edges.

With the Magnetic Lasso tool, you trace around an area, and the tool automatically "snaps" the selection border to the edge of an area based on differences in color and tonal values in adjoining pixels. For this reason, the tool usually works best on high-contrast images. Experiment with the settings on the options bar to get the best results.

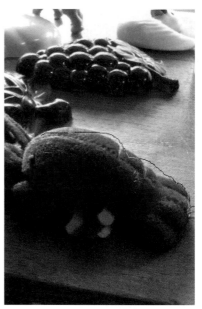

Figure 5.18 Select any area by tracing around it with the Lasso tool.

To select with the Lasso tool:

1. From the toolbar, choose the Lasso tool (or press L).

2. Keeping the mouse button pressed, drag all the way around an object or area in your image (**Figure 5.18**).

   When you release the mouse button, the open ends of the selection automatically join together (**Figure 5.19**).

✔ Tips

- To keep a selection active without keeping the mouse button pressed, hold down the Alt key before releasing the button.

- Use the Alt key to switch between the Polygonal Lasso and regular Lasso tools.

- Making lasso selections is much easier with a pressure-sensitive drawing tablet.

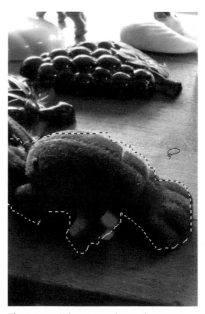

Figure 5.19 When you release the mouse button, the ends of the selection automatically join together.

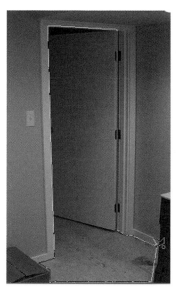

Figure 5.20 The Polygonal Lasso tool creates a border made of straight-line segments.

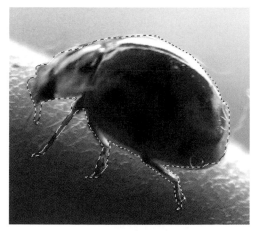

Figure 5.21 For selection with both freehand and straight lines, press Alt to switch between the regular Lasso and Polygonal Lasso tools.

To select with the Polygonal Lasso tool:

1. From the toolbar, choose the Polygonal Lasso tool (L).

2. Click points along the edge of the object to create straight-line segments for your selection (**Figure 5.20**).

3. Click back at the original starting point to join the open ends of the selection.

   You can also Ctrl+click or double-click anywhere on the image to close up the selection.

✔ Tips

- Be warned: The Polygonal Lasso tool can sometimes slip out of your control, creating line segments where you don't want them to appear. If you make a mistake or change your mind about a line selection, you can erase line-segment selections as long as you haven't closed the selection. Just press the Backspace or Delete key, and one by one the segments will be removed, starting with the most recent one.

- To use both the regular Lasso and Polygonal Lasso tools together, select the Lasso tool, and hold down the Alt key before releasing the mouse button. Alt-click creates new polygonal segments, while Alt-drag lets you draw freehand (**Figure 5.21**).

To select using the Magnetic Lasso tool:

1. From the toolbar, choose the Magnetic Lasso tool (L).

2. Click on or very close to the edge of the area you want to trace to establish the first fastening point (**Figure 5.22**).

3. Move the pointer along the edge you want to trace.

   The Magnetic Lasso tool traces along the selection border to the best of its ability and places additional fastening points along the way (**Figure 5.23**).

4. If the selection line jumps to the edge of the wrong object, place the pointer over the correct edge and click the mouse button to establish an accurate fastening point (**Figure 5.24**).

5. To close the selection line, click the starting point, or *do one of the following:*

   ▲ Ctrl+click.

   ▲ Double-click anywhere on the image.

   ▲ Press Enter.

✔ Tip

■ Press Alt+click to use the Polygonal Lasso tool while the Magnetic Lasso tool is selected. Press Alt+drag to use the Lasso tool.

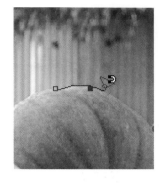

Figure 5.22
To start a selection border with the Magnetic Lasso tool, click the edge of the area you want to trace to create the first fastening point.

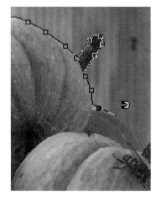

Figure 5.23
As you trace with the Magnetic Lasso tool, it places additional fastening points along the edge of the selection.

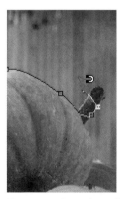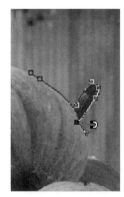

Figure 5.24 Sometimes the Magnetic Lasso tool jumps to another edge (left). To correct the path, just click the correct edge to bring the border back to the right location (right).

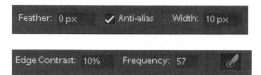

Figure 5.25 Look at the options bar while the Magnetic Lasso tool is selected; you'll find options that are unique to this tool.

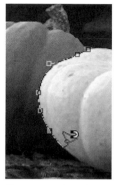
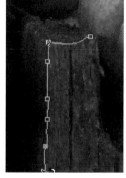

Figure 5.26 The Edge Contrast setting makes it easy to find an edge in high contrast areas (left, set to 80 percent) and low contrast areas (right, set to 5 percent).

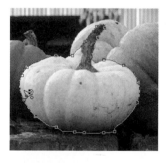

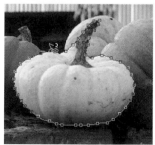

Figure 5.27
The Frequency option lets you determine how closely the fastening points are spaced: top is set to 7; bottom is set to 70.

To set Magnetic Lasso tool options:

1. Select the Magnetic Lasso tool.

2. Set any of the options visible on the options bar (**Figure 5.25**).

   ▲ Width sets the size of the area the tool scans as it traces the selection line.

   You can set this option to a value from 1 to 40 pixels. Wide widths work well for high-contrast images, and narrow widths work well for images with subtle contrast and small shapes that are close to each other.

   ▲ Edge Contrast establishes the amount of contrast required between shapes for an edge to be recognized and traced (**Figure 5.26**).

   This option is indicated by the percentage of contrast (from 1 to 100 percent). Try higher numbers for high-contrast images, and lower numbers for flatter, low-contrast images (just as with the Width option).

   ▲ Frequency specifies how close the fastening points are to each other.

   For Frequency, enter a number from 1 to 100. In general, you will need to use higher frequency values when the edge is very ragged or irregular (**Figure 5.27**).

   ▲ If you are using a stylus tablet, you can select Stylus Pressure to increase the stylus pressure and so decrease the edge width. That's right: With the button enabled, pressing harder on the stylus will yield a smaller, more precise edge.

SELECTING AREAS USING THE LASSO TOOLS

Making Selections by Color

The Magic Wand and Quick Selection tools allow you to make selections based on a selected color or tonal value. These tools can seem truly magical—or wildly unpredictable—at first. When you select an area of an image with either tool, it selects all of the pixels within a color or tonal range close to the pixel you've initially selected.

The Magic Wand tool provides options for setting tolerance (the range of color or tonal values included in the selection around the pixel where you're clicking or dragging), anti-aliasing (smoothing), contiguousness (whether the pixels need to be connected to that first selected pixel), and whether to include all layers in the selection.

The Grow and Similar commands, found in the Select menu, can be used with the Magic Wand to expand the selection area. The Grow command expands the range of adjacent pixels, and the Similar command expands the selection based on the pixel colors.

Although the Quick Selection tool doesn't offer the options available with the Magic Wand, it will often make an accurate selection based solely on the areas you mark with the brush.

To use the Magic Wand:

1. From the toolbar, choose the Magic Wand (or press W) (**Figure 5.28**).

2. On the options bar, choose whether to create a new selection, add to or subtract from an existing selection, or intersect with an existing selection (**Figure 5.29**). The default setting on the options bar creates a new selection.

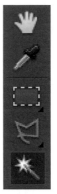

Figure 5.28
The Magic Wand icon is located just below the Lasso tool on the toolbar.

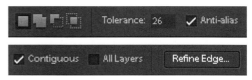

Figure 5.29 The Magic Wand options bar.

MEETING AGENDA

Date Scheduled _____ Time _____

Title _____

Purpose _____

Results Desired _____

Location _____

	SCHEDULED			ACTUAL			MEETING COST
Start	Stop	Total Hrs.	Start	Stop	Total Hrs.		

Persons Attending	✓	Value Per Hr.	Total
1			
2			
3			
4			
5			
6			
7			
8			
9			
10			

Items To Be Discussed	(Sequence→) ✓
1	
2	
3	
4	
5	
6	
7	
8	
9	
10	

Material Needed (Number each item)	Person Responsible
1	

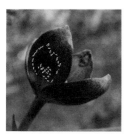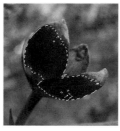

Figure 5.30 The Tolerance setting determines how wide a range of colors is included in the selection.

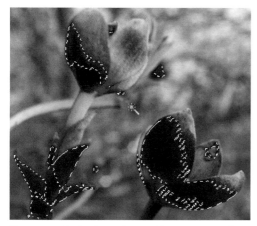

Figure 5.31 Uncheck Contiguous if you want to select similar colors throughout the image.

3. Select the tolerance (a range of pixels from 0 to 255) to establish how wide a tonal range you want to include in your selection.

The default tolerance level is 32 pixels. To pick colors or tonal values very close to the selected pixel, choose lower numbers. Entering higher numbers results in a wider selection of colors (**Figure 5.30**).

4. If you want your selection to have a smooth edge, select Anti-alias.

5. If you want only pixels adjacent to the original pixel to be included in the selection, select Contiguous (**Figure 5.31**).

6. If you want the selection to include pixels on all the layers, select All Layers (see Chapter 8 for more on working with layers).

7. Click a color or tone in the image. Based on your settings, a group or range of pixels will be selected.

✔ Tip

■ When you make your original selection with the Magic Wand, it takes a color "sample" from your image. You can adjust the sample size with the Eyedropper tool. The options bar lets you sample 1 pixel, or the average of a 3-by-3-pixel area (9 pixels total), or a 5-by-5-pixel area (25 pixels total). Whichever option is active determines how the Magic Wand establishes the sample color.

To expand the selection area:

1. From the toolbar, choose the Magic Wand tool.

2. Click a color or tonal value in the image.

3. From the Select menu, choose Grow to expand the selection of adjacent pixels.

   Each time you select Grow, the selection is expanded by the tolerance amount displayed on the Magic Wand options bar (**Figure 5.32**).

To include similar colors:

1. From the toolbar, choose the Magic Wand.

2. Click a color or tonal value in the image.

3. From the Select menu, choose Similar to expand the selection of nonadjacent pixels.

   The selection is extended through the image to similar tonal values using the tolerance amount set on the Magic Wand options bar (**Figure 5.33**).

✔ Tip

- You can also access the Grow command by right-clicking after you have made a selection with the Magic Wand. A contextual menu appears in the image window, which includes the Grow and Similar commands plus a number of other useful selection options (**Figure 5.34**).

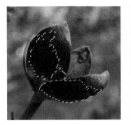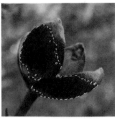

Figure 5.32 Making a selection at left covers just part of the desired image; choose Grow to expand to adjacent similarly colored areas.

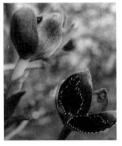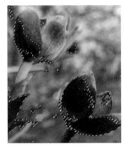

Figure 5.33 Choose Select > Similar to add pixels to your selection throughout the image.

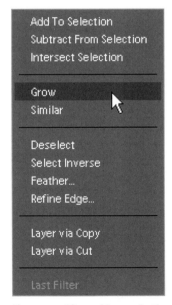

Figure 5.34 After making a selection with the Magic Wand tool, right-click to access selection options.

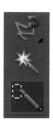

Figure 5.35
The Quick Selection tool.

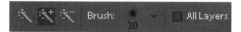

Figure 5.36 Buttons in the options bar supply different functions for the Quick Selection tool.

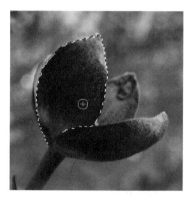

Figure 5.37 Painting through an area with the Quick Selection tool creates a new selection.

To use the Quick Selection tool:

1. From the toolbar, choose the Quick Selection tool (or press A) (**Figure 5.35**).

2. In the options bar, choose a brush size (**Figure 5.36**).

3. In the image window, click, or click and drag in the area where you want to make your selection. As you drag, the selection is created (**Figure 5.37**).

4. To add to the selection, drag an area outside the current selection (**Figure 5.38**).

5. To subtract from a selection, choose the Subtract from Selection button or hold down the Alt key, and then click (or drag) inside the selection area (**Figure 5.39**).

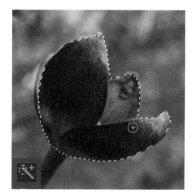

Figure 5.38 To add to a selection, paint in additional brushstrokes (Add to Selection is chosen by default).

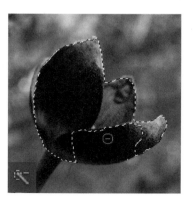

Figure 5.39 Use the Subtract from Selection button in the options bar to delete a portion of a selection.

Using the Selection Brush Tool

The Selection Brush tool lets you make a selection by painting over an error; it differs from the Quick Selection tool by selecting only the areas covered by the brush's "paint," instead of contiguous areas of similar tonal values.

The Selection Brush tool's options resemble those offered for the normal Brush tool. You can choose among a wide range of brush styles and sizes.

When you use the Selection Brush tool in the default Selection mode, simply click and drag through an area of your image to create a free-form, brushed selection. Unlike the other selection tools, the Selection Brush offers a Mask mode, which allows you to create a "protected" or unselected area. To work more easily with masked areas, you can control the opacity and color of the mask overlay. The two modes can be used together with great results. It's easier to make your initial selection in the default mode, and then switch to Mask mode to tune your selection.

To make a selection with the Selection Brush:

1. From the toolbar, choose the Selection Brush (or press A) (**Figure 5.40**).

2. The Mode menu on the options bar is set to Selection (**Figure 5.41**).

3. Choose a brush style and optionally choose values for the brush size and hardness (**Figure 5.42**).

    You can either enter values for the size and hardness, or drag the sliders (**Figure 5.43**) until you get the setting you want.

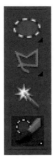

Figure 5.40
The Selection Brush.

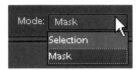

Figure 5.41 To make a selection, choose the Selection mode.

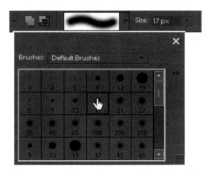

Figure 5.42 Choose from a wide variety of prebuilt brushes.

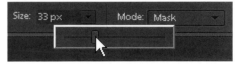

Figure 5.43 The brush size can be set from the options bar.

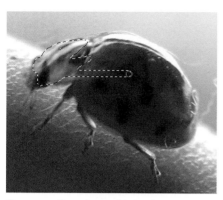

Figure 5.44 To make a selection, just "paint" over your image with the Selection Brush.

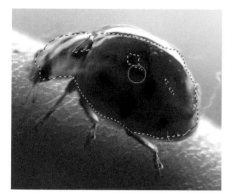

Figure 5.45 You can expand the selection by brushing around and through the original selection.

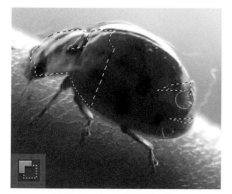

Figure 5.46 Use the Subtract from Selection button in the options bar to remove areas of your selection.

4. Drag the brush tool over your image to make a selection (**Figure 5.44**).

5. To expand your selection, brush on the edge of the selected area (**Figure 5.45**). To make a selection in another portion of your image, click and drag away from the original selection.

6. To subtract from your selection, choose the Subtract from Selection button in the options bar, and then click and drag through any portion of the selection (**Figure 5.46**).

✔ Tips

- Like other brushes, the Selection Brush tool works well with pressure-sensitive tablets that let you paint more naturally.

- A quick way to change the size of the Selection Brush is to press the bracket keys on your keyboard: [to reduce size and] to increase size.

USING THE SELECTION BRUSH TOOL

To make a mask with the Selection Brush:

1. Choose the Selection Brush tool.

2. From the Mode menu on the options bar, choose Mask (**Figure 5.47**).

3. Choose a brush style and optionally enter values for the brush size and hardness.

4. Set the overlay opacity with the slider, or enter a percentage in the text box (**Figure 5.48**).

5. Set the overlay color by clicking the Overlay Color box in the options bar, and then choose a color from the Color Picker.

   The default color is red, so if your selection area is also red it may be hard to see. Just choose a color that works best for each image.

6. Drag the brush tool over your image to make a mask (**Figure 5.49**).

   As soon as you select another tool, the mask overlay area changes to a selection border. The area is protected from any changes you apply to the image (**Figure 5.50**). If you want to modify the mask, select the Brush Selection tool again. The mask will automatically appear over the image, and you can continue to paint in additional masked areas.

✔ Tip

- The mask overlay is a very handy tool for inspecting your selections and can be used with any selection tool. Whenever you have an active selection, just click the Selection Brush tool and select the Mask option to see the masked area. When you're done viewing it in Mask mode, choose Selection from the Mode drop-down menu.

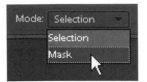

Figure 5.47 To make a mask, first select the Mask mode option.

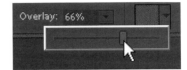

Figure 5.48 The opacity of your mask overlay can be set with the slider or entered into the text box.

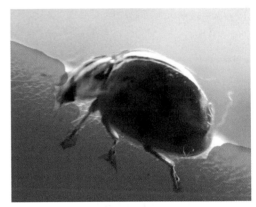

Figure 5.49 When you paint with the Mask option on, the area becomes filled with the mask overlay.

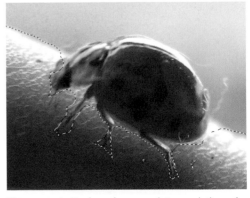

Figure 5.50 In Mask mode, you paint a mask through any areas that you *do not* want to be selected.

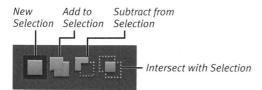

Figure 5.51 To add to the current selection, either click the Add to Selection icon on the options bar or hold down the Shift key while making another selection.

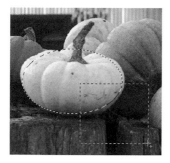

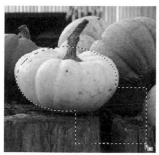

Figure 5.52 In this example, two selections are combined to form a single selection.

Adjusting Selections

You can probably tell by now that a little fine-tuning is needed to make selections just the way you want them. For example, imagine you're using the Magnetic Lasso tool to trace the outline of a face, but then realize you didn't include the ear in your selection. Rather than start again from scratch, you can add to or subtract from your selection until you've included every part of the image you want. Photoshop Elements even lets you select the intersection (or overlapping area) of two independent selections. This feature offers an effective solution for constructing interesting selection areas that would be difficult to create with a single selection tool.

To add to a selection:

1. Make a selection in your image with any of the selection tools.

2. With the selection still active, *do one of the following*:

   ▲ Using the same selection tool or after selecting another one, click the Add to Selection button (**Figure 5.51**) in the options bar.

   If the Add to Selection button is already highlighted, skip to step 3.

   ▲ Hold down the Shift key, and, if desired, select a different selection tool.

   A plus sign appears, indicating that you are adding to the current selection.

3. Make a new selection in your image. If you want to add to your existing selection, make sure your new selection overlaps the original. If you want to create an additional selection, make sure you click outside of your original selection. The new selection area is added to your first selection (**Figure 5.52**).

To subtract from a selection:

1. Make a selection with any of the selection tools.

2. With the selection still active, *do one of the following*:

   ▲ Select the Subtract from Selection button on the options bar, optionally choosing a different selection tool.

   ▲ Hold down the Alt key.

   A minus sign appears, indicating that you are subtracting from the current selection.

3. Drag the pointer through the area you want to subtract.

   The area you defined is removed from the selection (**Figure 5.53**).

To select the intersection of two selections:

1. Make a selection with any of the Marquee or Lasso selection tools.

2. With the selection still active, *do one of the following*:

   ▲ Select the Intersect with Selection button on the options bar and create a new selection that overlaps the current selection.

   ▲ Hold Alt+Shift and create a new selection that overlaps the current selection. An X appears, indicating that you are selecting an area of intersection.

3. A new selection area is formed based on the intersection of the two selections (**Figure 5.54**).

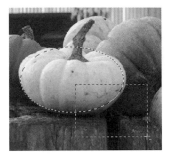

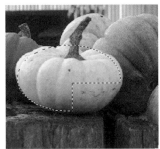

Figure 5.53 In this example, a pie-shaped cutout is left where the rectangle selection has been subtracted.

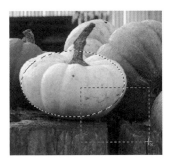

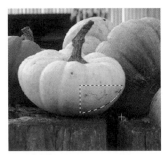

Figure 5.54 In this example, only the area of intersection remains.

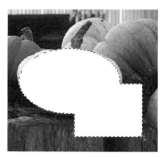

Figure 5.55 When you delete a selection, the selected area disappears, and your current background color shows through.

To deselect the current selection:

◆ From the Select menu, choose Deselect, or press Ctrl+D.

To reselect the last selection:

◆ Choose Select > Reselect, or press Shift+Ctrl+D.

To delete a selection:

Choose one of the following methods:

◆ From the menu bar, choose Edit > Cut, or press Ctrl+X.

◆ Press Backspace/Delete.

   When you delete a selection, the portion of the image within your selection disappears entirely, leaving a hole in your image (**Figure 5.55**). If you accidentally delete a selection, choose Undo from the Edit menu or press Ctrl+Z.

To hide a selection border:

◆ From the View menu, uncheck Selection, or press Ctrl+H.

   Sometimes, after you've made a selection, you want to hide the selection marquee while you edit the image; this prevents the selection border from obscuring your view. Be sure to press the same keyboard shortcut to display the selection once you're done—otherwise, you might lose track of it.

✔ Tip

■ You can *deselect* an entire selection at any time by pressing the Esc key.

ADJUSTING SELECTIONS

Softening the Edges of a Selection

Selections often work best when their edges are smooth, instead of hard. Anti-aliasing adds blended pixels to create a smooth edge instead of a stairstepped or jagged edge (**Figure 5.56**). Most selection tools offer an Anti-Alias check box in the options bar. That option is usually checked by default, and you almost always want to leave anti-aliasing enabled. When compositing images (combining several pieces into one), anti-aliasing smooths the border between elements.

Feathering blurs the edges of a selection. Set the amount of blurring on the options bar in the Feather box. Unlike anti-aliasing, which affects just the very edge of a selection, feathering creates a more dramatic, soft transition or halo effect around an image. Depending on the image selection, you may want to experiment with different feathering settings, because some detail is usually lost around the edges of a feathered selection.

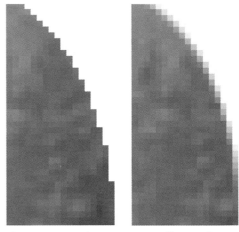

Figure 5.56 Anti-aliasing automatically smooths a selection edge by adding pixels that blend the color transition.

Refine Edge Combines Several Softening and Selection Tools

The Refine Edge dialog combines several softening and selection modification tools in one place (**Figure 5.57**). Refine Edge appears as a button in the options bar for several tools, but the dialog can be brought up via the Select menu for all selection tools as long as a selection has been made.

With the Preview button checked, changes are interactive as you combine Smooth, Feather, and Contract/Expand options. You can zoom in or out or pan the image.

The red Custom Overlay Color button provides a mask; double-click the button to set the overlay color.

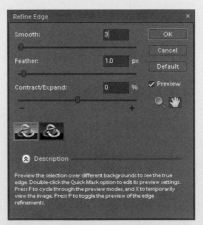

Figure 5.57 The Refine Edge dialog combines softening and selection options.

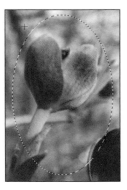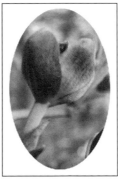

Figure 5.58 Select Anti-alias on the options bar before you make a selection to create a smooth edge, even on curved shapes.

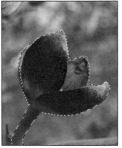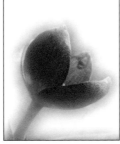

Figure 5.59 The dogwood blossom at left was highlighted through the Quick Selection tool, and then Inverse was chosen from the Select menu. A 25-pixel Feather was applied, and the background deleted to create the image at right.

To smooth jagged edges with anti-aliasing:

1. From the toolbar, choose any selection tool other than the Rectangular Marquee tool.

    The Rectangular Marquee tool's edges are composed of straight right angles, so no anti-aliasing is necessary. A rectangle selection's edge can still be softened with the Feather option.

    Anti-alias is checked by default on the options bar. If you unchecked the option, check it before making the selection.

2. Make a selection using the desired tool.

3. Cut or copy and then paste the selection into a new file.

    The resulting selection edge is automatically smoothed, with no jaggies (**Figure 5.58**).

To feather the edge of a selection:

1. From the toolbar, choose from any of the Marquee or Lasso tools.

2. On the options bar or in the Refine Edge dialog, select a value for the feather radius (from 0.1 to 250.0 pixels).

3. Make a selection.

    The resulting edge appears blurred, based on the number you entered for the Feather option (**Figure 5.59**).

✔ Tips

- You can apply feathering *after* you make a selection, unlike anti-aliasing. With your selection active, from the Select menu choose Feather or Refine Edge, and then enter a feather radius.

- You can also apply feathering effects to your image by applying the Vignette effect, available in the Effects palette. For more detail, see "Applying Filters and Effects" in Chapter 9.

Modifying Selection Borders

You can make subtle—or not so subtle—changes to a selection border with options found on the Select > Modify menu and in the Refine Edge dialog. The Border feature lets you change the width of the selection border. The Smooth command smooths out a jagged or irregular selection edge. To increase or reduce the size of a selection, use Expand or Contract. (In the Refine Edge dialog box, Expand/Contract is a slider from −100% to 100%.)

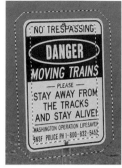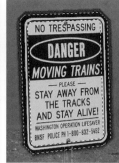

Figure 5.60 The Border command lets you control the width of a selection border. In this example, a 15-pixel border is selected at left, then filled with color at right.

To change the width of the border:

1. Make a selection in your image with any of the selection tools.

2. From the Select menu, choose Modify > Border or Refine Edge.

3. Enter a value for the border width.
   The selection border changes based on the number you enter (**Figure 5.60**).

To smooth the edge of a selection:

1. From the Select menu, choose Modify > Smooth or Refine Edge.

2. Enter a value for the radius of the smoothing effect.
   The radius values range from 1 to 100 and define how far away from the current edge the selection will move to create a new, smoother edge.

To expand or contract the selection area:

1. From the Select menu, choose Modify; then choose Expand or Contract.

2. Enter a value for the number of pixels you would like the selection to either grow (expand) or shrink (contract) (**Figure 5.61**).

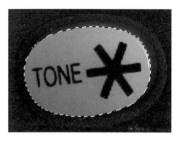

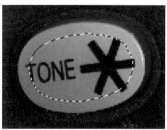

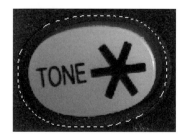

Figure 5.61 You can expand or contract the size of a selection border from the Modify menu.

FIXING AND RETOUCHING PHOTOS

How often have you thumbed through photo albums and found images you wished were better composed or lit more evenly? Or maybe you've sorted through shoeboxes from the attic, disappointed that time and age have taken their toll on those wonderful old photographs of your dad in his high school band uniform and your grandparents honeymooning at the lake. Until recently, there was no simple way to correct or repair photographs regardless of whether they were out of focus, water damaged, or poorly composed.

Happily, things have changed. In this chapter, you learn not only how to straighten and crop a crooked scan, but how to repair a damaged photo, enhance focus and image detail, and even eliminate that troublesome red-eye effect.

Cropping an Image

Professional photographers almost always use cropping techniques to achieve that perfect composition. In spite of all the wonderful advances in film and digital cameras, rarely is a picture taken with its subjects perfectly composed or its horizon line set at just the proper level. More often than not, subjects are off-center, and unwanted objects intrude into the edge of the picture frame. Photoshop Elements offers two simple and quick methods for cropping your images.

Figure 6.1
The Crop tool.

To crop an image using the Crop tool:

1. Select the Crop tool from the toolbox (C) (**Figure 6.1**).

2. In the image window, drag to define the area of the image you want to keep (**Figure 6.2**).

   The image outside the selected area is dimmed to indicate the portions that will be deleted.

3. If you want to modify your selection, move the pointer over one of the eight handles on the edges of the selection; then drag the handle to resize the selection (**Figure 6.3**).

4. When you're satisfied with your crop selection, double-click within the selection, press Enter, or click the Commit button on the lower corner of the selection (**Figure 6.4**).

   The image is cropped to the area you selected (**Figure 6.5**).

   If you're just not satisfied with your selection and want to start over, click the Cancel button.

✔ Tip

■ In the options bar, click the Clear button to remove any entries in the Width, Height, or Resolution text boxes.

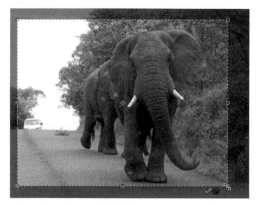

Figure 6.2 Elements highlights the image that will be preserved and dims the portions to be deleted.

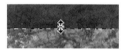 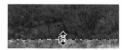

Figure 6.3 You can easily move and resize the area you choose to crop by dragging the handles around the perimeter of the cropping selection.

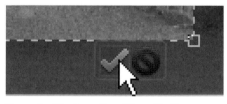

Figure 6.4 The Commit and Cancel buttons appear on the lower edge of the crop selection.

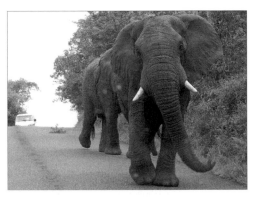

Figure 6.5 The final, cropped image.

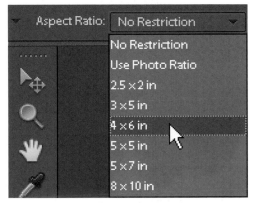

Figure 6.6 Use the Aspect Ratio drop-down menu to choose common photo dimensions.

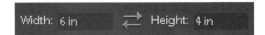

Figure 6.7 The Width and Height fields let you specify a custom aspect ratio.

To resize an image to specific dimensions using the Crop tool:

1. Follow steps 1–3 on the previous page to specify an area to crop.

2. From the Aspect Ratio drop-down menu, choose a common photo size (**Figure 6.6**).

   Or, in the options bar, enter a size in the Width and Height fields (**Figure 6.7**). The double-arrow button between the fields swaps values, making it easy to turn a horizontal crop area into a vertical one, and vice-versa.

3. If you need to change the image's resolution, edit the Resolution field; you can define it in pixels per inch or pixels per centimeter using the associated drop-down menu. However, see the sidebar on the next page for important information.

4. Double-click within the selection, press Enter, or click the Commit button to crop the photo.

✔ Tips

- If you're planning to print your photos using a commercial print service, be sure to crop your images to a standard size first. The images that digital cameras create don't match standard photo aspect ratios, which can lead to prints with black bars around the edges.

- You can define color and opacity options for the Crop tool shield (the dimmed area that surrounds your cropped selection) in the Display and Cursors area of the Preferences dialog. The default color is black, and the default opacity is 75%.

To crop an image using the Rectangular Marquee tool:

1. Select the Rectangular Marquee tool from the toolbox, or press M.

2. In the image window, drag to define the area of the image you want to keep (**Figure 6.8**).

3. From the Image menu, choose Crop. The image is cropped to the area you selected.

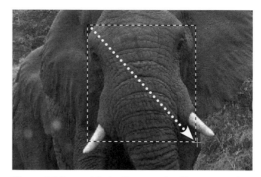

Figure 6.8 Drag with the Rectangular Marquee tool to define the part of the image you want to crop.

The Crop Tool Size and Resolution Options

Used together, the Crop tool's Aspect Ratio and Resolution options can lead you down a slippery slope, introducing unexpected image quality problems—foremost among them, unwanted resolution *upsampling*, which creates a fuzzy, ghosted, and generally out-of-focus effect. For more information on upsampling, see the "Downsampling vs. Upsampling" sidebar in Chapter 3, "Creating and Managing Images."

As an example, open a 4 x 5-inch image with a resolution of 150 pixels per inch. Select the Crop tool, choose "4 x 6 in" from the Aspect Ratio drop-down menu, and enter 150 in the Resolution field. Define the area you want to crop (which by definition will be a smaller area than the original 4 x 5 image), and then crop. The area you crop from the original image, no matter the selected size, will be forced up to 4 x 6, and will introduce upsampling (**Figure 6.9**).

You can use the Aspect Ratio drop-down menu to control the Width and Height ratios of your cropping selection; just leave the Resolution text box blank, and use the Image Size dialog (after you crop) to set the image resolution.

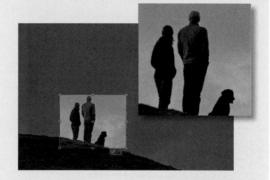

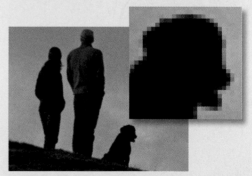

Figure 6.9 Be cautious when using the Crop tool's size and resolution options. In this example, an image was cropped with a final size defined that was larger than the original image (top). During cropping, the image was *upsampled*, sacrificing image quality (bottom). Both detail boxes are shown at 100% size.

Figure 6.10
The Straighten tool.

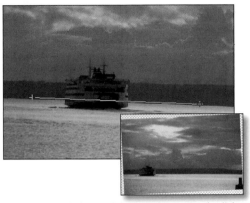

Figure 6.11 With the Straighten tool, you simply click and drag in a tilted photo (top) to align it perfectly (bottom).

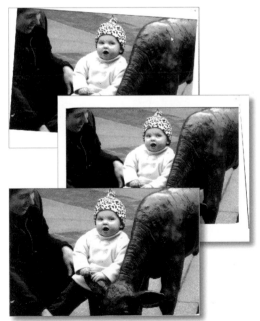

Figure 6.12 A scanned image (top) is automatically straightened (center) or straightened and cropped (bottom).

Straightening a Crooked Photo

Sometimes even your most carefully composed photos may be just a little off angle, with a not quite level horizon line or tilted portrait subjects. The nifty little Straighten tool makes short work out of getting your crooked photos back into alignment.

Or, perhaps you've scanned an image that shifted when you closed the scanner cover. Elements can automatically straighten it, with the option of cropping it to a clean rectangle.

To use the Straighten tool:

1. Select the Straighten tool from the toolbox, or press P (**Figure 6.10**).

2. Using a horizon line or other subject as a point of reference, click and drag from one side of the photo to the other.

   When you release the mouse button, your image rotates and aligns along the new horizontal plane you defined (**Figure 6.11**).

3. Use either the Crop or Marquee Selection tool to remove any extra border area introduced while straightening the photo.

To straighten a scanned image:

From the Image menu, choose one of the following:

◆ Rotate > Straighten and Crop Image.

◆ Rotate > Straighten Image.

   The Straighten and Crop Image command will do its best to both straighten the image and delete the extra background surrounding the image. The Straighten Image command simply straightens without cropping (**Figure 6.12**).

continues on next page

Both methods have their own sets of limitations. Rotate and Straighten works best if there is a space of at least 50 extra pixels or so surrounding the image. If this surrounding border is much smaller, Elements can have a difficult time distinguishing the actual photograph from the border and may not do a clean job of cropping.

Although you'll still need to manually crop your image after using the Straighten Image command, this method is probably a better choice, because you avoid the risk of Photoshop Elements indiscriminately cropping out areas of your image you may want to keep. For the surest control, however, straighten your images using the Crop tool as described in the next procedure.

To straighten a scanned image using the Crop tool:

1. Select the Crop tool from the toolbox.

2. In the image window, drag to select the area of the image you want to crop and straighten.

3. Move the pointer outside the edge of the selection area until it changes to a rotation pointer (**Figure 6.13**).

4. Drag outside of the selection until its edges are aligned with the image border.

5. Drag the selection handles, as necessary, to fine-tune the positioning; then press Enter (**Figure 6.14**).

    The image is cropped and automatically straightened.

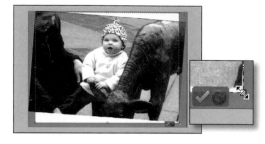

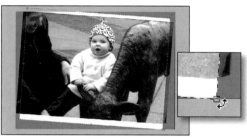

Figure 6.13 After you define a preliminary cropping selection (top), rotate the selection so it aligns with your image border (bottom).

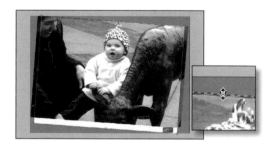

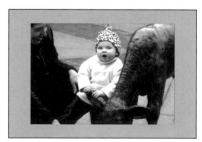

Figure 6.14 Make final adjustments to your cropping selection (top) before Elements automatically crops and straightens the image.

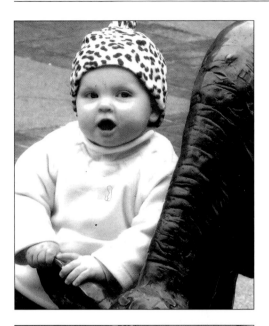

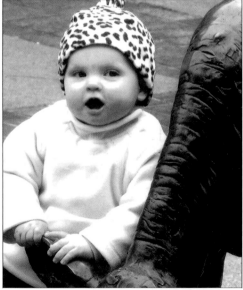

Figure 6.15 With just a little patience and the Clone Stamp and Healing Brush tools, imperfections caused by a poor scan or dust on the camera lens can be easily removed or repaired.

Repairing Flaws and Imperfections

Little maladies, such as torn edges, water stains, scratches, even specks of dust left on a scanner's glass or the camera's sensor, are the bane of the photo-retouch artist, and are problems all too common when you set to the task of digitizing and restoring old photographs. Even if you're shooting digitally, dust on the lens or the camera sensor can cause unwanted pixels and flaws. To the rescue come three similar but distinctly different repair and retouch tools.

The Clone Stamp tool will quickly become one of your favorite tools, not just for cleaning up and restoring photographs, but for any number of special effects and enhancements. It works on the simple principle of copying and duplicating (cloning) image pixels from one part of an image to another. Although ideal for repairing tears or holes in photographs, it can also be used to add or duplicate objects in a photograph. For example, you can create a hedgerow from one small bush or add clouds to a cloudless sky.

The Spot Healing Brush tool is the perfect tool for removing small imperfections like dust or tiny scratches. With a single click, the Spot Healing brush samples (copies) pixels from around the area of a trouble spot and creates a small patch that covers up the flaw and blends in smoothly with its surrounding area.

The Healing Brush tool operates like a combination of the Clone Stamp and Spot Healing Brush tools. As with the Clone Stamp tool, it first samples pixels from one area of your image to another. Then, like the Spot Healing Brush tool, it blends those pixels seamlessly with the area you want to repair (**Figure 6.15**).

To retouch an image with the Clone Stamp tool:

1. Select the Clone Stamp tool from the toolbox, or press S (**Figure 6.16**).

2. On the options bar, select a brush size using the brush Size slider (**Figure 6.17**).

   The brush size you choose will vary depending on the area you have available to clone from and the area you're trying to repair. Larger brush sizes work well for larger open areas like skies or simple, even-toned backdrops, whereas smaller brushes work well for textured surfaces or areas with a lot of detail.

3. Move the pointer over the area of your image you want to clone (the pointer becomes a circle, representing the brush size you've specified), and then hold down the Alt key.

   The pointer becomes a target (**Figure 6.18**).

4. Click once to select the area you want to sample; then, release the Alt key and move the pointer to the area to which you want the clone applied (**Figure 6.19**).

5. Hold down the mouse button, and drag to "paint" the cloned portion over the new area.

   The original image is replaced with a clone of the sampled image.

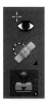

Figure 6.16
The Clone Stamp tool.

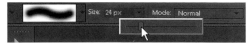

Figure 6.17 Choose any of Photoshop Elements' resizable brushes to apply your cloned repairs.

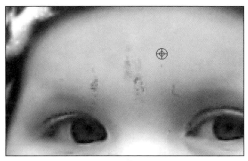

Figure 6.18 Clearly, someone needs to clean his scanner! Once you've found an area of your image you want to clone, hold down the Alt key; your pointer turns into a bull's-eye target. Click to set that area as the origin.

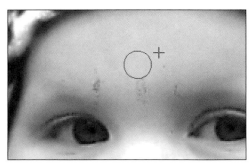

Figure 6.19 Drag the Clone Stamp tool over the portion of the image you want to replace. As you drag, crosshairs appear, providing a constant reference point of the cloned pixels as you paint over the image.

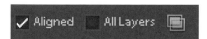

Figure 6.20 The Aligned option gives you control over where the Clone Stamp tool samples image pixels.

Figure 6.21 Using the image on the left as a source, the image in the middle was cloned with the Aligned option selected. Although the mouse button was released and depressed several times, the image was still copied *relative* to the initial sampling point. The image on the right was cloned with the Aligned option deselected. Notice that each time the mouse button was released and depressed, the clone again *started* from the initial reference point.

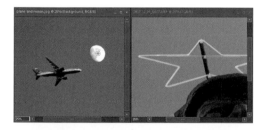

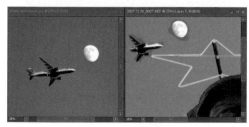

Figure 6.22 The Clone tool provides a controlled method for combining parts of one image with another.

To copy images from one picture to another with the Clone Stamp tool:

1. Select the Clone Stamp tool from the toolbox and then select a brush size from the options bar.

2. Still on the options bar, check that the Aligned option is selected (**Figure 6.20**).

   With the Aligned option selected, the Clone Stamp tool will always copy pixels *relative* to the initial sampling point, even if you release the mouse button and press it again to continue. With the Aligned option *deselected*, each time you release the mouse button and press to resume cloning, you will copy pixels *starting* from the initial sampling point (**Figure 6.21**).

3. Holding down the Alt key, click in the first picture to select the area you want to sample.

4. Click the second picture's image window to make it active, and then drag to paint a clone of the sampled image.

5. The original image in the second picture is replaced with a clone of the sampled image from the first (**Figure 6.22**).

✔ Tip

- Before experimenting with the Clone tool, it's good practice to first create a new, blank image layer. Creating a separate layer not only protects your original image by leaving it unchanged, but it gives you more creative flexibility. You can apply different cloned areas to different layers and then compare the effect of each by turning the layer visibility settings off and on. And if you apply different cloned areas on separate layers, you can experiment further by applying different blending mode and opacity settings to each clone. See Chapter 8, "Working with Layers."

To clean up small areas with the Spot Healing Brush tool:

1. Select the Spot Healing Brush tool from the toolbox, or press J (**Figure 6.23**).

2. On the options bar, select a healing method from the two radio buttons.

   ▲ Proximity Match samples pixels from around the edge of your brush shape to create the patch over the area you want to repair.

   ▲ Create Texture uses the pixels directly beneath the brush shape to create a soft, mottled texture.

3. On the options bar, select a brush size using the brush Size slider.

   Try to size your brush to fit snugly around the flaw you're covering.

4. Click and release the mouse button to apply the patch (**Figure 6.24**).

✔ Tip

■ Alternately, click and drag through a slightly larger area with the Spot Healing Brush tool.

Figure 6.23
The Spot Healing Brush tool.

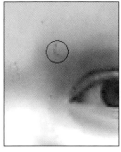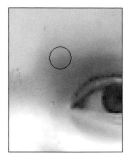

Figure 6.24 With a single mouse click, each dust speck is removed.

REPAIRING FLAWS AND IMPERFECTIONS

Clone and Healing Overlays

Photoshop Elements has an interesting retouching tool in its arsenal: the overlay. When using the Healing Brush or the Clone Stamp tools, set the origin point and then press Alt+Shift. A translucent overlay of the image appears; the mouse pointer remains fixed on the origin point, so you can see what will be drawn when you click the mouse button (**Figure 6.25**). With this approach, you don't have to click blindly and hope that the edit you're about to make is the one you envisioned.

To make the overlay appear whenever the tool is selected, click the Overlay Options button in the options bar (just to the right of the All Layers check box) and enable the Show Overlay check box.

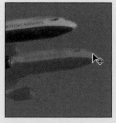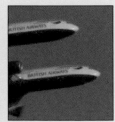

Figure 6.25 The overlay lets you preview what will be drawn (left) when you start drawing (right).

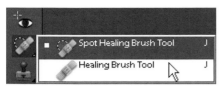

Figure 6.26 The Healing Brush tool.

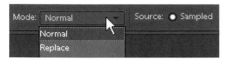

Figure 6.27 Although several healing modes are available, most often the Healing Brush tool works best in Normal mode.

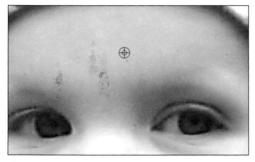

Figure 6.28 Once you've found an area of your image to use as a patch, hold down the Alt key and click to select it. Your pointer turns into a bull's-eye target.

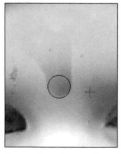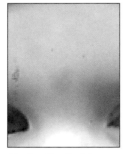

Figure 6.29 As you draw, the Healing Brush picks up the pixels relative to the origin point, just like the Clone Stamp tool (left). After you release the mouse button, Elements blends the values in the area (right).

To remove flaws with the Healing Brush tool:

1. In the toolbox, select the Healing Brush tool from beneath the Spot Healing Brush tool (**Figure 6.26**).

2. From the Mode drop-down menu on the options bar, check that Normal is selected (**Figure 6.27**).

   Normal mode blends sampled pixels with the area you're repairing to create a smooth transition with the area surrounding the repair. Replace mode does little more than duplicate the behavior of the Clone Stamp tool. For information on the other effect modes available from the drop-down menu, see "About Opacity and Blending Modes" in Chapter 8.

3. On the options bar, select a brush size using the brush Size slider.

   The brush size you choose will vary depending on the area you have available to sample from and the area that you're trying to repair.

4. Move the pointer over the area of your image you want to sample and hold down the Alt key. The pointer becomes a target (**Figure 6.28**).

5. Click once to select the area you want to sample; then release the Alt key and move the pointer to the area you want to repair.

6. Hold down the mouse button and drag to "paint" the sampled image over the new area (**Figure 6.29**).

   The sampled image blends with the repair area to cover any flaws and imperfections.

REPAIRING FLAWS AND IMPERFECTIONS

Applying Patterns

Although some of Photoshop Elements' patterns can be a little gimmicky, others, like many of the fabric and rock textures, can be useful when you're trying to repair or retouch a damaged or aged photograph. For example, you might use one of the abstract stone patterns to camouflage a particularly damaged background in an old photo that would be difficult to salvage by any other method. Photoshop Elements provides a default set of patterns plus seven additional sets containing objects as varied as flowers, stone faces, and textured artist's surfaces. Patterns can be applied using two methods. If you have a large area of the same tonal value or color, you can use the Paint Bucket tool. On the other hand, if you have a smaller area made up of varying colors or textures, use the Pattern Stamp tool.

To apply a pattern to a selected area with the Paint Bucket tool:

1. Select the Paint Bucket tool from the toolbox, or press K (**Figure 6.30**).

2. On the options bar, click the Pattern check box.

3. Still on the options bar, click to open the pattern picker (**Figure 6.31**).

4. Click to choose from the list of default patterns, or click the down-arrow button to the right of the thumbnail image to open the Pattern palette menu.

5. Select from the list of pattern sets in the bottom section of the menu.

   The pattern picker displays the new pattern library.

6. Return to the image window and click in the area where you want to apply the pattern. The pattern is painted in the image (**Figure 6.32**).

Figure 6.30
The Paint Bucket tool.

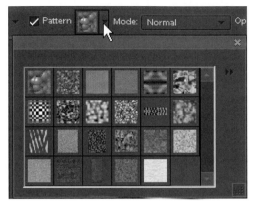

Figure 6.31 You can choose from a variety of patterns in the pattern picker on the options bar.

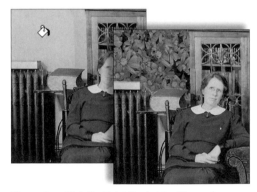

Figure 6.32 Click the Paint Bucket tool in any large area where you want to apply a pattern. Here, a floral pattern was selected to create brand-new living room wallpaper.

APPLYING PATTERNS

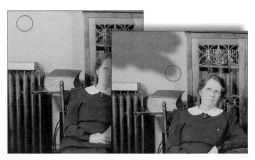

Figure 6.33 Position the pattern brush anywhere in your image to paint a pattern.

Mount a Photo on Canvas

You can create an interesting textured effect for almost any photo by using patterns from the Artist Surfaces set.

1. In the Layers palette, create a new layer above your original photo layer.

2. From the Pattern palette menu in the options bar, choose the Artist Surfaces pattern set, and then choose from one of the artist surfaces.

3. With the pattern layer selected, apply a blend mode (try Multiply) to combine the photo and pattern layers.

4. If you like, adjust the pattern layer's opacity setting.

Your photo will appear to be printed on the textured artist surface (**Figure 6.34**).

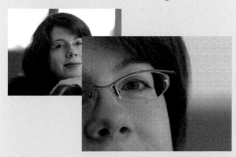

Figure 6.34 Any photo can be made to appear rendered on a variety of other fine art surfaces.

To apply a pattern with the Pattern Stamp tool:

1. In the toolbox, select the Pattern Stamp tool from beneath the Clone Stamp tool.

   If you hold the Alt key while clicking the Clone Stamp tool in the toolbox, you can toggle between the Clone Stamp and Pattern Stamp tools. Or, if the Clone Stamp tool is already selected, you can select the Pattern Stamp tool from the options bar.

2. On the options bar, select a brush size using the brush Size slider.

   If you like, you can also make opacity and blending changes.

3. Pick a pattern by following steps 3 through 5 in the previous procedure.

4. Once you've chosen a pattern, return to the image window, hold down the mouse button, and then drag to paint the pattern in your image (**Figure 6.33**).

✔ Tips

- The Paint Bucket tool fills areas based on tonal value and color, so you'll have the most success filling areas composed of similar values, such as blank walls or clear, cloudless skies. You can adjust the behavior of the Paint Bucket tool by entering different values in the Tolerance text box on the options bar, but the results are a little unpredictable, and the process involves some trial and error.

- In addition to the Pattern palette's default mode of Small Thumbnail, you can view patterns as Text Only, Large Thumbnail, Small List, or Large List. As a further aid, if Show Tool Tips is selected in the General Preferences dialog, simply hover over any pattern thumbnail for a second or two to reveal a small pop-up descriptive name of that pattern.

Correcting Red Eye

When you're in an indoor or darkened space, your pupils grow larger to let in more light. The pupils can't shrink fast enough to compensate for a camera's flash, so when that light reflects off the back of the eye, it causes red eye. Many newer cameras have flashes that flicker before the picture is actually snapped, giving the subject's pupils a chance to contract and greatly reduce the effects of red eye. But chances are you still have some older photos lying around you'd like to repair. The Red Eye Removal tool offers an effective way to remove red eye, simply by changing pixels from one color to another.

To remove red eye from a photograph:

1. Select the Red Eye Removal tool from the toolbox, or press Y (**Figure 6.35**).

2. On the options bar, set the Pupil Size slider to match the proportional size of the pupil (the red part of the eye that you want to turn black) to the colored portion of the eye. Then, on the options bar, use the Darken Amount slider to control the darkness of the retouched pupil (**Figure 6.36**).

   Although these settings are not inconsequential, the defaults of 50 percent work fine in the majority of cases I've tried.

3. If necessary, zoom in on the area you want to correct; then click and drag to draw a selection over the colored portion of one eye (**Figure 6.37**).

4. Release the mouse button to remove the red eye effect. If you're not quite satisfied with the results the first time, press Ctrl+Z to undo the operation, and then repeat steps 2 through 4, revising the option bar settings or changing the size of the selection before you click and drag.

Figure 6.35
The Red Eye Removal tool.

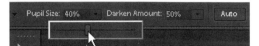

Figure 6.36 Two sliders on the options bar help you to adjust red eye removal.

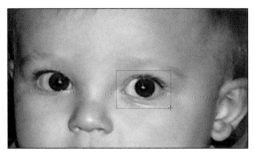

Figure 6.37 To remove red eye, draw a selection around the eye and release the mouse button.

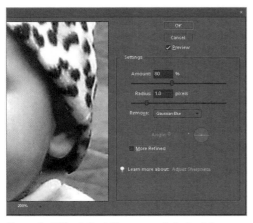

Figure 6.38 The Adjust Sharpness dialog's sliders adjust the degree of sharpening you apply.

Original
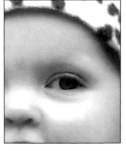

Amount: 80%
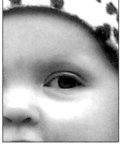

Original
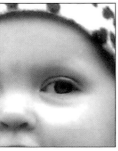

Amount: 150%
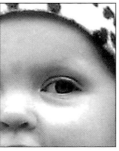

Figure 6.39 The Amount slider controls the percentage of sharpness applied to your image. The difference here is most pronounced around the eyelid and in the pattern on the hat. Also note that the sharpening appears too aggressive in the 150% version when zoomed-in so close, but at normal size may look just fine; feel free to experiment quite a bit to achieve your desired image.

Sharpening Image Detail

Generally speaking, you probably want most of your photos to be in focus—which can be surprisingly difficult to achieve, depending on how zoomed-in you were, surrounding movement, or even just plain shaky fingers (maybe cut back on the caffeine). Even then, photos may not quite "pop" the way you'd like them to. In addition, any time you resize an image by resampling, pixels may be lost in the process, and so you also lose some degree of image detail.

Elements offers an Auto Sharpen command (under the Enhance menu), but you may want more control. Instead, look to the Adjust Sharpness command, which finds pixels with different tonal values and then slightly increases the contrast between those adjoining pixels, thereby creating a sharper edge. The resulting correction can help to enhance detail and bring blurred or fuzzy areas throughout an image into clearer focus.

To sharpen an image:

1. From the Enhance menu, choose Adjust Sharpness to open the Adjust Sharpness dialog (**Figure 6.38**).

2. Make sure the Preview box is checked; then drag the following sliders to adjust the image's sharpness:

   ▲ The Amount slider sets the percentage of contrast applied to the pixels and so determines the degree of sharpness you apply. For high-resolution images (those above around 150 pixels per inch), set the Amount slider to between 150 and 200 percent. For lower-resolution images, use settings somewhere around 30 to 80 percent (**Figure 6.39**).

continues on next page

SHARPENING IMAGE DETAIL

▲ The Radius slider determines the number of pixels surrounding the contrasting edge pixels that will also be sharpened. Although the radius can be set all the way to 64, you should never have to enter a value much higher than 2, unless you're trying to achieve a strong, high-contrast special effect (**Figure 6.40**).

▲ The More Refined check box offers higher quality, but requires more processing time and power. If you're experimenting with the settings, keep this option disabled until you reach the level of sharpening you want.

▲ The Remove drop-down menu offers three types of correction: Gaussian Blur applies the effect to the entire image; Lens blur detects edges in its sharpening; and Motion Blur works to reverse the blur caused by camera movement. If Motion Blur is enabled, adjust the Angle setting to match the angle of the movement (**Figure 6.41**).

▲ Use the preview area to see a detailed view of your image as you apply the changes. You can move to a different area of an image by holding down the mouse button and dragging with the hand pointer in the preview screen. You can also zoom in or out of an area using the minus and plus buttons below the preview.

3. When you're satisfied with the results, click OK to close the dialog and apply the changes.

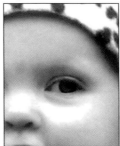
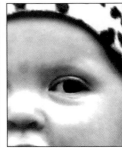

Original   Amount: 80%   Radius: 10.0 pixels

Figure 6.40 The Radius slider controls the number of pixels included in any sharpened edge. Smaller numbers include fewer pixels, and larger numbers include more pixels (exaggerated here for effect).

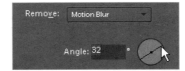

Figure 6.41 If the blur is caused by movement of the camera or subject, Motion Blur can compensate.

Adjust Sharpness vs. Unsharp Mask

If you've used Photoshop or another image editor in the past, you may be familiar with the Unsharp Mask command (under the Enhance menu). It provides the same controls as the Remove: Gaussian Blur option of the Adjust Sharpness dialog, and I suspect Adobe kept it in Elements for people who've been using that feature for years. The Adjust Sharpness feature, however, adds compensation for motion blur, which I find to be more common. Depending on the severity of the blur, Adjust Sharpness can salvage a shot that otherwise would have to be rejected.

SHARPENING IMAGE DETAIL

Figure 6.42
The Blur tool.

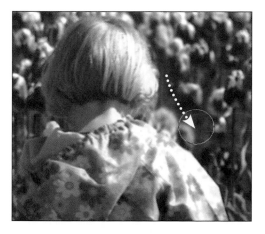

Original   *After blur tool applied*

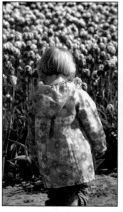 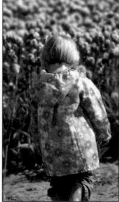

Figure 6.43 Drag the brush through the area you want to blur. You can resize the brush as you work on larger and smaller areas.

Enhancing Image Detail

The Adjust Sharpness command works best on entire images or large portions of images. A couple of other tools are better suited for making sharpening and focus adjustments in smaller, more specific areas of an image. Not surprisingly, the Blur tool softens the focus in an image by reducing the detail, and the Sharpen tool helps bring areas into focus. For instance, you can create a sense of depth by blurring selected background areas while keeping foreground subjects in focus, or enhance the focus of a specific foreground subject so that it better stands out from others.

To blur a specific area or object:

1. Select the Blur tool from the toolbox, or press R (**Figure 6.42**).

2. On the options bar, select a brush size using the brush Size slider.

   If you want, you can also select a blend mode and enter a Strength percentage. The higher the percentage, the more the affected area is blurred.

3. Move the brush pointer to the area of your image you want to blur; then hold down the mouse button and drag through the area (**Figure 6.43**).

   As you drag, the area is blurred.

✔ Tip

■ Working on a portrait? Another tool to consider is the Surface Blur filter (Filter > Blur > Surface Blur), which smooths surface areas like skin without blurring edges. It's an easy way to minimize wrinkles and other sharp details in faces.

To sharpen a specific area or object:

1. Select the Sharpen tool from the toolbox, or press R to toggle through the enhance tools to the Sharpen tool (**Figure 6.44**).

2. On the options bar, select a brush size.

   If you prefer, choose a blend mode and enter a Strength percentage. The higher the percentage, the more the affected area is sharpened.

3. Move the brush pointer to the area of your image you want to sharpen; then hold down the mouse button and drag through the area (**Figure 6.45**).

   As you drag, the area is sharpened.

✔ Tip

■ Use the Blur and Sharpen tools together when you want to draw attention to a particular person or object. First, use the Blur tool to soften the focus and detail of the subjects you want to appear to recede into the background. Then use the Sharpen tool to bring the subject of primary interest into sharp focus.

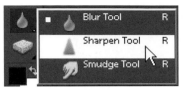

Figure 6.44 The Sharpen tool.

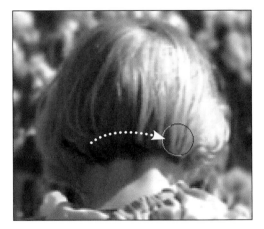

Original *After sharpen tool applied*

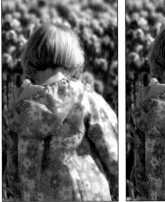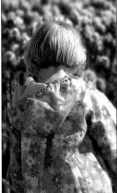

Figure 6.45 I can pull more detail out of the girl's hair and coat by dragging the Sharpen tool over that area.

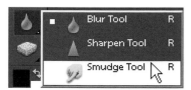

Figure 6.46 The Smudge tool.

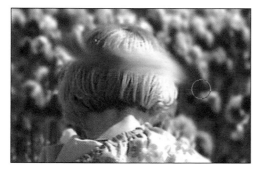

Figure 6.47 The Smudge tool can easily do more harm than good, so use it sparingly.

Blending with the Smudge Tool

The Smudge tool is one of those specialty tools that's a little hard to classify. Traditionally, it's grouped with the Blur and Sharpen tools in the toolbox and is often used for retouching tasks. The Smudge tool's closest cousin may be the Blur tool, because it can also be used to soften edges and transitions in an image. Its real strength lies in its ability to push and pull image pixels around in your picture. Drag the tool through an area, and its pixels smear and blend with the adjacent pixels as if you were pulling a brush through freshly applied paint. Use the Smudge tool in backgrounds and other areas where you may need to smooth flaws or imperfections and where retaining detail isn't critical. With a little practice, you can also create some convincing painterly effects by varying the length and direction of the brushstrokes. As with the Blur and Sharpen tools, the Smudge tool's effects can be adjusted with controls on the options bar.

To use the Smudge tool:

1. Select the Smudge tool from the toolbox, or press R to toggle through the enhance tools to the Smudge tool (**Figure 6.46**).

2. On the options bar, select a brush size using the brush Size slider.

   Just as with the Blur and Sharpen tools, you can select a blend mode and enter a Strength percentage. The higher the percentage, the more the affected area is smudged.

3. Move the brush pointer to the area of your image you want to smudge; then hold down the mouse button and drag through the area (**Figure 6.47**).

   As you drag, the area is softened and blended.

Smudge, not Sludge

The Smudge tool tends to produce a more artificial effect than the other retouching tools, so use it with moderation. Unless your intent is to create a wet paint effect in a large portion of your image, limit use of the Smudge tool to repairing or smoothing small, unobtrusive areas. You don't want a small repair to become the focus of attention.

Using the Tonal Adjustment Tools

In traditional photography, technicians control darkness and lightness values on specific parts of an image by masking one area of film while exposing another. In the process, selected areas are either *burned in* (darkened) or *dodged* (lightened). The Burn and Dodge tools replicate this effect without the bother of creating masks. Instead, simply drag an adjustable tool's brush pointer through the area you want to affect. If one portion of an image is dramatically overexposed or washed out, and another portion is underexposed, the Dodge and Burn tools can be used to target and correct just those specific problem areas.

The Sponge tool increases or decreases the intensity of the color. Use the Sponge tool to bring colors back to life in badly faded, older photographs, or work in the opposite direction, pulling the color out of a newer photo and creating an antique effect.

To lighten a portion of an image with the Dodge tool:

1. Select the Dodge tool from the toolbox, or press O to toggle to the Dodge tool (**Figure 6.48**).

2. On the options bar, select a brush size using the brush Size slider. Choose a brush size appropriate to your image. For most images, a brush size between 20 to 40 pixels is a good start.

   Using the Range and Exposure settings, you can also select a specific tonal range to lighten (shadows, midtones, or highlights) and control the amount of lightness applied (**Figure 6.49**).

3. Move the brush pointer to the area of your image you want to lighten; then hold down the mouse button and drag through the area (**Figure 6.50**).

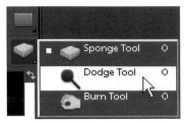

Figure 6.48 The Dodge tool.

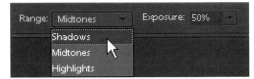

Figure 6.49 Select the part of the tonal range you most want to affect with Photoshop Elements' tonal adjustment tools. With both the Dodge and Burn tools, you can choose to limit your changes to just the shadow, midtone, or highlight areas.

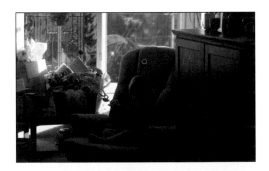

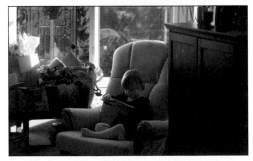

Figure 6.50 Drag the Dodge or Burn brush through any area to lighten or darken the pixels while preserving image detail. Here, I've used the Dodge tool to lighten the child and chair, keeping the tones in the window (which would get blown out if I were to lighten the entire image).

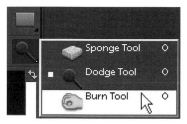

Figure 6.51 The Burn tool.

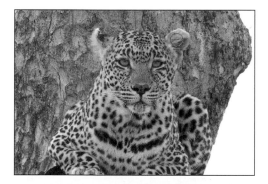

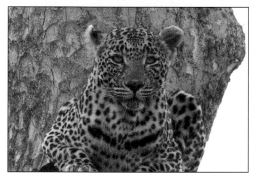

Figure 6.52 In this image, the leopard is washed out and blends into the background (top). The Burn tool added some much needed form and dimension by darkening the pixels in the shadow and midtone areas (bottom).

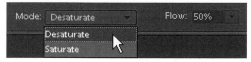

Figure 6.53 On the options bar, choose whether you want the Sponge tool to add or subtract color.

To darken a portion of an image with the Burn tool:

1. Select the Burn tool from the toolbox, or press O to toggle through the tonal adjustment tools to the Burn tool (**Figure 6.51**).

2. In the options bar, select a brush size using the brush Size slider.

   If you like, you can also select a specific tonal range to darken (shadows, midtones, or highlights) and control the amount of darkness applied with the Exposure setting.

3. Move the brush pointer to the area of your image you want to darken; then hold down the mouse button and drag through the area (**Figure 6.52**).

To adjust the color saturation with the Sponge tool:

1. Select the Sponge tool from the toolbox, or press O to toggle through the tonal adjustment tools to the Sponge tool.

2. On the options bar, select a brush size using the brush Size slider.

3. From the Mode drop-down menu on the options bar, select whether you want to saturate (add) or desaturate (subtract) color (**Figure 6.53**).

   You can also adjust the amount of color to be added or subtracted using the Flow percentage slider.

4. Move the brush pointer to the area of your image where you want to change the color's intensity; then hold down the mouse button and drag through the area.

USING THE TONAL ADJUSTMENT TOOLS

Erasing Backgrounds and Other Large Areas

The Background Eraser tool is an intelligent (and really quite amazing) little feature. Not only does it remove the background from around very complex shapes, but it does so in a way that leaves a natural, softened, anti-aliased edge around the foreground object left behind. Additionally, because the Background Eraser tool always erases to transparency, if you use it to remove the background from even a flattened layer, it automatically converts that layer to a floating, transparent one. This allows you to easily place a new background behind a foreground image, or to move it into a different photo composition altogether.

To use the Background Eraser tool:

1. Select the Background Eraser tool from beneath the Eraser tool in the toolbox (**Figure 6.54**).

   Alternatively, you can press E to select the Eraser tool and then press E again to toggle to the Background Eraser tool.

2. On the options bar, select a size using the brush Size slider.

3. From the Limits drop-down menu, select one of the limit modes (**Figure 6.55**).

   Contiguous mode erases any pixels within the brush area that are the same as those currently beneath the crosshairs, as long as they're touching one another.

   Discontiguous mode erases all pixels within the brush area that are the same as those beneath the crosshairs, even if they're not touching one another.

4. Select a Tolerance value using the Tolerance slider (**Figure 6.56**). The value controls which pixels are erased according to how similar they are to the pixels

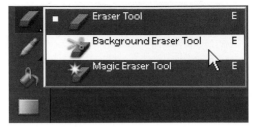

Figure 6.54 The Background Eraser tool.

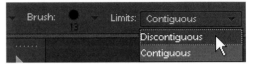

Figure 6.55 The Limits drop-down menu controls which pixels beneath the brush are sampled and erased.

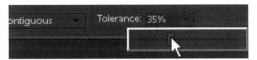

Figure 6.56 You use the Tolerance slider to increase or decrease the number of pixels sampled based on their similarity to one another.

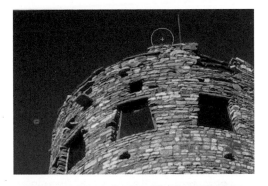

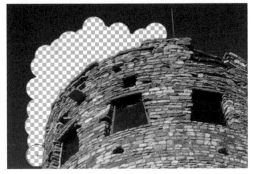

Figure 6.57 Begin by placing the crosshairs of the brush in the background portion of the image (top), then drag the brush along the outside edge of the foreground object to erase the background (bottom). Continue around the edge of the foreground object until it's completely separated from the background.

beneath the eraser crosshairs. Higher Tolerance values increase the range of colors that are erased, and lower values limit the range of colors erased.

5. In the image window, position the eraser pointer on the edge where the background and foreground images meet, and then drag along the edge.

The background portion of the image is erased, leaving behind the foreground image on a transparent background (**Figure 6.57**). The brush erases only pixels similar to those directly below the crosshairs, so the entire background can be completely erased while leaving the foreground image intact.

✔ Tips

- It's okay if the circle (indicating the brush size) overlaps onto the foreground image, but be sure to keep the crosshairs over just the background area. The Background Eraser tool, of course, doesn't really know the difference between background and foreground images, and is simply erasing based on the colors selected, or *sampled*, beneath the crosshairs. If the crosshairs stray into the foreground image, that part of the image will be erased, too.

- There's a third eraser tool—the Magic Eraser tool—that I've chosen not to cover here because, frankly, it doesn't work very well. It operates on the same principle as the Magic Wand tool by deleting like pixels based on color or tonal value. That's all well and good, but you're not given any feedback or opportunity to modify your selection. You just click, and poof—a large area of color is gone. Since the erasure typically is either not quite enough or a little too much, you undo, reset the tolerance, try again, undo—well, you get the idea.

Removing a Foreground Image from Its Background

The Magic Extractor works much the same way as the Background Eraser tool, but distinguishes itself with speed and added control. Using brushes, mark and identify first the foreground image you want to save, and then the background image you want to delete. A set of additional tools helps you to fine-tune your foreground and background selections, and a number of options are available for preview and for final touch-up.

To use the Magic Extractor tool:

1. From the Image menu, choose Magic Extractor to open the Magic Extractor dialog (**Figure 6.58**).

2. From the tool area on the left side of the dialog, select the Foreground Brush tool (**Figure 6.59**).

3. Use the brush Size slider, if necessary, to adjust the size of your brush, and then use the brush to mark the foreground area of the image—the area of the image you want to preserve.

    You can mark the foreground with a series of either dots or scribbles, or a combination of the two. The idea is to use the brush to get a good cross-sampling of all the different pixel colors and tones in the foreground (**Figure 6.60**).

4. Select the Background Brush tool, and in the same manner, mark the area of the image you want to remove.

5. Click the Preview button to see the results of your work (**Figure 6.61**).

    Use the Zoom and Hand tools to get a closer look at the transitions between the foreground image and the background.

6. If necessary, use one of the touch-up tools to modify or clean up the transi-

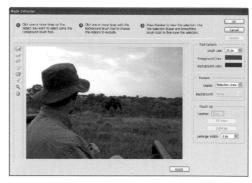

Figure 6.58 Open the Magic Extractor dialog from the Image menu.

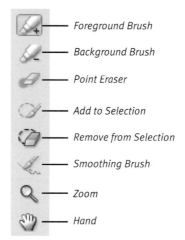

Figure 6.59 The Magic Extractor tool set.

- Foreground Brush
- Background Brush
- Point Eraser
- Add to Selection
- Remove from Selection
- Smoothing Brush
- Zoom
- Hand

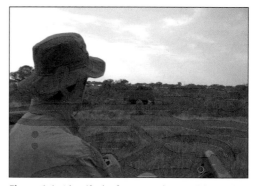

Figure 6.60 Identify the foreground area with a series of dots and scribbles.

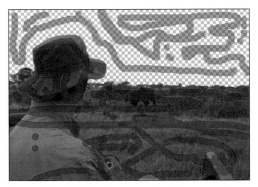

Figure 6.61 Click Preview to see the changes you've made to your image in the preview window.

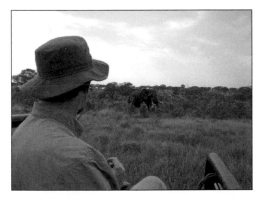

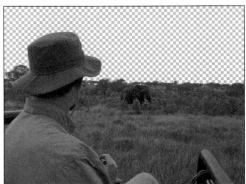

Figure 6.62 The Magic Extractor identified the foreground and background areas of the image, and then deleted the background.

tions between the foreground image and background:

▲ The Point Eraser tool removes portions of marks you've made. When you remove a portion of a mark from the background area, for instance, you're telling the Magic Extractor that you don't want to erase pixels of a particular tonal or color range.

▲ The Add to Selection tool allows you to paint back in areas of the foreground image that may have been mistakenly removed along with the background.

▲ The Remove from Selection tool works like an eraser to remove areas of the foreground image.

▲ The Smoothing Brush softens the transition between the foreground image and transparent background by adding a halo of deleted background color to the edge of the foreground image.

7. If necessary, use the options in the Touch Up area of the dialog to further refine the foreground image.

8. Click OK to finish (**Figure 6.62**).

✔ Tip

■ Within the Magic Extractor dialog, you can only Undo (Ctrl+Z) the action of two tools: the Remove from Selection tool and the Smoothing Brush tool. But if you're not happy with the results you're getting, you can start over from scratch by either clicking the Reset or Cancel buttons. Clicking the Reset button will undo every action in the Preview window, but will leave the dialog open, whereas clicking Cancel will exit the dialog altogether without applying any changes.

Removing Objects from a Scene

You've probably seen the photo on the Web or forwarded via e-mail from a friend: A couple in full wedding attire are exchanging vows on the beach, the ocean meeting the sky in the background, and...what's that? Yes, a topless sunbather is walking into the frame, ruining an otherwise romantic wedding photo. In Elements 7, however, that photo would be easily salvageable.

The new Photomerge Scene Cleaner lets you take a collection of similar images and selectively "paint out" objects you'd prefer weren't in the photo. Select two or more images that contain an element you want to remove; scenes where people are moving are ideal, because Elements takes areas from the background and superimposes them over the person you wish to hide. (In fact, the early name for Scene Cleaner was "Tourist Remover.")

To remove objects from a scene:

1. Open two or more photos of the scene you want to clean in the Editor, and select them in the Project Bin.

2. Choose File > New > Photomerge Scene Cleaner; or, go to the Guided Edit pane and click Scene Cleaner under the Photomerge heading.

   The first image appears in the Source pane on the left, with an empty Final pane on the right.

3. Choose the image that will be the basis for the finished photo and drag it to the Final pane (**Figure 6.63**).

4. Click a photo in the Project Bin that contains background in the area where you want to remove an object from the Final image (**Figure 6.64**).

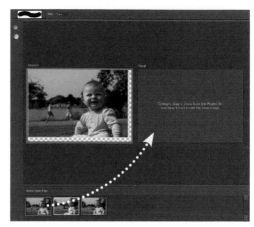

Figure 6.63 Drag the photo you want to use as a base into the Final pane.

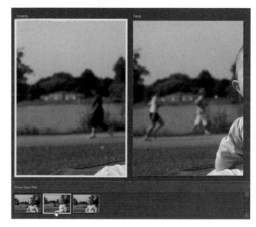

Figure 6.64 I need to remove the two runners in the Final image, so I click a photo that has an empty area corresponding to where one of the runners is. (I've zoomed in here to see the runners better.)

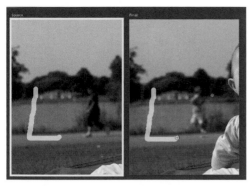

Figure 6.65 Drawing over one runner in the Final image grabs the corresponding pixels from the Source, removing the runner. Notice that I also included the runner's shadow.

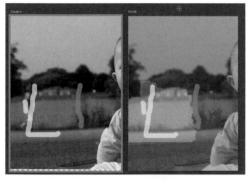

Figure 6.66 Clicking the Show Regions check box displays the areas Elements is using.

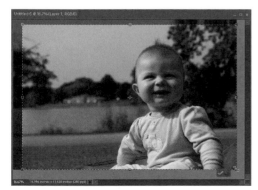

Figure 6.67 You may need to crop the final photo to remove artifacts left over from blending the images.

5. With the Pencil tool selected, draw over the object to be removed in the Final image (**Figure 6.65**). Elements copies that area from the selected Source image to make the object vanish.

Repeat steps 4 and 5 to remove other objects from the scene. (Move the mouse pointer off the Final image to preview it without pencil strokes.) The ink color corresponds to the outline surrounding each source image, so you can easily tell which areas are being used. You can also click the Show Regions check box to view the patchwork Elements created (**Figure 6.66**).

6. To fine-tune the effect, you may need to use the Eraser tool to erase some of your pencil marks in the Final image.

7. Click Done. Elements saves the image in a new layered file.

✔ Tips

- Depending on how well the source images lined up, you may need to crop the final image to remove blending irregularities (**Figure 6.67**).

- Elements attempts to align the source images based on their contents, but sometimes things end up a little off. If that's the case, click the Advanced Options expansion triangle to reveal the Alignment tool, which you can use to mark three points the images share. Click the Align Photos button to realign them.

- Click the Pixel Blending check box to get a higher-quality, but slower and more processor-intensive, result.

- A tool like Photomerge Scene Cleaner is a great reason to take multiple shots of a scene while you're shooting. With digital photography, you can fire off lots of exposures and end up with plenty of choices.

REMOVING OBJECTS FROM A SCENE

Compositing Images

Combining multiple images to create a single merged image is called *compositing*. You can combine different digital photos or scanned images to create effects that range from subtle to spectacular to silly. For example, you can replace a landscape's clear blue sky with a dramatic sunset, create complex, multilayered photo collages, or replace the face of the Mona Lisa with that of your Uncle Harold.

To replace part of an image with another image:

1. Open an image that contains an area you want to replace. I'll call this the "target" image.

   In this example, the sky isn't as dynamic as it could be (**Figure 6.68**). Since the edges are well defined, the image is a good candidate for the Background Eraser tool.

2. From the toolbox, select the Background Eraser tool; then adjust its brush size and tolerance values.

3. Position the Background Eraser tool along the outside edge of the foreground shape (the tower). Making sure that the brush crosshairs are over the background (sky), drag along the edge to erase the background. Continue to erase the background until the area is completely transparent (**Figure 6.69**).

4. Open the image you want to use to replace the transparent pixels in your original image. I'll call this the "source" image.

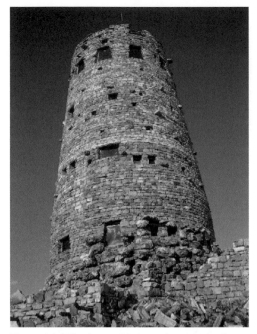

Figure 6.68 I'll enhance this image by replacing its background with something more dynamic.

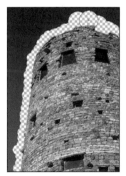 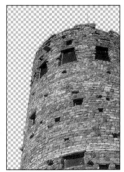

Figure 6.69 Use the Background Eraser tool to remove the sky and create a transparent background.

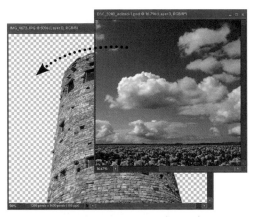

Figure 6.70 Drag the source image (the sky) into the target image (the tower).

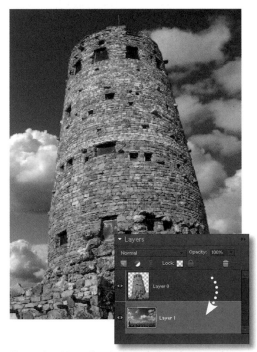

Figure 6.71 Move the sky layer below the tower layer on the Layers palette and adjust the position in the image window.

5. Select the Move tool and drag the source image into the target image (**Figure 6.70**).

In the example, the sky image is larger than the empty background area, which allows flexibility in positioning the new sky in the composition.

If you like, you can also use the selection tools to select just a portion of the source image, then drag just that selection into the target image.

6. On the Layers palette, drag the source layer below the target layer (**Figure 6.71**). (For more information about layers, see Chapter 8.)

7. In the image window, use the Move tool to adjust the position of the source image until you're satisfied with the composition.

✔ Tips

■ It's always good to save a copy of your composition retaining the layers in case you want to make further adjustments. Layered files should be saved as Photoshop Elements (PSD) files.

■ Instead of using the Background Eraser tool, you could have just as easily used the Magic Extractor in Step 3 to clear the background.

COMPOSITING IMAGES

Merging Portions of Multiple Photos

My instructions were simple: get a good photo of my niece and nephew together. It sounds easy, but you can't assume that a five-year-old and his little sister will sit still. If it weren't for my camera's ability to shoot three frames per second, I think I'd still be trying to get the shot.

Elements makes that quandary much easier with Photomerge, an impressive feature that lets you combine areas of multiple photos into one nearly seamless composition.

To merge portions of multiple photos:

1. Open two or more similar photos in the Editor.

2. Select the photos you want to use in the Project Bin. (If you don't initially, Elements will ask you to do so.)

3. Choose File > New > Photomerge Group Shot; or, in the Edit pane, click the Guided heading and then click Group Shot under Photomerge (**Figure 6.72**).

   The first image appears in the Source pane on the left, with an empty Final pane on the right.

4. Drag one of the images to the Final pane (**Figure 6.73**). This image is the end result, so it should have the fewest imperfections (such as people's heads turned away from the camera, motion blur, or other issues).

5. Click to select a photo in the Project Bin that contains an element (replacing someone's face, for example) you want merged into the Final pane. The photo appears in the Source pane (**Figure 6.74**).

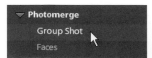

Figure 6.72 Choose the feature in the Guided Edit pane.

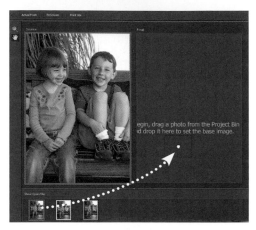

Figure 6.73 Drag the photo you want to use as a base into the Final pane. In this case, the boy's facial expression is my favorite of the three, so I'm building on the first image.

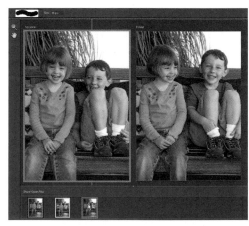

Figure 6.74 I like the girl's expression in the third image, so I've clicked it in the Project Bin to load it into the Source pane. Elements uses colored borders to help you track which photo is which.

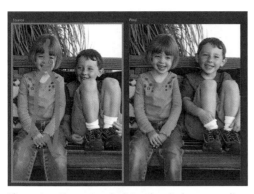

Figure 6.75 Elements calculates the pixels surrounding the areas I've drawn and merges them into the Final image.

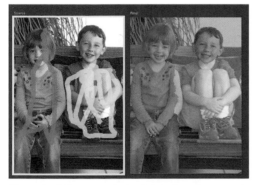

Figure 6.76 I drew over the boy's legs from the second image to merge them into the Final image. I've also enabled the Show Regions option to see how Elements has patched the photo together.

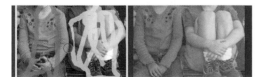

Figure 6.77 In the previous figure, the girl's left arm ended up deformed as a result of the merge. To remedy, I used the Eraser tool to shave some of the yellow line on the boy's right arm.

6. Select the Pencil tool (if it's not already selected) and, in the Source pane, draw over the area you want to transfer to the Final image (**Figure 6.75**). When you release the mouse button, Elements incorporates that area into the Final image. Repeat Steps 5 and 6 for other areas you want to merge (**Figure 6.76**).

7. Elements does an amazing job of automatically merging images, but it's not perfect. If you need to adjust some areas, use the Eraser tool to edit the drawing lines in the Source pane (**Figure 6.77**).

8. Click Done to exit the Photomerge interface. Elements saves the image in a new layered file.

✔ Tips

■ After you exit Photomerge, you may still need to perform some clean-up editing on the image in the Full Edit mode. The merged image appears on a new layer above the Source image. Use the Clone Stamp tool (or the other tools covered in this chapter) to fine-tune the image.

■ Elements attempts to align the source images based on their contents, but sometimes things end up a little off—due to different image sizes, slightly different camera angles, and so forth. If that's the case, click the Advanced Options expansion triangle to reveal the Alignment tool, which you can use to mark three points the images share. Click the Align Photos button to realign them.

■ Click the Pixel Blending check box to get a higher-quality, but slower and more processor-intensive, result.

■ The Faces option under Photomerge works similarly to Group Shot, but requires you to set alignment points first. It's great rainy-day fun!

Using the Smart Brush

In Chapter 4, I touched on the Touch Up edits found in the Guided Edit mode, which let you select an area and apply common fixes such as intensifying a blue sky or brightening a person's teeth (see "Making Touch Up Edits"). Those tools are simplified front ends for the Smart Brush found in Full Edit mode.

The Smart Brush applies many more effects—called Smart Paints—than the four offered in the Guided Edit pane, and you can also edit the appearance of a Smart Paint effect after you've applied it.

What's behind the magic? Each Smart Paint application is a new adjustment layer; a layer mask defines the area where the effect is applied (see Chapter 8 for more on working with layers).

To apply a Smart Paint effect:

1. With an image open in Full Edit mode, select the Smart Brush tool from the toolbox (**Figure 6.78**) or press F.

2. In the Smart Paint menu that automatically appears, choose an effect; click the drop-down menu at top to list categories of effects (**Figure 6.79**), and then click a Smart Paint style to use it.

3. Paint over an area of your photo. Elements creates a selection and applies the Smart Paint effect (**Figure 6.80**).

   You can adjust the brush size using the Brush pop-up menu in the options bar.

✔ Tip

- When you apply a new Smart Paint to an image, a new selection is created. To switch easily between multiple Smart Paint areas, click the layer pin that appears. Right-clicking the pin brings up options for refining the area, deleting the effect, or hiding the selection border.

Figure 6.78
The Smart Brush tool.

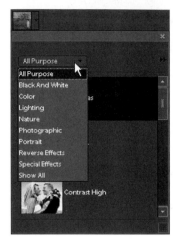

Figure 6.79 The Smart Paint menu and category drop-down menu list the various Smart Brush effects.

Adjustment layer pin

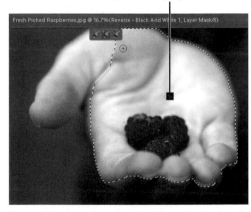

Figure 6.80 Paint the area to be affected by the Smart Paint effect (Reverse–Black And White shown here).

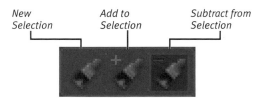

New
Selection   Add to
Selection   Subtract from
Selection

Figure 6.81 The selection tools appear above the Smart Paint area.

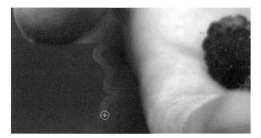

Figure 6.82 Use the Detail Smart Brush tool to draw directly on the layer mask for a more precise selection.

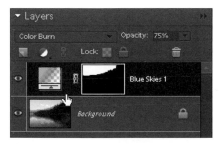

Figure 6.83 Smart Paints are actually just adjustment layers.

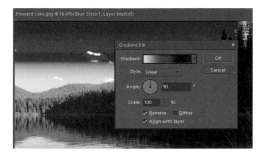

Figure 6.84 The Blue Skies Smart Paint effect applies a gradient fill to the selected area, which you can edit (but please, not like this, I beg you).

To edit a Smart Paint selection area:

◆ Once you start painting, the brush is in Add to Selection mode so additional areas you paint are added to the selection.

◆ To apply the Smart Paint to a different area of the image, click the New Selection button and begin painting.

◆ To deselect part of the Smart Paint area, click the Subtract from Selection button in the Options bar or in the floating toolbar that accompanies the selection (**Figure 6.81**).

◆ Click the Refine Edge button on the options bar to feather, contract or expand, or smooth the edge. The Inverse check box inverts the selection.

◆ To fine-tune the selection, switch to the Detail Smart Brush tool (press F again). The selection border disappears, letting you add to, or subtract from, the mask that defines the area (**Figure 6.82**).

To change Smart Paint settings:

◆ In the Layers palette, double-click the adjustment layer that corresponds with the Smart Paint effect (**Figure 6.83**).

The dialog that appears depends on the effect you chose; for example, Blue Skies applies a gradient to the area, so the Gradient Fill dialog appears. You can then edit the gradient (**Figure 6.84**).

✔ Tip

■ Some Smart Paints, such as the Black and White Yellow Filter, are not editable. Double-clicking the layer reveals that the effect was created in the full version of Photoshop. That actually means Elements has no interface or capability to edit the effect, even though the program is clearly capable of applying it.

Creating Panoramas

With Photoshop Elements, you can create wide, panoramic images that would be difficult to capture with a single shot from a standard camera. The Photomerge Panorama command analyzes your individual photos and assembles them into a single panoramic image (**Figure 6.85**).

Taking pictures for panoramas

If you're getting ready to snap some scenic photos and know you want to assemble them into a panorama later, making a few camera adjustments will make it easier to assemble a seamless panorama.

◆ Use a consistent zoom level when taking the pictures.

◆ Use a consistent focus. If your subject matter is far away, set your camera's focus to infinity, if that option is available.

◆ Use consistent exposure. A panorama with widely varied lighting will be difficult to merge seamlessly. Set your camera's exposure manually or lock the exposure setting if possible. Photomerge can make slight adjustments for images with different exposures, but it is not as effective when the image exposure varies greatly.

◆ If possible, use a tripod. You can take pictures for a panorama with a handheld camera, but you might find it difficult to keep all of the images perfectly level.

◆ Overlap sequential images by about 15 to 40 percent (**Figure 6.86**). Photomerge looks for similar detail in the edges of your images to match consecutive pictures. Try to capture as much detail throughout the frame to give Photomerge more reference points to match up.

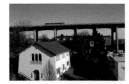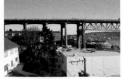
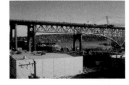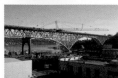
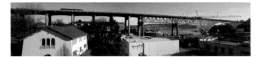

Figure 6.85 Photomerge combines several separate photos into a single panoramic picture.

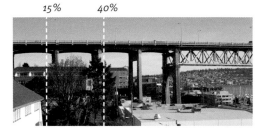

Figure 6.86 The more your images overlap, the better your chances of successfully merging them. Try for an overlap of between 15 and 40 percent.

✔ Tips

■ Try taking *two* versions of panorama images: one with the camera held horizontally and one with the camera held vertically. See which option makes a better panorama.

■ You're not limited to creating horizontal panoramas. You can also create vertical panoramas of tall subjects, such as skyscrapers or redwood trees.

■ Some digital cameras include a feature that helps you compose multiple overlapping photos when you shoot.

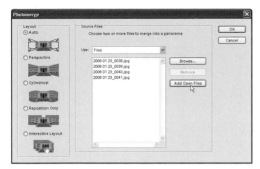

Figure 6.87 Browse for photos to merge in the Photomerge dialog.

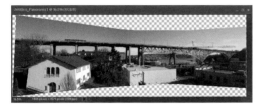

Figure 6.88 When you click OK, your merged images open in a new Elements file.

Assembling images into a panorama

To create a panoramic image, you select the images you want to merge and then let Photomerge work its magic.

To create a panorama:

1. Open the images you want to merge in the Editor, or select them in the Organizer.

   If you want to make any adjustments, such as tonal corrections or cropping, make your corrections first, *before* you begin assembling the images.

2. From the File menu, choose New > Photomerge Panorama. The Photomerge dialog appears (**Figure 6.87**).

3. Click the Add Open Files button to use the images from Step 1. If you need to delete a file from the list, select it and then click the Remove button.

   If you want to add more images, click the Browse button to open the Open dialog; then navigate to the folder containing the images you want to merge.

4. Choose a panorama style from the Layout column based on your source images. For example, you'd choose Cylindrical if you shot a 360-degree revolution around one point.

   The Interactive Layout option works differently than the rest, as you'll see on the following pages; for now, don't choose it.

5. When you have all of the images you want in the Source Files list, click OK.

   Photoshop Elements automatically opens the images in the Source Files list (if they're not already open), and with a little behind-the-scenes trickery, merges them into a single image (**Figure 6.88**).

continues on next page

✔ Tips

- You may see an alert message telling you that some images can't be assembled. If Photomerge can't find enough common details in your images, it will ignore those files. See the next page for a solution.

- Once you click OK to create your panorama, there's no returning to the Photomerge dialog to make further adjustments. If you're not happy with the way your panorama rendered, you'll need to start over. Refer to the following topics for further instruction on how to make additional adjustments to your panorama before you click the OK button.

- If seams are still visible in the panorama, try touching up those areas with the Clone tool.

- Use the Crop tool to remove those rough edges and give your panorama a nice, crisp rectangular border (**Figure 6.89**).

- Before you print your final panorama, take the time to examine its size in the Image Size dialog (from the File menu, choose Resize > Image Size). Depending on the size and resolution of the images you've used, your panoramas can quickly grow to exceed the standard paper stock sizes for your printer (which are usually no larger than 8.5 x 14 or 11 x 17 inches). Once you've determined the final image dimensions, use either the Image Size dialog or the controls in the Print Preview dialog to resize your image so it will fit on whatever paper stock you have available.

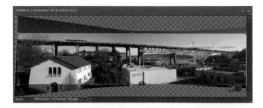

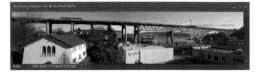

Figure 6.89 After creating the panorama, you can use the Crop tool to trim the image.

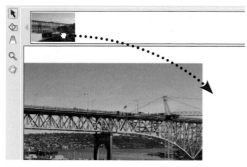

Figure 6.90 Drag or double-click an image in the Lightbox to move it to the work area.

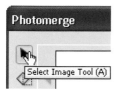

Figure 6.91
The Select Image tool.

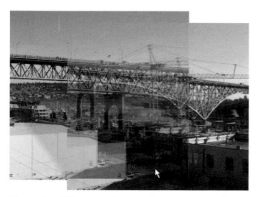

Figure 6.92 When you drag one image over another, the top image becomes semitransparent, allowing you to align the images.

Adjusting images using the Interactive Layout

When you choose the Interactive Layout option in the initial Photomerge dialog, Elements opens a new window where you can fine-tune the composition before it's built.

To reposition images in the panorama:

1. If one of your images is in the Lightbox area (just above the main preview area), add it to the work area by dragging it from the Lightbox (**Figure 6.90**).

   If you want to remove an image from the panorama, you can also drag images from the work area back into the Lightbox.

   Once all the images are in the work area, they still may not be lined up perfectly.

2. Check that the Select Image tool is highlighted in the Photomerge dialog (**Figure 6.91**).

3. Drag the image over the image with which it should merge. As you drag, the image becomes partially transparent so you can more easily line it up with the one below it (**Figure 6.92**).

4. When the two images match up, release the mouse button.

   If Snap to Image is selected in the dialog, any two overlapping images will automatically try to match up with one another. If Snap to Image is not selected, Photomerge allows you to align the overlapping image manually.

   Turning off Snap to Image allows you to move the images in small increments if they are not matching up exactly. You may also need to rotate an image slightly to make it match up with its neighbor correctly.

continues on next page

CREATING PANORAMAS

5. Select the Rotate Image tool, and then drag to rotate the selected image if needed (**Figure 6.93**).

The Photomerge dialog offers several options for moving through its work area while composing your panoramas, including its own built-in navigator.

6. To navigate through the work area, *do one of the following:*

▲ Select the Move View tool (the hand icon) in the dialog and drag in the work area.

▲ In the Navigator, drag the view box. This changes the view in the work area (**Figure 6.94**).

▲ Use the scroll bars at the bottom and right edges of the work area.

7. To change the zoom level in the work area, *do one of the following:*

▲ Select the Zoom tool in the dialog and click in the work area to zoom in.

▲ Hold down the Alt key while clicking to zoom out.

▲ Move the slider under the thumbnail in the Navigator.

▲ Click the Zoom icons under the thumbnail in the Navigator section of the dialog.

✔ Tip

■ You may see some tonal variation as a result of merging the images in the Interactive Layout (as in the images on the next page). However, Elements smooths those when the final panorama is constructed.

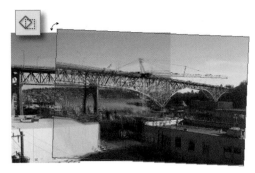

Figure 6.93 You can rotate images to help align them in the work area.

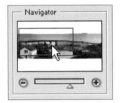 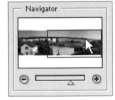

Figure 6.94 Drag the view box in the Navigator to change the view in the work area.

CREATING PANORAMAS

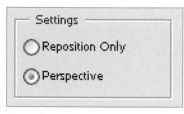

Figure 6.95 Click the Perspective radio button to add exaggerated perspective to your merged composition.

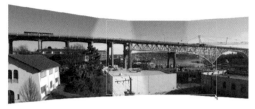

Figure 6.96 When you select the Perspective setting, Photomerge adjusts and distorts the images to create the illusion of a vanishing point. Here, the vanishing point image is identified by the light blue outline.

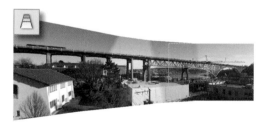

Figure 6.97 When you change the Vanishing Point image, the other images adjust and distort in response to change the perspective.

Enhancing perspective

Even the most sophisticated camera lenses tend to flatten what little depth or perspective is present in the landscapes or objects they capture. Photomerge Panorama lets you restore that lost perspective to create a more natural-looking panoramic image. In addition, you can adjust the vanishing point (the point where natural perspective recedes into the distance) to help draw attention to a specific area or object in your panorama.

To add perspective to a panorama:

1. In the Settings section of the dialog, select the Perspective option (**Figure 6.95**).

   The outside edges of the panorama are distorted, creating a more dramatic, and sometimes more realistic, perspective view (**Figure 6.96**). The middle of the center image is designated as the vanishing point, and the outside images appear to recede into its center. The vanishing point image is identified by a blue outline when it's selected.

2. To make a different image the vanishing point image, first select the Set Vanishing Point tool.

3. Click a different image in the work area. The panorama changes the perspective to make it look as if the other images now recede into the new Vanishing Point image (**Figure 6.97**).

4. If the perspective option doesn't give you the effect you'd hoped for, select the Reposition Only option in the Settings section of the dialog to return your panorama to its original state.

   You can also remove the perspective from your panorama by dragging the Vanishing Point image to the Lightbox.

CHANGING AND ADJUSTING COLORS

7

Almost any photograph can benefit from some simple color or lighting corrections. For example, you might find that a vivid sunset you photographed ends up looking rather dull and ordinary, or that a portrait taken outdoors is too dark to discern any details. Luckily, you're never stuck with a roll of inferior images. Photoshop Elements provides a powerful set of color correction tools, with both manual and automatic adjustments, so you can fine-tune your images as much as you want.

In this chapter, I'll review Photoshop Elements' color-correction tools and discuss which tools you may want to use, and when you'll most likely want to use them. I'll also show you how to help colors display and print accurately (also known as *color management*) and how to correct colors and tonal values in your images. Along the way, I'll shed some light on why what may appear to be the most obvious color-enhancement options are not always the best choices for improving the color in an image.

About Color Models and Color Modes

No matter how your images got into the computer, whether from a scanner, a digital camera, or copied from a stock art CD, the version of the image stored on your hard disk can only *approximate* the colors of the original scene. A computer is only capable of dealing with numbers, so it somehow has to come up with numerical equivalents of the colors perceived by our eyes.

Computers use number systems, called *color models,* to display and reproduce color. One of the most common is the RGB color model. In this model, the color of each pixel is described as combinations of different amounts of the colors red, green, and blue. These colors were chosen because the cells in our eyes that respond to color (called cones) come in three types; some are sensitive to red, some to green, and some to blue. Therefore, the RGB model tries to characterize colors in a way that's similar to the way the human eye perceives them.

It's important to remember that color models, at best, can only *approximate* the colors in your image. No color model is as sensitive as the human eye.

Color Modes

A color *mode* specifies which color model will display and print your images. Photoshop Elements includes four color modes—RGB, Grayscale, Bitmap, and Indexed. (Another common mode, CMYK, is not supported by Elements; it's primarily a color mode for print publishing.)

◆ **RGB mode.** RGB stands for red, green, and blue, which are the three color channels your eye perceives (**Figure 7.1**). These are also the three color phosphors used in your computer monitor to display color. The combination of these channels

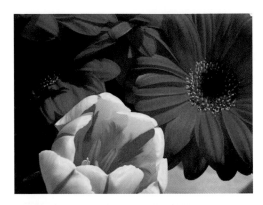

Red

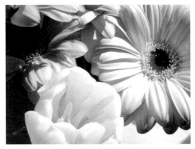

Green

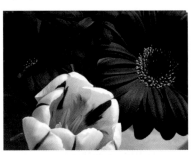

Blue

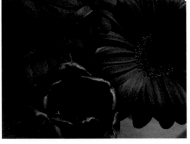

Figure 7.1 An RGB image is made up of three separate color channels: Red, Green, and Blue. (Each channel contains only its color's hues, which are represented in grayscale when viewed separately like this.)

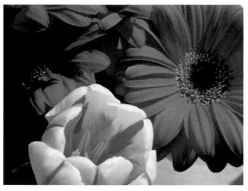

Figure 7.2 Grayscale mode converts the color channels to shades of gray.

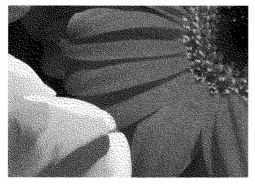

Figure 7.3 You can convert any grayscale image to a bitmapped image (here enlarged to 100 percent to show the texture).

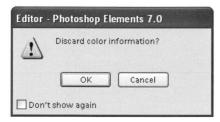

Figure 7.4 Converting from RGB to grayscale discards the color information.

creates the full-color image you see. Many selection and correction options allow you to adjust these colors independently.

◆ **Grayscale mode.** A grayscale image is made up of 256 unique shades of gray (**Figure 7.2**). Converting from RGB to Grayscale reduces the image to just one color channel, so the resulting image file size is about one third of the RGB version. If you're looking to create a black and white photo, however, see "Converting to Black and White," later in this chapter.

◆ **Bitmap mode.** An image converted to Bitmap mode really *is* a black-and-white image, because during the conversion, each pixel is rendered as black or white (**Figure 7.3**).

◆ **Indexed mode.** The indexed color version of an image is limited to a maximum of 256 colors, and is used when you're preparing images strictly for viewing on computer monitors. In most cases you won't convert photos to this mode but will instead use the Save for Web dialog (see Chapter 12).

To change color mode:

1. From the Image menu, select Mode and choose one of the color modes. The Bitmap and Indexed Color options present you with conversion options; the Grayscale option displays a dialog asking if you want to discard the color information (**Figure 7.4**).

2. Click OK.

✔ Tip

■ Before converting your file to another color mode, it's a good idea to save a "master" version of your photo first. That way, no matter what changes you make to your image, you always have the original, unaltered version.

Managing color

You've learned some color basics, but before going any further, you may want to take a couple of steps to ensure that the color you see on your monitor will be reasonably accurate when you decide to print or send images to the Web. Fortunately, color management in Elements is simple and doesn't require any labor-intensive chores on your part.

You should first make sure the colors you see on the monitor are reasonably accurate and represent what others will see on their monitors. Calibrating your monitor is a particularly good idea if you have an older monitor or have inherited it from a friend or relative (you don't know what they might have done to the monitor settings). If you have a newer monitor, it probably came with an accurate calibration from the factory.

If you're using a CRT monitor, you can use Adobe Gamma to calibrate it; you'll find it on the Photoshop Elements installation CD in the Goodies\Software\Adobe Gamma folder.

However, Adobe Gamma doesn't work with LCD monitors. Instead, turn to tools such as Datacolor's Spyder (`spyder.datacolor.com`) or the free Microsoft Color Control Panel Applet for Windows XP (download from `http://www.microsoft.com/prophoto/downloads/colorcontrol.aspx`).

If you prefer, you can also choose color settings optimized for either Web graphics or color printing.

Color Management Is an Imperfect Science

As you start selecting and adjusting colors in Photoshop Elements, it's important to understand that the term *color management* can be a little misleading.

Color management operates under the assumption that we're creating artwork at our calibrated monitors under specific, controlled lighting conditions, and that our desktop printers work at peak performance at all times. In other words, it assumes controlled, uncompromised perfection.

At the time of this writing, the late afternoon sun is casting some lovely warm reflections off the blinds of the window and onto the wall directly behind my computer monitor, and is competing for attention with the glow from the 40-watt, soft-white bulb in my desk lamp. Therein lies the problem: the vast majority of Photoshop Elements users are working in similarly imperfect conditions.

In addition to trying to make a perfect science out of a host of imperfect variables, color management all but ignores one of the most imperfect sciences of all: our very human, very subjective perception. I may print out an image I find perfectly acceptable, whereas you may look at the same image and decide to push the color one way or another to try to create a different mood or atmosphere. That's what makes everything I create so different. That's what makes it art. And that's (at least in part) what makes color management an imperfect science. So, as you read through this chapter, keep in mind that your images will never look *precisely* the same when viewed by different users on different monitors. And that's perfectly all right.

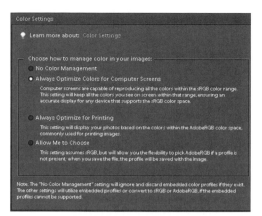

Figure 7.5 Choose a color management option best suited to the final output of your image.

About Color Profiles

The choices you make in the Color Settings dialog affect only the *display* of an image onscreen and won't affect how an image is printed. The Always Optimize for Printing option, for instance, will simulate the AdobeRGB color spectrum on your monitor but will not assign the AdobeRGB *color profile* to an image. A color profile is information embedded in an image and stored in the background until it's required (usually by a printer). The color profile helps to interpret the RGB color information in an image and convert it to a color language that a printer can understand, and so reproduce the most accurate color possible. You can assign a color profile to an image at any time regardless of the option you've set in the Color Settings dialog. With an image open, simply choose Convert Color Mode from the Image menu. From the Convert Color Profile submenu, you can Remove an unwanted profile (sRGB, for example) and apply the profile more suitable for printing: AdobeRGB.

To choose color settings:

◆ From the Edit menu, choose Color Settings.

The Color Settings dialog appears with three color management options plus the option to choose No Color Management (**Figure 7.5**).

▲ **Always Optimize Colors for Computer Screens** displays images based on the sRGB (standard RGB) color profile and is the default setting. It's a good all-around solution, particularly if you are creating images to be viewed primarily onscreen.

▲ **Always Optimize for Printing** displays color based on the AdobeRGB profile. Although the image you see onscreen may display with only subtle color differences (as compared to sRGB), you will generally get truer, more accurate color when you send the image to print.

▲ **Allow Me to Choose** will default to sRGB, but if the image contains no color profile, you'll have the option of choosing AdobeRGB.

Converting to Black and White

Taking a color photograph and making it black and white (well, technically *grayscale*) can involve more than just draining the color. The RGB values can be adjusted to highlight different tones in the final image, the contrast can be changed—edits you could perform separately later. But the Convert to Black and White dialog rolls them into one place and throws in some handy presets, too.

To convert an image to black and white:

1. Open the image you want to convert in the Editor.

2. From the Enhance menu, choose Convert to Black and White (or press Alt+Ctrl+B) to open the similarly-named dialog (**Figure 7.6**).

3. Optionally, choose a preset from the Select a style list that matches the type of image you're editing (**Figure 7.7**).

4. If you want to change the black and white photo's appearance, use the Adjustment Intensity sliders (**Figure 7.8**).

5. When you're satisfied with the result in the preview, click OK. The photo is converted to black and white (**Figure 7.9**).

✔ Tip

■ Duplicate the layer the image is on in the Layers palette before you open the Convert to Black and White dialog, and then apply the command to that layer. The feature applies only to the active layer, not the entire image as if you had switched to Grayscale mode.

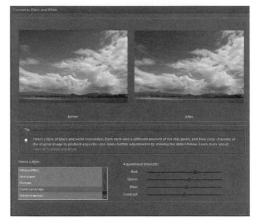

Figure 7.6 The Convert to Black and White dialog includes many adjustments you likely would have made anyway.

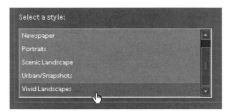

Figure 7.7 Elements includes several preset styles that can get you started.

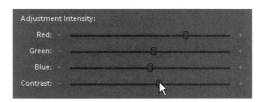

Figure 7.8 Experiment with the Adjustment Intensity sliders to get the look you want.

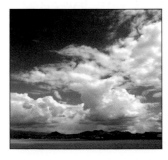

Figure 7.9 You may not be Ansel, but you're getting there.

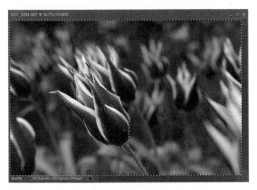

Figure 7.10 Select the area you want to convert to grayscale.

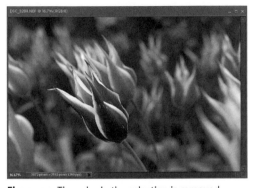

Figure 7.11 The color in the selection is removed.

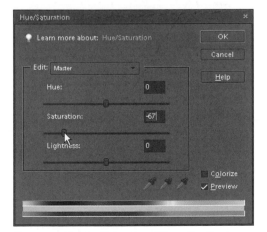

Figure 7.12 Use the Saturation slider in the Hue/Saturation dialog to control the amount of color you remove from an image.

Removing Color

Unlike converting to black and white (which removes all color information from an image), you can use the Remove Color command to remove color from just a portion of an image. This feature can be used to great effect for highlighting or dimming specific areas, creating neutral fields in which to place type, or as a first step before applying a colorization or color tint effect.

To apply the Remove Color command:

1. Using any of the selection or marquee tools, select the area of your image from which you want to remove the color (**Figure 7.10**).

2. From the Enhance menu, choose Adjust Color > Remove Color, or press Shift+Ctrl+U.

   All color is removed from the selected areas of the image and replaced by levels of gray (**Figure 7.11**).

✔ Tip

■ You can control how much color to remove from an image or selection by using the Saturation slider in the Hue/Saturation dialog. From the Enhance menu, choose Adjust Color > Adjust Hue/Saturation, or press Ctrl+U to open the dialog. Then, move the Saturation slider to the left until you achieve the desired effect (**Figure 7.12**). The value 0 on the saturation scale represents normal color saturation, whereas –100 (all the way to the left) represents completely desaturated color, or grayscale.

About Tonal Correction

Tonal correction tends to be one of the least understood (and thus most intimidating) features of Elements. Mention *levels* and *histograms* and *white points* to even some seasoned graphics professionals, and you'll see their eyes begin to glaze. That's a shame, because there's really no magic involved. Once understood, tonal correction can be one of the simplest and most instantly gratifying steps toward improving an image.

In plain terms, correcting tonal range simply comes down to adjusting brightness and contrast. Elements offers several ways to make automatic brightness and contrast adjustments. But the most precise and intuitive method is by using the Levels dialog, and the heart of the Levels dialog is the histogram.

Understanding histograms

The **histogram** is a graphic representation of the tonal range of an image. The lengths of the bars represent the number of pixels at each brightness level: from the darkest, on the left, to the lightest, on the right. If the bars on both sides extend all the way to the left and right edges of the histogram box, the darkest pixels in the image are black, the lightest pixels are white, and the image is said to have a *full tonal range* (**Figure 7.13**). If, as in many images, the bars stop short of the edges, the darkest and lightest pixels are some shade of gray, and the image may lack contrast. In extreme circumstances, the bars may be weighted heavily to the left or right, with the tonal range favoring either the shadows or highlights (**Figure 7.14**). Whatever the tonal range, the brightness and contrast of an image can be adjusted using sliders located beneath the histogram in the Levels dialog (see "Adjusting Levels Manually" later in this chapter).

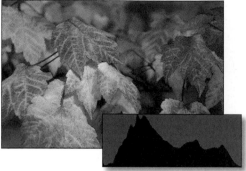

Figure 7.13 A photo displaying full tonal range and its accompanying histogram. Note how the histogram extends all the way to the left and right, indicating that pure blacks are present in the darkest shadow areas and pure whites are present in the lightest highlight areas. The fairly uniform peaks and valleys throughout the middle portion of the histogram also indicate sufficient pixel data present in the midtones.

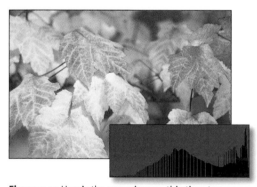

Figure 7.14 Here's the same image, this time too bright and with insufficient contrast. Note the lack of data on the left end, indicating a lack of black pixels, and the abundance of data on the right, indicating very light tones.

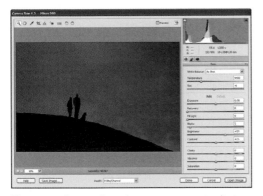

Figure 7.15 Camera Raw gives you an opportunity to adjust the raw, unedited image data.

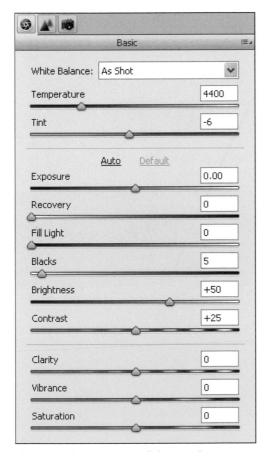

Figure 7.16 The Camera Raw dialog contains many adjustment tools for correcting an image before it's opened in the Editor.

Adjusting Camera Raw Photos

Many digital cameras save photos in camera raw format, which is the unedited data captured by the camera's image sensor; each manufacturer uses its own proprietary specifications, so you'll see files ending in .NEF, .CRW, or others. Camera raw gives you more options for adjusting an image—the camera hasn't already made choices for sharpening or tonal balance for you.

Unlike changes made in the Editor, however, the modifications you make in the Camera Raw dialog are saved alongside your image, so you can go back and tweak the raw settings later if you want.

To adjust camera raw images:

1. Choose an image in the Organizer and open it in the Editor, or open a file directly in the Editor. If the file is in camera raw format, the Camera Raw dialog appears (**Figure 7.15**).

2. If you want to give the dialog first crack at the image, click Auto above the adjustment sliders. Otherwise, edit the settings by dragging each slider (**Figure 7.16**). Here's a breakdown of what they do:

   ▲ **White Balance.** The Temperature and Tint sliders make the photo warmer or cooler. (The Auto button doesn't apply to White Balance settings.)

   ▲ **Exposure** brightens or darkens the image.

   ▲ **Recovery** pulls detail out of blown-out (very bright) areas.

   ▲ **Fill Light** brightens midtones without overexposing the image.

   ▲ **Blacks** pushes darker areas to black.

continues on next page

▲ **Brightness** raises or lowers the overall illumination.

▲ **Contrast** applies contrast to the image's midtones.

▲ **Clarity** sharpens the image by detecting and working on edges, as opposed to sharpening everything.

▲ **Vibrance** applies saturation but doesn't allow colors to become clipped (blown out).

▲ **Saturation** increases or decreases the color intensity of the image as a whole.

More controls are available in the detail tab (click the icon with two triangles):

▲ **Sharpening** offers the same type of controls discussed in Chapter 6; the settings are applied to the entire image.

▲ **Noise Reduction** works to remove the digital spottiness caused by shooting in low-light situations or at high ISO settings. The Luminance slider applies to grayscale noise, while the Color slider affects chroma noise, or noise made up of multiple colors.

3. The Camera Raw dialog also includes several tools found in the Editor (**Figure 7.17**); if you need to rotate the image, for example, you may as well do it here.

4. Click the Open Image button to apply the adjustments and open the file in the Editor (**Figure 7.18**).

✔ Tips

■ The clipping indicators can warn if areas are too white or too black (**Figure 7.19**).

■ If you're planning to apply sharpening in the Editor later, don't make those adjustments in the Camera Raw dialog.

■ Hold Alt and click Open Image to save a new copy with the raw edits applied.

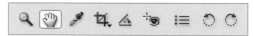

Figure 7.17 The following tools are available if you want to make the adjustments here (left to right): Zoom, Move, Eyedropper (for identifying white point), Crop, Straighten, Fix Red-Eye, Preferences (for the Camera Raw dialog), and Rotate counter-clockwise and clockwise.

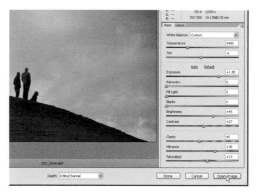

Figure 7.18 When you're happy with the results, click the Open Image button.

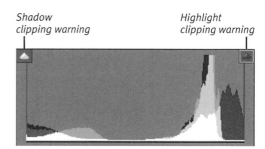

Shadow clipping warning

Highlight clipping warning

Figure 7.19 The clipping icons warn when darks or whites are too heavy; click an icon to view the affected areas in the image.

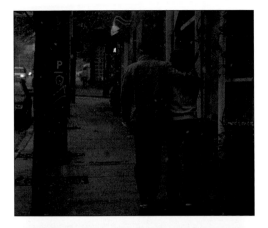

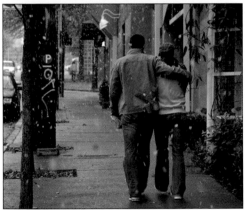

Figure 7.20 The photo on the top lacks sufficient tonal range, particularly in the highlight and lighter midtone areas. The photo on the bottom, corrected with the Auto Levels command, reveals more detail in both the shadow and highlight areas because the pixels have been distributed across the full tonal range.

Adjusting Levels Automatically

Photoshop Elements gives you the option of applying a quick fix to image levels and contrast with the Auto Levels and Auto Contrast commands. Although I recommend working with the histogram in the Levels dialog, the auto commands can be a good jumping-off point before launching into more controlled, manual image correction. The auto commands tend to be most successful when applied to photographs that contain an *average tonal range*; one where most of the image detail is concentrated in the *midtones*. Midtones are those tonal values that fall about halfway between the darkest and lightest values. Midtone areas tend to contain more image information—more visible detail, that is—than extremely dark or light areas. Photographs with predominant midtones—whether in grayscale or in color—are usually the best candidates for auto correction. Severely overexposed or underexposed images may be beyond help. If the camera or scanner didn't capture the detail in the first place, it's not there to be corrected.

To apply Auto Levels to an image:

1. From the Enhance menu, choose Auto Levels, or press Shift+Ctrl+L.

   Photoshop Elements instantly adjusts the image's tonal range (**Figure 7.20**).

2. If you're not happy with the result, select Edit > Undo Auto Levels, or press Ctrl+Z.

Get Smart

Finessing an image's levels and other settings gives you an enormous amount of power to correct tonal ranges—but maybe you don't have the time or desire to be a slave to the sliders. The Auto Smart Fix command under the Enhance menu does it all for you. If you don't like the result, you can build from there or start over and tackle each setting yourself.

To apply Auto Contrast to an image:

1. From the Enhance menu, choose Auto Contrast, or press Alt+ Shift+Ctrl+L (**Figure 7.21**).

   Photoshop Elements instantly adjusts the image's contrast (**Figure 7.22**).

2. To undo, choose Edit > Undo Auto Contrast, or press Ctrl+Z .

✔ Tips

■ As mentioned earlier, the auto commands work best in specific circumstances (as when the image's tonal range favors the midtones) and should be used sparingly. The Auto Levels command, in particular, can yield some surprising and unexpected color shifts. In some instances it seems to overcompensate by swapping out one undesirable color cast for another, whereas in others it may ignore the color altogether and throw the contrast way out of whack. Give these auto commands a try, but be prepared to commit that Undo keyboard shortcut to memory.

■ If you're looking for adjustments without all the detail, the Quick Fix environment groups a cross-section of some of the more commonly used commands and functions into one convenient, interactive workspace. See Chapter 4 for more information.

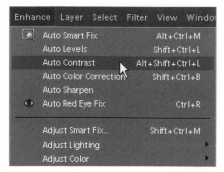

Figure 7.21 Choose Enhance > Auto Contrast to apply an instant contrast fix to your image.

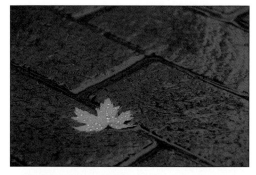

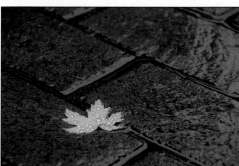

Figure 7.22 The photo on the top lacks sufficient contrast, so detail is lost in both the shadow and highlight areas. The photo on the bottom, corrected with Auto Contrast, reveals detail not present in the original.

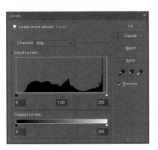

Figure 7.23
The Levels
dialog.

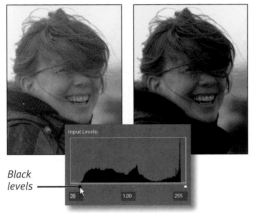

Black
levels

Figure 7.24 Moving the left slider underneath the left edge of the histogram spreads the darker pixels more evenly into the dark areas of the midtones and shifts the darkest pixels to black.

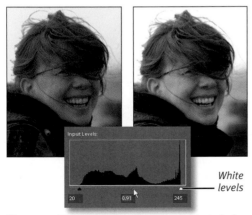

White
levels

Figure 7.25 The right slider affects the lightest pixels in the image. Moving the right slider underneath the right edge of the histogram spreads the lighter pixels more evenly into the light areas of the midtones and shifts the lightest pixels to white, resulting in more detail in the highlight areas.

Adjusting Levels Manually

The Levels dialog can do more to improve the overall tonal quality of your image than any other workspace in Photoshop Elements. Many images, whether scanned or imported from a digital camera, don't contain the full tonal range, and as a result lack sufficient contrast. That lack of contrast translates into loss of detail, usually most noticeably in the shadow and highlight areas. Using the histogram and sliders in the Levels dialog, you darken the darkest pixels and lighten the lightest ones to improve contrast, then adjust the brightness levels in the midtones.

To adjust the tonal range:

1. From the Enhance menu, choose Adjust Lighting > Levels, or press Ctrl+L to open the Levels dialog (**Figure 7.23**).

2. Select the Preview box and drag the slider on the left until it rests directly below the left edge of the histogram (**Figure 7.24**). The image darkens as the darkest pixels in the image move closer to black.

3. Drag the slider on the right until it rests directly below the right edge of the graph (**Figure 7.25**). The image lightens as the lightest pixels move closer to white.

4. Drag the middle slider to the left or right to adjust the brightness level of the pixels that fall in the midtones.

5. Click OK to close the Levels dialog.

✔ Tip

■ What about the Brightness/Contrast command? I never use it. Unlike Levels, which affects pixels in specific tonal ranges, Brightness/Contrast indiscriminately lightens or darkens pixels across the entire tonal range, typically creating more problems than it solves.

ADJUSTING LEVELS MANUALLY

167

Adjusting Lighting

Overexposed background images and under-exposed foreground subjects are a common problem for most amateur photographers. Much like the Levels command, the Shadows/Highlights dialog operates on pixels in specific tonal ranges while leaving the other tonal ranges alone.

To lighten detail in shadow:

1. From the Enhance menu, choose Adjust Lighting > Shadows/Highlights.

   The Shadows/Highlights dialog appears (**Figure 7.26**).

2. In the Shadows/Highlights dialog, *do one or all of the following*:

   ▲ Drag the Lighten Shadows slider to the right to lessen the effect of the shadows, or to the left to introduce shadow back into the image.

   ▲ Drag the Darken Highlights slider to the right until you're satisfied with the detail in the foreground or other brightly lit areas.

   ▲ Drag the Midtone Contrast slider to the right to increase the contrast, or to the left to decrease the contrast.

3. Click OK to close the Shadows/Highlights dialog and apply the changes (**Figure 7.27**).

✔ Tips

■ I've found in many (if not most) images imported from a digital camera, the Shadows/Highlights dialog defaults work surprisingly well on their own, requiring just minor slider adjustments.

■ In any case, use the Midtone Contrast slider sparingly. A little goes a long way, and adjustments of more than plus or minus 10% can quickly wash out or flatten an image's details.

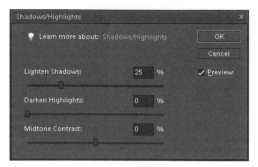

Figure 7.26 The Shadows/Highlights dialog.

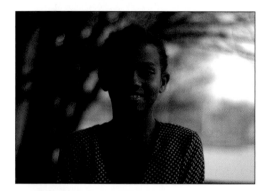

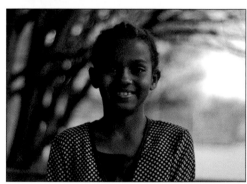

Figure 7.27 The top photo is underexposed in the foreground, so detail in the girl's face is hidden in shadow. In the bottom photo, making adjustments with the Lighten Shadows and the Midtone Contrast sliders selectively brightens and enhances detail in both her face and shirt.

ADJUSTING LIGHTING

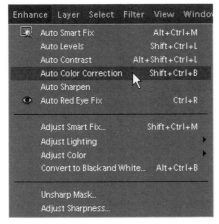

Figure 7.28 Choose Auto Color Correction from the Enhance menu to automatically remove color cast from your image.

Adjusting Color

Color cast refers to a general shift of color to one extreme or another: An image can be said to have a yellow or red cast, for instance. Although sometimes introduced into images intentionally (to create a certain mood or effect), color casts are usually unhappy accidents. They can result from any number of circumstances, from a scanner in need of calibrating to tired chemicals in a film developer's lab. Even light from a fluorescent bulb can create unwanted color shifts in photographs.

Thankfully, Elements gives you several ways to deal with color cast: a wonderful little automatic menu command, a dialog that allows you to manually color-correct an image by adding and subtracting color values in small increments, a dialog for adjusting color curves, and a feature that can dramatically improve skin tones.

To adjust color with the Auto Color Correction command:

◆ From the Enhance menu, choose Auto Color Correction, or press Shift+Ctrl+B (**Figure 7.28**).

That's it. Photoshop Elements performs some elegant, behind-the-scenes magic, examining the image's color channels and histogram and performing a little math, and *voilà*—no more color cast.

✔ Tip

■ I use this feature all the time before applying any other image correction. I'm constantly amazed at how well this simple menu command works, and usually give it a try even if I don't perceive a color cast. It almost always offers some degree of improvement to the color.

ADJUSTING COLOR

To adjust color using color curves:

1. From the Enhance menu, choose Adjust Color > Adjust Color Curves to open the Adjust Color Curves dialog.

2. To go with one of Elements' suggestions, click one of the styles at left (**Figure 7.29**). You can also drag the sliders under Adjust Sliders to manually tweak highlights, midtone brightness and contrast, or shadows. The points on the color curve to the right represent each setting.

3. Click OK to apply the color changes.

To adjust color in an image based on skin tones:

1. From the Enhance menu, choose Adjust Color > Adjust Color for Skin Tone to open the Adjust Color for Skin Tone dialog.

2. Check that the Preview check box is selected, and then move the cursor onto the photo until it becomes an eyedropper. Click with the eyedropper on any part of a person's skin (**Figure 7.30**).

   Photoshop Elements adjusts the color in the entire image, but pays special attention to the skin tones.

3. If you're not satisfied with the results, click a different area of skin, or use the sliders to fine-tune the color change (**Figure 7.31**).

4. Click OK to close the dialog and set the color changes.

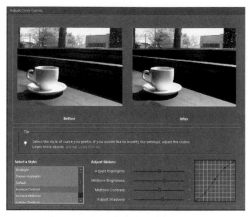

Figure 7.29 The Adjust Color Curves provides one more way of fine-tuning an image's color.

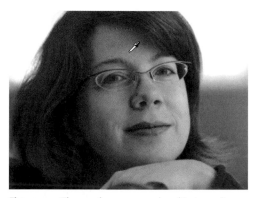

Figure 7.30 The eyedropper samples skin tones in a photo and then makes a best-guess color correction.

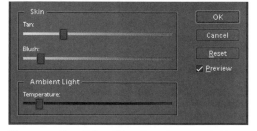

Figure 7.31 Use dialog sliders to make manual skin tone corrections.

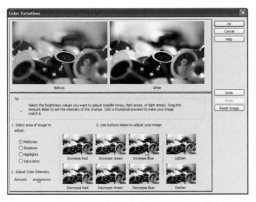

Figure 7.32 The core of the Color Variations dialog is the lower, thumbnail button area. Each time you click a thumbnail you apply a slight color shift to your image. The thumbnails can be clicked any number of times and in any combination.

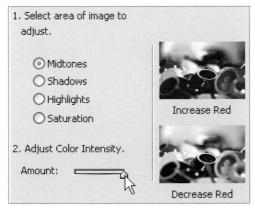

Figure 7.33 The Amount slider is a bit of a brute force mechanism, but it works well with trial and error.

To remove color cast with the Color Variations dialog:

1. From the Enhance menu, choose Adjust Color > Color Variations.

2. Determine the color cast of your image.

   Because Elements doesn't offer any help in determining color cast, you're pretty much on your own here. Look for clues to color cast in objects or areas you are familiar with and can make good, educated guesses on. Ask yourself if that bright blue sky is looking a little yellow, or if those leafy greens have a little pink tinge to them, and then work from there.

3. In the lower portion of the dialog, click the thumbnail with the description that best describes what you need to do (Increase Red, Decrease Blue, and so on) while referring to the After view in the top half of the dialog (**Figure 7.32**).

4. Continue to click any combination of thumbnails, as many times as necessary, until the After view looks satisfactory.

5. Click OK to close the Color Variations dialog and view your corrected image.

✔ Tips

- To a large degree, using the Color Variations dialog is a matter of trial and error, and to a lesser degree a rather subjective process (**Figure 7.33**). And as much as I'd like to provide some little hints or formulas, experience and experimentation are the real keys to success with this dialog.

- If you find yourself completely lost, or just want to start over, click the Before thumbnail in the upper-left corner, or the Reset Image button along the right side to reset the entire dialog.

Replacing Color

The Replace Color command does just what you would expect it to do, and does it very well indeed. In a nutshell, it allows you to select a specific color, either across an entire image or in an isolated area of an image, and then change not only the color but its saturation and lightness values as well. Eyedropper tools let you add and subtract colors to be replaced, whereas a slider control softens the transition between the colors you choose and those around them. I've seen this used to great effect on projects as varied as experimenting with different color schemes before painting a house's trim to changing the color of a favorite uncle's tie so that it no longer clashes with his suit.

To replace color across an entire image:

1. From the Enhance menu, choose Adjust Color > Replace Color.

2. In the Replace Color dialog, click the Selection radio button under the image preview box (**Figure 7.34**).

   When the Replace Color dialog is open, your pointer will automatically change to an eyedropper tool when you move it over your image.

3. With the eyedropper tool, click in the image to select the color you want to change (**Figure 7.35**).

   The color selection appears as a white area in the image preview of the Replace Color dialog (**Figure 7.36**).

4. To expand the selection and include similar colors, drag the Fuzziness slider to the right. To contract the selection and exclude similar colors, drag the Fuzziness slider to the left.

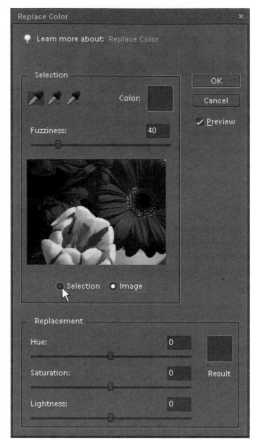

Figure 7.34 Options under the image preview box let you choose whether to view your color selections or just the image.

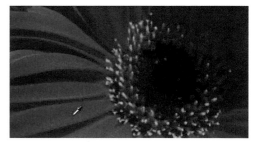

Figure 7.35 Click the actual image in the image window to make a color selection.

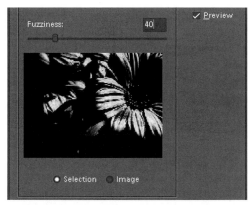

Figure 7.36 The image preview area of the Replace Color dialog shows selected colors as white or shades of gray.

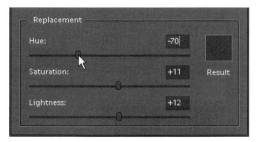

Figure 7.37 Drag the Hue, Saturation, and Lightness sliders until you capture the right color effect. You may have to experiment a little until you get it just right.

You may want to expand or contract your selection beyond the limits of the Fuzziness slider. If parts of a selection fall too heavily in shadow or highlight, or have very reflective surfaces, you may need to make additional color selections or deletions.

5. To add a color to the selection, Shift+click the eyedropper tool in another area of the image. To subtract a color from the selection, press Alt+click.

The dialog contains separate add and subtract eyedropper tools, but the keyboard shortcuts provide a much more efficient way to modify your color selections.

6. With the Preview check box selected, drag the Hue, Saturation, and Lightness sliders (**Figure 7.37**) until you achieve the desired color effect.

These sliders operate just like the ones in the Hue/Saturation dialog. The Hue slider controls the actual color change; the Saturation slider controls the intensity of the color, from muted to pure; and the Lightness slider controls the color's brightness value, adding either black or white.

7. Click OK to close the Replace Color dialog and view your corrected image.

To replace color in a specific area of an image:

1. In the image window, make a selection around the area to which you want to apply the color change (**Figure 7.38**).

2. From the Enhance menu, choose Adjust Color > Replace Color.

3. In the Replace Color dialog, click the Image button under the image preview. A detail view of your selection appears. When the Replace Color dialog is open, your pointer automatically changes to an eyedropper tool.

4. With the eyedropper tool, click in the image preview box of the Replace Color dialog to select the color you want to change (**Figure 7.39**).

5. Click the Selection radio button to toggle to the Selection view.

6. To add or subtract a color from the selection, click the Image button to toggle back to that view; then use the keyboard shortcuts, as described in the previous procedure, to adjust the selection.

7. Use the Fuzziness slider to further fine-tune your selection (**Figure 7.40**).

8. With the Preview check box selected, drag the Hue, Saturation, and Lightness sliders until you achieve the desired color.

9. Click OK to apply your changes.

✔ Tip

■ If you prefer, you can always choose to make your color selection in the actual image in the image window, just as I did in the previous procedure. But if the selections you're making are small, relative to the total size of your image, it's often easier to work within the confines of the Replace Color dialog.

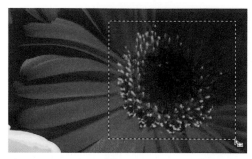

Figure 7.38 Any selections you make are reflected in the Replace Color dialog.

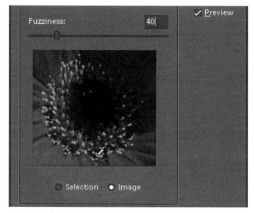

Figure 7.39 Click the image within the Replace Color dialog to make a color selection.

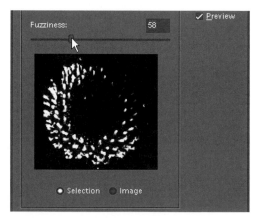

Figure 7.40 When the Selection radio button is clicked, the image in the preview box changes to show the selected colors as white or shades of gray.

REPLACING COLOR

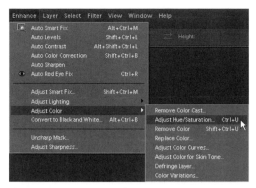

Figure 7.41 Open the Hue/Saturation dialog to access the Colorize option.

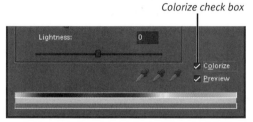

Figure 7.42 Click the Colorize check box to add a colored tint to any image.

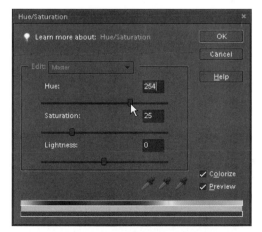

Figure 7.43 The position of the Hue slider determines the color your tinted image will be.

Adding a Color Tint to an Image

Using a technique called *colorization*, you can add a single color tint to your images, simulating the look of a hand-applied color wash or the warm, antique glow of an old sepia-toned photograph. You can apply the effect to any image, even if it was originally saved as grayscale, as long as you first convert it to RGB. In addition to colorizing an entire image, you can use layers and layer modes to tint specific areas or objects. Because the shades of color you apply are determined by the image's original tonal values, photographs with good brightness and contrast levels make the best candidates for colorizing.

To colorize a large area of an image:

1. Using any of the selection or marquee tools, select the area of your image you want to colorize. If you want to colorize an entire image, it's not necessary to make a selection.

2. From the Enhance menu, choose Adjust Color > Adjust Hue/Saturation, or press Ctrl+U to open the Hue/Saturation dialog (**Figure 7.41**).

3. With the Preview check box selected, click the Colorize check box (**Figure 7.42**). Clicking the Colorize check box converts all the color in the image to a single hue.

4. Drag the Hue slider right or left until you arrive at the color you like (**Figure 7.43**).

5. Drag the Saturation slider to adjust its values. Dragging to the left moves the color's saturation value closer to gray, whereas dragging to the right moves its value closer to a fully saturated color.

continues on next page

6. Drag the Lightness slider to adjust the color's brightness values.

Dragging to the left dims the color's brightness value, shifting it closer to black, whereas dragging to the right brightens its value, shifting it closer to white.

7. Click OK to close the Hue/Saturation dialog. Your image (or selection) is now composed of different values of the single color hue you selected.

✔ Tip

■ When you're applying a color tint to just a portion of your image, I recommend making a selection and then creating a new Hue/Saturation adjustment layer in the Layers palette (**Figure 7.44**). See "Making Color and Tonal Changes with Adjustment Layers" in Chapter 8 for more information.

Hue/Saturation adjustment layer

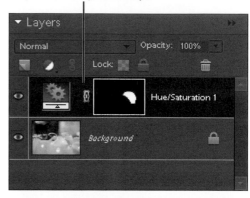

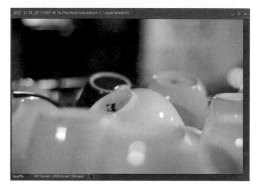

Figure 7.44 When selectively colorizing your image, you'll get more flexibility by using an adjustment layer.

WORKING WITH LAYERS

8

Photoshop Elements allows you to work on individual image layers. You can create and name new layers, and then reorder, group, and even merge selected layers together.

In this chapter, you'll learn how layers are created, and then explore several methods and techniques to help you take advantage of one of Elements' most powerful and creative features.

The chapter concludes with a comprehensive look at the Undo History palette. This helpful palette tracks and displays a record of every action you make (from selections, to layer creation, to retouching), and then lets you easily undo any action and return to different states in the history of your image creation.

Understanding Layers

When you first import or scan an image into Photoshop Elements, it consists of one default layer. In many cases, you'll probably want to make a few simple changes to your photo and will have no need for multiple layers. But when you begin working with some of the more involved and complex image manipulation and retouching tools, you'll find that layers can make things a whole lot easier.

Layers act like clear, transparent sheets stacked one on top of another, and yet, when you view a final image, they appear as one unified picture (**Figure 8.1**). As you copy and paste selections, you may notice these operations automatically create new layers in your image. You can edit only one layer at a time, which allows you to select and modify specific parts of your photo without affecting the information on other layers. This is the real beauty of layers: the ability to work on and experiment with one part of your image while leaving the rest of it completely untouched. One exception is the adjustment layer, which lets you make color and tonal corrections to individual *or* multiple layers without changing the actual pixels.

Layers appear in your image in the same order as they appear in the Layers palette. The top layer of your image is the first layer listed on the Layers palette, and the background layer is positioned at the bottom of the list.

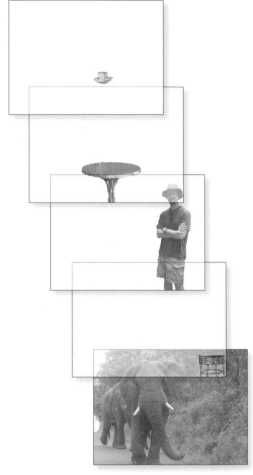

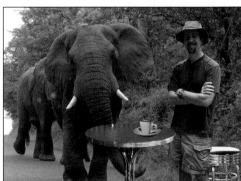

Figure 8.1 Layers act like clear acetate sheets, where transparent areas let you see through to the layers below. (It's a good thing I showed the layers, or else you might think the photo was undoctored!)

Using the Layers Palette

Show or hide layers

New Layer icon

Create Adjustment Layer icon

Lock icons

More button

Active layer

Delete Layer icon

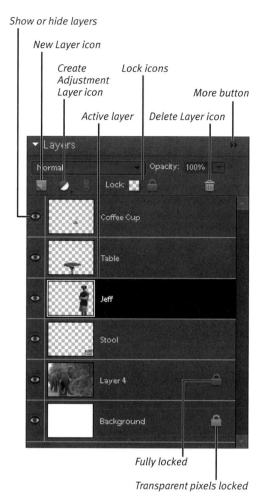

Fully locked

Transparent pixels locked

Figure 8.2 The Layers palette shows stacked layers exactly as they're arranged in your image. This palette gives you complete control over the stacking order of your layers, whether they're visible or hidden.

When you launch Photoshop Elements for the first time, the Layers palette automatically appears in the lower-right corner of your screen in the palette bin. You can use the Layers palette from within the palette bin, or drag it out into the work area.

From within the Layers palette, you can select which layer to make the active layer, display and hide layers, and lock layers to protect them from unintentional changes (**Figure 8.2**). You can also change layer names, set the opacity (transparency) of individual layers, and apply blending modes.

The palette menu offers quick access to many of the same commands found on the Layer menu, plus options for changing the appearance of the palette thumbnails.

To view the Layers palette:

Do one of the following:

◆ Choose Window > Layers.

◆ Click the disclosure triangle on the Layers palette tab in the palette bin.

◆ Choose Window > Reset Palette Locations to return all the palettes to their default locations, including Layers, which appears in the lower right.

To view the Layers palette menu:

◆ Click the More button in the top-right corner of the Layers palette (**Figure 8.3**).

Once the Layers palette menu is open, you can select a command from the menu.

✔ Tips

■ To change the appearance of the layer thumbnail views, choose Palette Options from the Layers palette menu and click the size you want (**Figure 8.4**). The smaller the icon, the more layers you're able to view at one time on the palette. So if you find yourself working on images with a lot of layers, the smallest thumbnails may work best.

■ When the Layers palette is floating, the More button actually includes the word "More." But when when it's docked, the button appears as just two right-facing triangles.

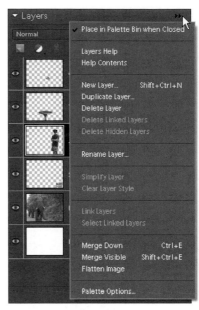

Figure 8.3 Click the More button to display the Layers palette menu.

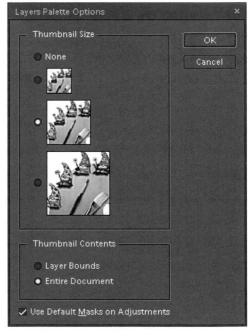

Figure 8.4 Choose the size of the thumbnail views from the Layers Palette Options menu.

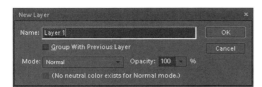

Figure 8.5 Default layer names are Layer 1 for the first layer you create, Layer 2, Layer 3, and so on. You can enter a new name when creating a layer, or you can rename it later.

New Layer icon

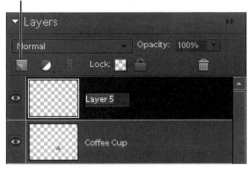

Figure 8.6 Click the New Layer icon to quickly create a new, blank layer.

✔ Tips

- You can also quickly create a new layer by clicking the New Layer icon near the top of the Layers palette (**Figure 8.6**). The new layer appears as the top layer in the palette with the default blending and opacity modes applied. To rename the new layer, double-click its name in the Layers palette and enter a new name.

- To work more easily on your image, you can choose to show or hide any of its layers from the Layers palette menu.

Layer Basics

To begin working with layers, you need to master just a few fundamental tasks. You can start by creating and naming a new layer, and then adding an image (or portion of an image) to it.

Once you've constructed an image file of multiple layers, you need to select the individual layer before you can work on that layer's image. Keep in mind that any changes you make will affect only the selected, or *active* layer, and that only one layer can be active at a time.

To create a new layer:

1. From the Layer menu or from the Layers palette menu, select New > Layer, or press Shift+Ctrl+N.

2. In the New Layer dialog, choose from the following options:

   ▲ Rename the layer with a more meaningful and intuitive name. The default names are Layer 1, Layer 2, Layer 3, and so on (**Figure 8.5**).

   ▲ Choose a blending mode for the layer. The default blending mode is Normal, meaning that no change will be applied to the layer. You can experiment with other blending modes directly from the Layers palette.

   ▲ Choose the level of opacity for the layer. Opacity can also be adjusted at any time from the Layers palette.

   ▲ Group the new layer with the previous (or lower) layer. The Group feature in the Layers palette produces an effect like masking, where the lower layer in the group acts as a window for the upper layer's image to show through. For a detailed description of layer grouping, see "Creating Masking Effects with Layer Groups" later in this chapter.

To select a layer:

Do one of the following:

◆ On the Layers palette, click the Layer thumbnail or name to make that layer active (**Figure 8.7**).

If you've imported an image from a digital camera or scanner, by default it will have only one layer—the background layer, which is selected by default.

◆ Select the Move tool and click directly on a layer image in the image window. A border with selection handles appears around the layer image to indicate that it's selected (**Figure 8.8**).

To show or hide a layer:

◆ On the Layers palette, click the eye icon to hide the layer (the eye disappears). Click again and the eye reappears, making the layer visible again in the image window (**Figure 8.9**).

✔ Tips

■ When you try to select or make changes to an area in your image, you might encounter weird and unexpected results. For example, your selection can't be copied, or you apply a filter but nothing happens. More often than not, this is because you don't have the correct layer selected. Just refer to the Layers palette to see if this is the case. Remember that the active layer is always highlighted in the Layers palette.

■ You can quickly show or hide multiple layers simply by clicking and dragging through the eye column.

■ To quickly display just one layer, Alt-click its eye icon. The other layers become hidden. Alt-click again to show all layers.

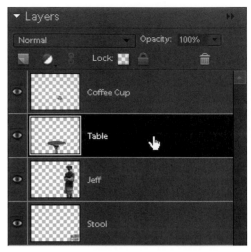

Figure 8.7 Click the layer name or thumbnail to make it the active (editable) layer.

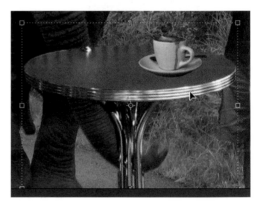

Figure 8.8 When you click a layer image in the image window, a bounding box appears to show you that it is the selected, active layer.

Hidden   *Visible*

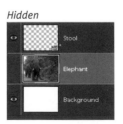 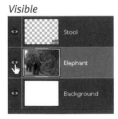

Figure 8.9 Click the eye icon to hide a layer; click again to make the layer visible.

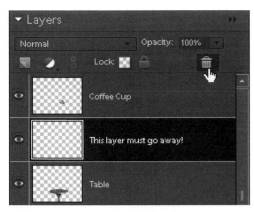

Figure 8.10 Clicking the Trash icon also removes the selected layer.

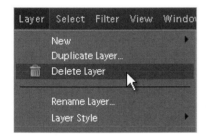

Figure 8.11 Choose Layer > Delete Layer from the Layer menu (or Layers palette menu) to delete a selected layer.

To delete a layer:

1. Select a layer on the Layers palette.

2. *Do one of the following:*

   ▲ With the layer selected, click the Trash icon on the Layers palette (**Figure 8.10**) and then click Yes in the dialog that appears.

   ▲ From the Layer menu or from the Layers palette menu, choose Delete Layer (**Figure 8.11**).

   ▲ Drag the layer to the Trash icon on the Layers palette.

Background Layers

When you import a photo from a digital camera or scanner, the photo appears on the *background* (or base) layer in Photoshop Elements. In fact, when you open an image file from just about any source, chances are it has been flattened and contains only a background layer. This layer cannot be reordered (that is, its relative position or level cannot be moved), and it cannot be given a blending mode, or assigned a different opacity.

When you create a new image and choose Transparent for its background, the bottom layer is called *Layer 1*. This layer can be reordered, and you can change its blending mode or opacity just as with any other layer.

A simple *background* layer can never be transparent, but that's okay if you're not concerned with changing opacity or applying blending modes. However, if you want to take advantage of the benefits transparency offers, start by creating an image with transparent background contents, or convert an existing *background* layer to a regular layer.

Changing the Layer Order

The layer stacking order determines which layers are on top of others, and plays a big role in determining how your image looks. As you build a composition, you may decide you want to change the layer order, either to help you work more easily on a particular layer, or to get a particular result or effect. The actual, visible overlapping of elements is determined by the layer order, so you may need to reorder layers frequently when you work on complex images.

Elements provides two main ways to change the stacking order of your layers. The most common and versatile approach is to drag the layer within the Layers palette. The second way is to select the Layer > Arrange menu and then choose commands such as Bring to Front and Send to Back—a method similar to what you use to arrange objects in a drawing program.

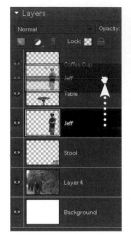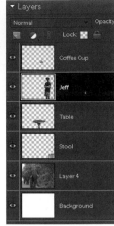

Figure 8.12 Drag a layer up or down on the Layers palette to change its stacking order.

To change the layer order by dragging:

1. On the Layers palette, select the layer you want to move.

2. Drag the layer up or down in the Layers palette (**Figure 8.12**).

   You will see a thick double line between the layers, indicating the new layer position.

3. Release the mouse button when the layer is in the desired location.

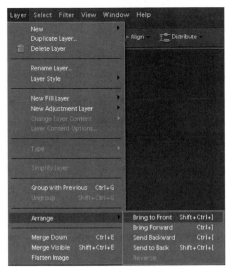

Figure 8.13 You can also change a layer's position using the options on the Layer > Arrange menu.

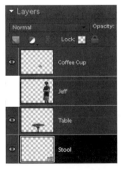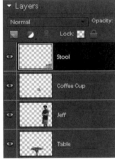

Figure 8.14 The Bring to Front command moves the layer to the top level in your image.

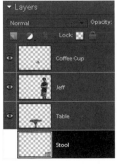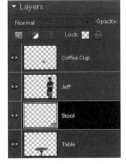

Figure 8.15 The Bring Forward command moves the layer up just one level.

To change the layer order by arranging:

1. Select the layer you want to move on the Layers palette.

2. From the Layer menu, choose Arrange, and then select one of the following options from the submenu; or use the keyboard shortcuts noted for each (**Figure 8.13**).

   ▲ **Bring to Front** (Shift+Ctrl+]) moves the layer to the top of the Layers palette and the image (**Figure 8.14**).

   ▲ **Bring Forward** (Ctrl+]) moves the layer up by one step in the stacking order (**Figure 8.15**).

   ▲ **Send Backward** (Ctrl+[) moves the layer down by one step in the stacking order.

   ▲ **Send to Back** (Shift+Ctrl+[) makes the layer the bottom layer on the Layers palette.

   You can also Shift-click to select two layers in the Layers palette, and select Reverse to swap their order in the layer stack.

✔ Tip

■ If your image contains a background layer and you choose the Send to Back command, you'll find that the background layer stubbornly remains at the bottom of your Layers palette. By default, background layers are locked in place and can't be moved. To get around this, just double-click and rename the background layer to convert it to a functional layer. Then you can move it wherever you like.

Managing Layers

As you add layers to an image, Elements assigns them a default numerical name (Layer 1, Layer 2, and so on). As your image becomes more complex, it's much easier to find a cloud image on a layer called *clouds* than it is to remember that the clouds are on Layer 14, for example.

You can also link layers together, so that any changes, such as moving and resizing, happen to two or more layers together.

And you can protect layers from unwanted changes by locking them. All layers can be fully locked, so that no pixels can be changed, or you can lock just the transparent pixels, so that any painting or other editing happens only where opaque (nontransparent) pixels already are present. This partial locking is useful if you've set up your image with areas that you know you want to preserve as transparent (like for a graphic you want to incorporate into a Web page). And locking an image protects it in other ways, too: You can move a locked layer's stacking position on the Layers palette, but the layer can't be deleted.

To rename a layer:

1. Double-click the layer's name on the Layers palette to display the text cursor and make the name editable (**Figure 8.16**).

2. Enter a new name for the layer and press the Enter key. The new name appears on the Layers palette.

To link layers:

1. Ctrl-click to select the layers in the Layers palette that you want to link together.

2. Click the Link icon near the top of the Layers palette. The link icon will appear in each linked layer, to the right of the layer name (**Figure 8.17**).

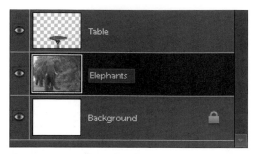

Figure 8.16 To rename a layer, just double-click its name on the Layers palette.

Link icon

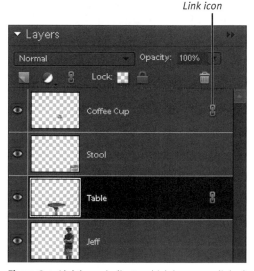

Figure 8.17 Link icons indicate which layers are linked together.

MANAGING LAYERS

Lock All

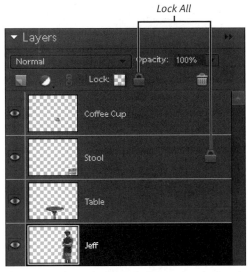

Figure 8.18 The Lock All icon indicates that the layer's pixels are completely locked.

To lock all pixels on a layer:

1. Select the layer on the Layers palette.

2. Click the Lock All icon near the top of the Layers palette.

   The Lock All icon appears to the right of the layer name on the Layers palette (**Figure 8.18**).

To lock transparent pixels on a layer:

1. Select the layer on the Layers palette.

2. Click the Lock Transparent Pixels icon near the top of the Layers palette.

   The Lock Transparent Pixels icon appears to the right of the layer name on the Layers palette (**Figure 8.19**).

Lock Transparent Pixels

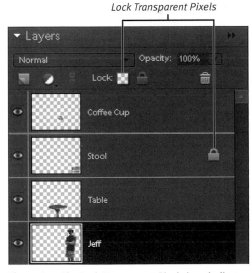

Figure 8.19 The Lock Transparent Pixels icon indicates that the transparent pixels are locked.

MANAGING LAYERS

Merging Layers

Once you begin to create projects of even moderate complexity, the number of layers in your project can add up fairly quickly. Although Elements lets you create an almost unlimited number of layers, there are a couple of reasons why you may want to consolidate some or all of them into a single layer (**Figure 8.20**). For one thing, it's just good housekeeping. It doesn't take long before the Layers palette begins to fill, and you find yourself constantly scrolling up and down in search of a particular object or text layer. And every layer you add drains a little more from your system's memory. Continue to add layers, and, depending on available memory, you may notice a decrease in your computer's performance.

Photoshop Elements offers three approaches to merging image layers. You can merge just two at a time, merge multiple layers, or flatten your image into a single background layer.

To merge one layer with another:

1. On the Layers palette, identify the two layers you want to merge, and then select the topmost of the two.

   Photoshop Elements will merge two layers only when one is stacked directly above the other. If you want to merge two layers that are separated by one layer or more, you'll need to rearrange their order in the Layers palette before they can be merged.

2. From the More menu on the Layers palette, choose Merge Down (**Figure 8.21**), or press Ctrl+E. The two layers are merged into one.

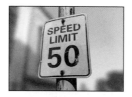
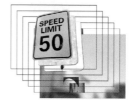
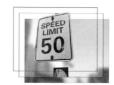

Figure 8.20 The top image is a composite of a number of layers from a 3D rendering program: a background layer, the pole, the sign's shadow on the pole, and three layers for the sign itself. To simplify the file, the three sign layers were merged into a single layer, and the pole and the shadow were combined (lower right). The finished image will look the same, but because it's composed of fewer layers, its file size will be significantly smaller.

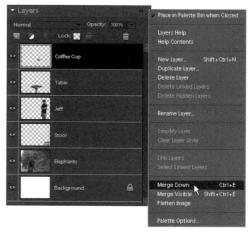

Figure 8.21 Combine a single layer with the layer below it by using the Merge Down command.

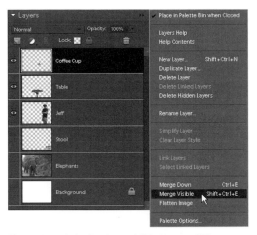

Figure 8.22 Only the three visible layers will be merged into one using the Merge Visible command.

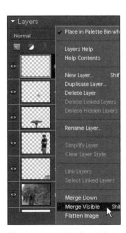 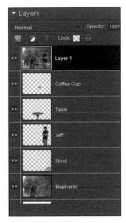

Figure 8.23 On the left, a new layer has been created at the top of the Layers palette. If you hold down the Alt key while selecting Merge Visible from the palette menu, all visible layers are merged and copied to the new layer, as shown on the right.

To merge multiple layers:

1. On the Layers palette, identify the layers you want to merge, checking that the Visibility (eye) icon is on for just the layers you want to merge.

2. From the More menu on the Layers palette, choose Merge Visible (**Figure 8.22**), or press Shift+Ctrl+E.

   All of the visible layers are merged into one layer.

✔ Tip

■ You can create a new layer and then place a merged *copy* of all of the visible layers on that layer by holding the Alt key while choosing Merge Visible from the Layers palette's More menu. The visible layers themselves aren't merged and so remain separate and intact (**Figure 8.23**). This technique offers you a way to capture a merged snapshot of your current file without actually merging the physical layers. It can be a handy tool for brainstorming and comparing different versions of the same layered file. For instance, take a snapshot of a layered file, change the opacity and blending modes of several layers, and then take another snapshot. You can then compare the two snapshots to see what effect the different settings have on the entire file.

MERGING LAYERS

To flatten an image:

1. In the Layers palette, click the More button to open the palette menu.

2. From the palette menu, select Flatten Image.

3. If any layers are invisible, a warning box appears asking if you want to discard the hidden layers. If so, click OK.

   The entire layered file is flattened into one layer (**Figure 8.24**).

✔ Tip

- If there's any chance you may eventually want to make revisions to your layered image, always create a duplicate file before flattening so the layers are safely preserved in your original. Once you've flattened, saved, and closed a file, there's no way to recover those flattened layers.

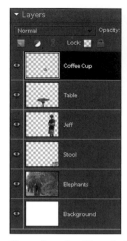
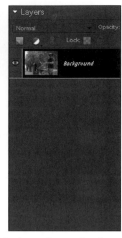

Figure 8.24 Combine all of the layers in a project into a single layer by using the Flatten Image command.

MERGING LAYERS

Removing a Halo from an Image Layer

Often when you create a new image layer from a selection, you'll find you've inadvertently selected pixels you didn't want to include. This is a particularly common problem when you're trying to remove an image from its background using the Magic Wand or Quick Selection tools. On close inspection, what you thought was a clean selection actually includes a *halo* of colored background pixels.

Once you've pasted your selection into its new layer, choose Adjust Color from the Enhance menu, and then choose Defringe Layer from the Adjust Color submenu. In the Defringe dialog, enter a pixel width to control how much of the border of your image you want to affect—for high-resolution images, I usually start around 5. Then, just click OK to see the results in the image window (**Figure 8.25**). If you're not happy with the results, undo the operation by pressing Ctrl+Z, then repeat the steps, entering a new pixel width in the Defringe dialog.

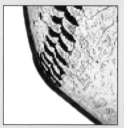
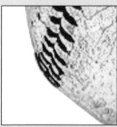

Figure 8.25 When zoomed in, it's apparent that the old, weathered baseball I've cut and pasted carried with it a halo of the background it was resting on (left). After applying Defringe, the colored halo has disappeared (right).

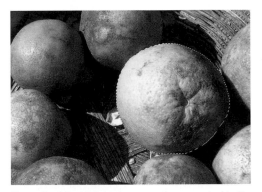

Figure 8.26 Any selected area can be converted to its own layer.

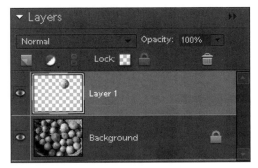

Figure 8.27 Copying a selection to a new layer leaves the original selection unchanged.

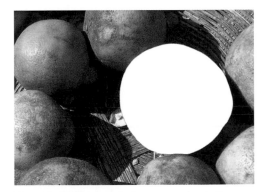

Figure 8.28 The Layer via Cut command cuts the selected pixels to a new layer. (The new layer has been hidden here to demonstrate that it's actually cut, not copied.)

Converting and Duplicating Layers

You now know you can create a new layer using the Layer > New command; in addition, Elements creates layers in all sorts of sneaky ways. For example, whenever you copy and paste a selection into an image, it's automatically added to your image on a brand new layer.

When you start editing an image, you'll often find it convenient to create a selection and convert it to a layer to keep it isolated and editable within your photo. It's also quite easy to duplicate a layer, which is useful when you want to copy an existing layer as is, or use it as a starting point and then make additional changes.

The background layer is unique and by default can't be moved, but sometimes you will need to move it, change its opacity, or apply a blending mode. To do any of those things, you'll need to convert it to a regular layer. And sometimes you'll want to convert an existing layer to the background. Although these conversions are not necessary for most simple photo projects, they are quite common when you combine or make composite images.

To convert a selection to a layer:

1. Make a selection using any of the selection tools (**Figure 8.26**).

2. From the Layer menu, choose New; then perform one of the following commands:
   - ▲ **Layer via Copy** (Ctrl+J). The selection is copied to a new layer, leaving the original selection unchanged (**Figure 8.27**).
   - ▲ **Layer via Cut** (Shift+Ctrl+J). The selection is cut to a new layer, leaving a gaping hole in the original layer, with the current background color showing through (**Figure 8.28**).

To duplicate a layer:

1. Select the layer on the Layers palette.

2. Duplicate the layer using *one of the following methods:*

   ▲ If you want to create a new name for the layer, choose Layer > Duplicate Layer.

   The Duplicate Layer dialog appears, where you can rename the layer (**Figure 8.29**). Note that you can also get to this dialog from the Layers palette menu.

   ▲ If you're not concerned with renaming the layer right now, just drag the selected layer to the New Layer icon on the Layers palette (**Figure 8.30**).

   The new layer appears above the original layer with a "copy" designation added to the name (**Figure 8.31**).

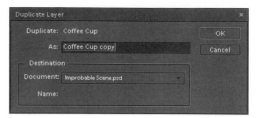

Figure 8.29 Use the Duplicate Layer dialog to rename your new duplicate layer.

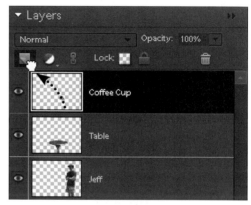

Figure 8.30 You can also duplicate a layer by dragging any existing layer to the New Layer icon on the Layers palette.

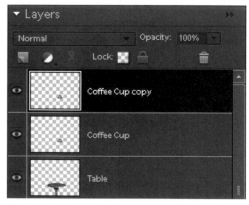

Figure 8.31 The new layer appears right above the original layer on the Layers palette.

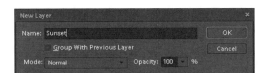

Figure 8.32 You can convert the background to a layer and rename it during the conversion.

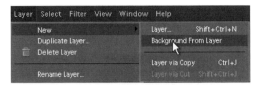

Figure 8.33 You can convert a layer to a background by choosing Layer > New > Background From Layer.

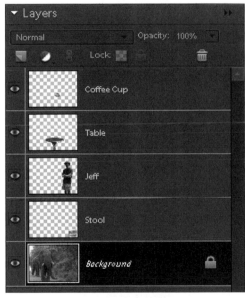

Figure 8.34 New background layers always appear at the bottom of the Layers palette.

To convert a background to a layer:

1. From the Layer menu, choose New > Layer from Background.

2. If desired, type a new name for the layer and click OK (**Figure 8.32**).

To convert a layer to a background:

1. Select a layer on the Layers palette.

2. From the Layer menu, choose New > Background From Layer (**Figure 8.33**).

3. The new background appears at the bottom of the Layers palette (**Figure 8.34**).

✔ Tips

- You can also convert the background by double-clicking the background on the Layers palette, which brings up the same New Layer dialog.

- The Type and Shape tools also each automatically generate a new layer when you use them, keeping those elements isolated on their own unique layers.

- The Background From Layer command won't work if you already have an existing background layer in your Layers palette. Why? Because no image can have two background layers at the same time. To get around this, create a duplicate of the current background layer (you can rename it later). You can then safely delete the background layer, and follow steps 1–2 to convert a regular layer into a background.

CONVERTING AND DUPLICATING LAYERS

Copying Layers Between Images

It's extremely easy to copy layers from one Elements document to another. If you're used to the drag-and-drop technique, you'll be glad to know this method works well for copying layers as well as selections. Remember, as you copy and paste selections they end up on their own layers. So, layers often contain unique objects you can easily share between photos.

To drag and drop a layer from the Layers palette:

1. Open the two images you plan to use.

2. In the source image, select the layer you want to copy by clicking it in the Layers palette.

3. Drag the layer's name from the Layers palette into the destination image (**Figure 8.35**).

   The new layer appears both in the image window and on the Layers palette of the destination image (**Figure 8.36**). When you drag a layer from one image into another, the original, source image is not changed. The layer remains intact.

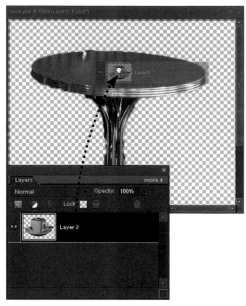

Figure 8.35 To copy a layer, just drag it from the Layers palette and drop it directly onto another image.

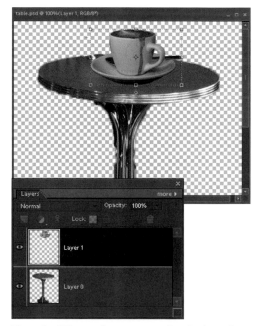

Figure 8.36 The new layer appears directly above the previously selected (active) layer in the destination image and in the Layers palette.

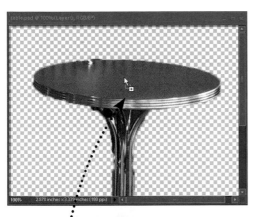

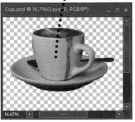

Figure 8.37 The Move tool lets you select and duplicate a layer from within the image window.

To drag and drop a layer using the Move tool:

1. Open the two images you plan to use.

2. Select the Move tool, and then in the source image window, select the layer you want to copy by clicking it.

   You can also select the layer by clicking its thumbnail in the Layers palette.

3. With the Move tool still selected, drag the actual image layer from the source image window to the destination image (**Figure 8.37**).

   The copied layer appears on the Layers palette immediately above the previously active layer.

To copy and paste a layer between images:

1. In the source image, select the layer you want to copy from by clicking it either in the Layers palette or the image window.

2. Choose Select > All to select all of the pixels on the layer, or press Ctrl+A.

3. Choose Edit > Copy to copy the layer to the clipboard, or press Ctrl+C.

4. In the destination image, choose Edit > Paste, or press Ctrl+V.

   The contents of the copied layer will appear in the center of the destination image.

✔ Tip

- In some cases, the layer in your source image may be larger than the destination image, in which case not all of the layer will be visible. Just use the Move tool to bring the desired area into view.

Transforming Layers

You can also scale (resize), rotate, and distort layer images. They can be altered either numerically, by entering specific values on the options bar, or manually, by dragging their control handles in the image window. Constrain options, such as proportional scaling, are available for most transformations, and a set of keyboard shortcuts helps to simplify the process of adding distortion and perspective.

To scale a layer image:

1. Click a layer in the Layers palette to activate it; then from the Image menu, choose Transform > Free Transform, or press Ctrl+T. The options bar displays the scale and rotation text boxes and the reference point locator (**Figure 8.38**).

2. On the options bar, click to set a reference point location.

   The reference point determines what point your layer image will be scaled to: toward the center, toward a corner, and so on (**Figure 8.39**).

3. If you want to scale your layer image proportionately, click the Constrain Proportions check box.

4. Enter a value in either the height or width text box. The layer image is scaled accordingly.

5. At the lower-right corner of your layer image, click the Commit Transform button (**Figure 8.40**), or press Enter.

✔ Tip

■ You can scale a layer image manually by selecting it with the Move tool and then dragging any one of the eight handles on the selection border. Constrain the scaling by holding down the Shift key while dragging one of the four corner handles.

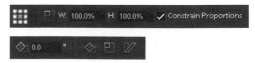

Figure 8.38 Precise scale and rotation values can be entered for any shape.

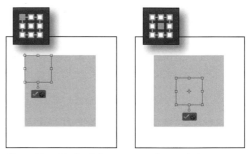

Figure 8.39 Both of these rectangles are being reduced in size by about half. The one on the left is scaled toward its upper-left corner, and the one on the right is scaled toward its center.

Figure 8.40 The Commit Transform button scales the layer image to the size you define.

TRANSFORMING LAYERS

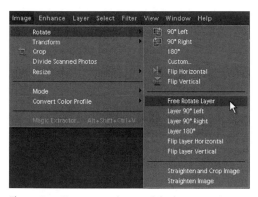

Figure 8.41 You can apply any of the layer rotation menu commands to a layer image.

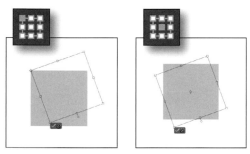

Figure 8.42 Both of these squares are being rotated about 20 degrees. The one on the left is rotated around its upper-left corner, and the one on the right is rotated around its center.

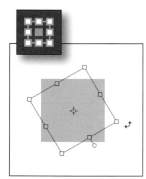

Figure 8.43
Rotate any layer image manually by dragging it around its reference point with the rotation pointer.

To rotate a layer image:

1. Click a layer in the Layers palette; then from the Image menu, choose Rotate > Free Rotate Layer (**Figure 8.41**).

   The options bar changes to show the scale and rotation text boxes and the reference point locator.

2. On the options bar, click to set a reference point location (**Figure 8.42**).

3. Enter a value in the rotate text box. The image will rotate accordingly.

4. Click the Commit Transform button, or press Enter.

✔ Tips

■ To rotate the image in 90- or 180-degree increments or to flip it horizontally or vertically, choose Image > Rotate; then choose from the list of five menu commands below the Free Rotate Layer command.

■ You can rotate a layer image manually by selecting it with the Move tool and then moving the pointer outside of the selection border until it becomes a rotation cursor (**Figure 8.43**). Drag around the outside of the selection border to rotate the image. In addition, you can constrain the rotation to 15-degree increments by holding down the Shift key while dragging the rotation cursor.

■ If you simply want to reposition a layer image in the image window, click anywhere inside the image with the Move tool and then drag the image to its new position.

To distort a layer image:

1. Click a layer in the Layers palette to make it active. From the Image menu, choose Transform; then choose Skew, Distort, or Perspective (**Figure 8.44**).

2. On the options bar, check that the reference point location is set to the center.

   The reference point can, of course, be set to any location, but the center seems to work best when applying any of the three distortions.

3. Drag any of the layer image's control handles to distort the image.

   Dragging the control handles will yield different results depending on the distort option you choose (**Figure 8.45**).

4. On the options bar, click the Commit Transform button, or press Enter.

5. Click the Commit Transform button a second time (or press Enter) to deselect the image layer and hide the selection border.

To align or distribute layer objects:

1. Select two or more layers in the Layers palette; the Distribute command requires three or more selected layers.

2. Select the Move tool from the toolbox.

3. From the options bar, click the Align or Distribute drop-down menu and choose how you'd like the layer objects repositioned (**Figure 8.46**).

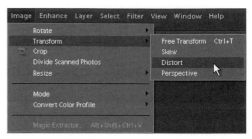

Figure 8.44 Choose one of the three specific transformation commands.

Figure 8.45 The same square layer image transformed using Skew (left), Distort (center), and Perspective (right).

Before

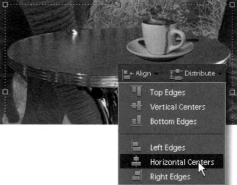

After

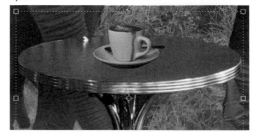

Figure 8.46 You can align or distribute objects on different layers.

TRANSFORMING LAYERS

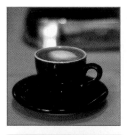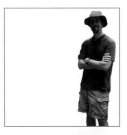
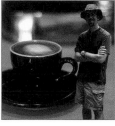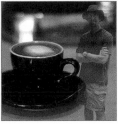

Figure 8.47 Two separate layers (top) compose this image of me and a giant coffee cup. The lower-left image displays the top layer with an opacity setting of 100 percent. The lower-right image displays the top layer with an opacity setting of 50 percent.

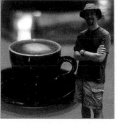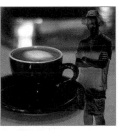

Figure 8.48 The image on the left contains no blending modes; the image on the right displays the top layer with the Difference blending mode applied.

About Opacity and Blending Modes

One of the most effective and simple ways to enhance your layered image is to create the illusion of combining one layer's image with another by blending their pixels. This differs from merging layers because the layers aren't actually combined, but rather appear to mix together. Photoshop Elements provides two easily accessible tools at the top of the Layers palette that can be used alone or in tandem for blending multiple layers together: the Opacity slider and the Blending Modes drop-down menu. The Opacity slider controls the degree of transparency of one layer over another. If a layer's opacity is set at 100 percent, the layer is totally opaque, and any layers beneath it are hidden. If a layer's opacity is set to 30 percent, 70 percent of any underlying layers are allowed to show through (**Figure 8.47**).

Blending modes are a little trickier. Whereas Opacity settings strictly control the opaqueness of one layer over another, blending modes act by mixing or blending one layer's color and tonal value with the one below it. The Difference mode, for example, combines one layer's image with a second, and treats the top layer like a sort of negative filter, inverting colors and tonal values where dark areas blend with lighter ones (**Figure 8.48**).

To set a layer's opacity:

1. On the Layers palette, select the layer whose opacity you want to change (**Figure 8.49**).

2. To change the opacity, *do one of the following*:

   ▲ Enter a percentage in the Opacity text box, which is located at the top of the Layers palette.

   ▲ Click the arrow to activate the Opacity slider and then drag the slider to the desired opacity (**Figure 8.50**).

✔ Tips

■ You can change the opacity settings in 10-percent increments directly from the keyboard. With a layer selected on the Layers palette, press any number key to change the opacity: 1 for 10 percent, 2 for 20 percent, and so on. Also, as in Photoshop, pressing two number keys in rapid succession will work—e.g., 66 percent. If this technique doesn't seem to be working, make sure you don't have a painting or editing tool selected in the toolbox. Many of the brushes and effects tools can be sized and adjusted with the number keys, and if any of those tools are selected, they take priority over the Layers palette commands.

■ A background layer contains no transparency, so you can't change its opacity until you first convert it to a regular layer (see "To convert a background to a layer" earlier in this chapter).

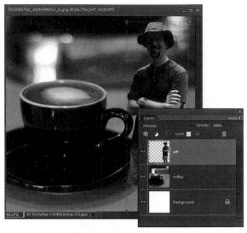

Figure 8.49 The top layer is selected on the Layers palette. Its opacity is set at 100 percent.

Opacity slider

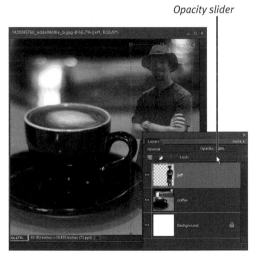

Figure 8.50 You can change a layer's opacity from 0 to 100 percent by dragging the Opacity slider.

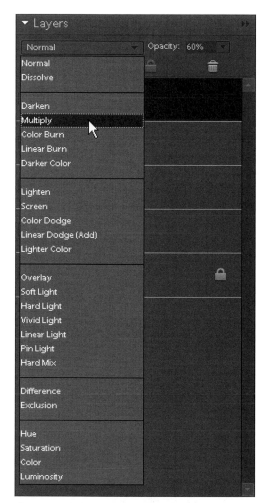

Figure 8.51 Select a blending mode from the Layers palette's Blending Mode menu.

To apply a blending mode to a layer:

1. On the Layers palette, select the uppermost layer to which you want to apply the blending mode.

Remember, blending modes work by mixing (blending) the image pixels of one layer with the layers below it, so your project will need to contain at least two layers in order for a blending mode to have any effect.

2. Select the desired blending mode from the Blending Mode drop-down menu (**Figure 8.51**).

The image on the layer to which you've applied the blending mode will appear to mix with the image layers below.

✔ Tip

■ You can apply only one blending mode to a layer, but it's still possible to apply more than one blending mode to the same image. After assigning a blending mode to a layer, duplicate the layer and then choose a different blending mode for the duplicate. There are no hard-and-fast rules to follow, and the various blending modes work so differently with one another that getting what you want is largely an exercise of trial and error. But a little experimentation with different blending mode combinations (and opacities) can yield some very interesting effects that you can't achieve any other way.

ABOUT OPACITY AND BLENDING MODES

Creating Masking Effects with Layer Groups

Layer groups provide a simple and quite intuitive way to create a sophisticated masking effect in Photoshop Elements. Any object placed on a layer, including photographic images and lines of editable text, can be used as the basis for masking any number of layer objects above it. Think of the lower, or *base* layer, as a window through which the upper layers are allowed to show through. So, for example, you could have a favorite fishing trip photo framed within the shape of a boat or fish, or a photograph of the sky placed within the word "CLOUDS" (**Figure 8.52**). Once grouped, any layer within the group can be repositioned independently of the others, or the entire group can be linked and moved as one.

To create a layer group:

1. On the Layers palette, identify the layer you want to use as your base layer (**Figure 8.53**).

Your layers must be arranged so that the layer (or layers) you want to group are directly above the base layer.

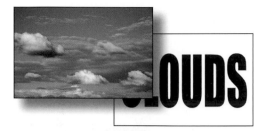

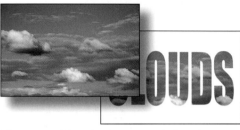

Figure 8.52 This project is composed of two layers: a photograph of clouds and the CLOUDS text layer. The cloud photo completely covers the text layer in the image on the left, but when grouped with the text layer, the clouds peek through only where the text is visible.

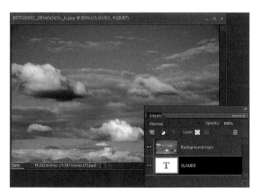

Figure 8.53 In this figure, the CLOUDS text layer serves as the base layer. It will soon be grouped with the sky layer (Background copy), which is selected directly above it.

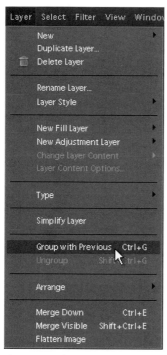

Figure 8.54 Choose Group with Previous to create a layer group.

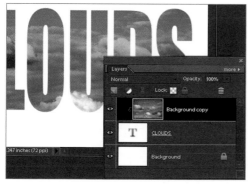

Figure 8.55 A Grouped Layer icon appears after a layer group is created.

2. Still on the Layers palette, select the layer above the base layer; then from the Layer menu choose Group with Previous (**Figure 8.54**), or press Ctrl+G.

The two layers are now grouped, and the upper layer is visible only in those areas where the base layer object is present.

On the Layers palette, the base layer's name is underlined, and the grouped layer's name and thumbnail are indented. An icon, placed to the left of the thumbnail, further identifies grouped layers (**Figure 8.55**).

To ungroup layers:

1. On the Layers palette, select the base layer.

2. From the Layer menu, choose Ungroup, or press Shift+Ctrl+G.

✔ Tip

■ For a faster way to create a layer group, Alt-click the space between the two layers.

CREATING MASKING EFFECTS WITH LAYER GROUPS

Applying Effects with Layer Styles

With Layer styles, you can add editable effects to individual layers within an image, and you can be as conservative or as wild as your heart desires. For example, you can add a subtle drop shadow to an object, or you can go in the opposite direction and set your friend's hair ablaze with the Fire layer style. Beveled edges, glowing borders, and even custom textures can all be applied to any object or text layer. The Layer Styles options in the Effects palette contains a series of style sets, grouped as galleries and accessed from the palette's drop-down menu. Once you've applied a layer style, you can choose to keep it as an active element of a layer and return to and adjust it at any time; or you can choose to merge the layer object and style together to simplify the layer.

To apply a layer style:

1. On the Layers palette, choose the layer to which you want to apply the layer style (**Figure 8.56**).

2. To open the Effects palette, *do one of the following*:
   ▲ From the Window menu, choose Effects.
   ▲ Click the disclosure triangle on the Effects palette tab in the palette bin.

3. Click the Layer Styles icon at the top of the palette (**Figure 8.57**).

4. From the Library drop-down menu, choose a style set (**Figure 8.58**). The set you choose presents a gallery from which you can select a specific style.

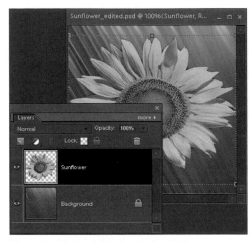

Figure 8.56 Select a layer to apply a layer style.

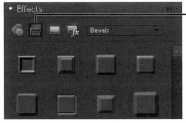

Layer Styles icon

Figure 8.57 The Effects icons allow you to select Filters, Layer Styles, and Photo Effects (or All) from the same palette.

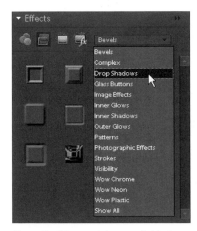

Figure 8.58 Layer styles are divided into different style sets.

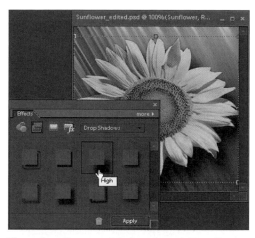

Figure 8.59 Choose a style from the palette gallery and click Apply to make the style active.

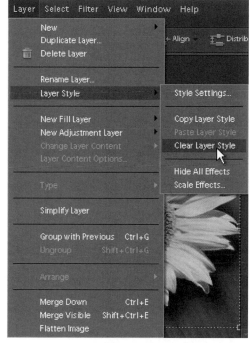

Figure 8.60 Clear all styles on a layer with the Clear Layer Style menu command.

5. In the style gallery, click the style you want to apply to your layer.

6. Click the Apply button (or double-click the chosen style). The style is applied to the layer object (**Figure 8.59**), and a Layer Style icon appears next to the layer name on the Layers palette.

To remove a layer style:

◆ From the Layer menu, choose Layer Style > Clear Layer Style (**Figure 8.60**). The Clear Layer Style command will remove all styles from the layer, no matter how many have been applied.

✔ Tips

■ Multiple layer styles can be assigned to a single layer; however, only one layer style from each set can be assigned at a time. In other words, you can assign a drop shadow, bevel, and outer glow style to the same layer all at once, but you can't assign two different bevel styles at the same time.

■ Layer styles can be applied only to images or text on a regular, transparent layer. If you try to apply a style to a background layer, a warning box asks if you want to first make the background a layer. Click OK and the background is converted to a layer; your chosen layer style will be applied automatically.

■ Elements allows you to apply a layer style to a blank layer, but the layer style won't have any effect until text or an image is placed on the layer. When you place something on a layer with a previously assigned layer style, it will display with the layer style's attributes: drop shadow, beveled edge, and so on.

To edit a layer style:

Layer Style icon

1. On the Layers palette, double-click the Layer Style icon to the right of the layer name (**Figure 8.61**). The Style Settings dialog opens.

2. Make sure the Preview box is selected; then refer to the image window while dragging the Size, Distance, and Opacity sliders (**Figure 8.62**).

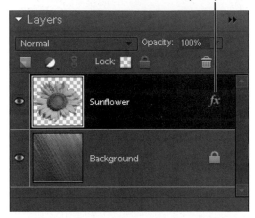

Figure 8.61 When a layer style is applied, a Layer Style icon appears to the right of the layer name.

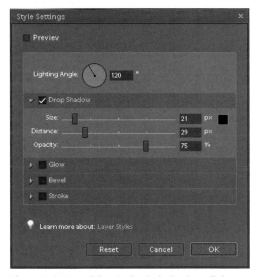

Figure 8.62 Use sliders in the Style Settings dialog to modify the shadow, glow, bevel, and stroke styles.

The Style Settings Dialog

Not all of the layer styles can be adjusted. But using a series of sliders, a wheel, check boxes, and radio buttons, you *can* make adjustments to drop shadows, inner and outer glows, bevels, and stroke styles. Here's a quick tour of the Style Settings dialog controls (**Figure 8.63**).

Except for Lighting Angle and Bevel, each section contains a slider to determine how opaque the effect appears, as well as a color well for changing the effect's color. The distance and size slider values are all based on units of pixels. Click a style's check box to enable it.

◆ The Lighting Angle wheel controls the direction of the light source when a bevel or shadow style is applied. Changing the light angle will change which beveled surfaces are in highlight and which are in shadow, and will also control where a drop shadow falls behind an object (**Figure 8.64**).

◆ The Drop Shadow's Distance slider quite simply controls the distance that a drop shadow is placed from an object. The larger the number, the more shadow is exposed from behind an object. If the distance is set to 0, the shadow is centered directly under the object and isn't visible. The Size slider determines how large the shadow appears.

◆ The Inner Glow Size slider lets you increase or decrease the amount of glow radiating in from the edges of an object.

◆ The Outer Glow Size slider lets you increase or decrease the amount of glow radiating out from the edges of an object.

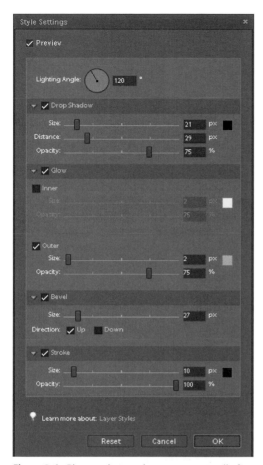

Figure 8.63 Please, please, please, never use all of these effects at once! I'm just showing all options.

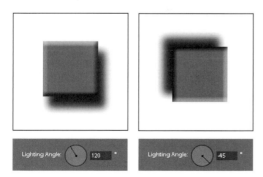

Figure 8.64 The Lighting Angle wheel sets a light source for any bevel or drop shadow styles you apply, and can be set to light any object from any angle.

continues on next page

THE STYLE SETTINGS DIALOG

- The Bevel Size slider controls the amount of beveled edge on your object. An inside bevel of 3 will be almost imperceptible, whereas larger values create an increasingly more pronounced bevel effect.

- The Bevel Direction radio buttons control the appearance of a bevel style. If the Up button is selected, the bevel will appear to extrude or come forward; if the Down button is selected, the bevel will appear to recede (**Figure 8.65**).

- The Stroke effect draws a solid line around elements on the layer. The size slider sets the line's width.

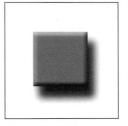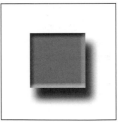

Figure 8.65 When the bevel direction is set to Up, the object bevel appears to come forward (left). When the bevel direction is set to Down, the object bevel appears to recede into the distance (right).

Once you've applied a layer style, you can return to it at any time to modify it, but you also have the option of merging the layer style with its layer by *simplifying*. In effect, simplifying is like flattening an individual layer. Simplifying a layer permanently applies a layer style to its layer and can help to reduce the complexity and file size of your project.

To simplify a layer:

1. On the Layers palette, click to select the layer you want to simplify.

2. From the palette menu on the Layers palette, choose Simplify Layer (**Figure 8.66**). The layer style is merged with the layer, and the Layer Style icon disappears from the layer on the Layers palette.

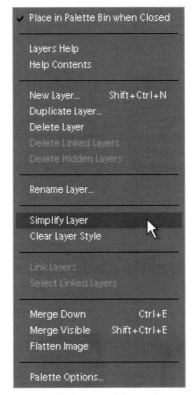

Figure 8.66 Once a style is set the way you like it, you can permanently apply it to a layer object by simplifying the layer.

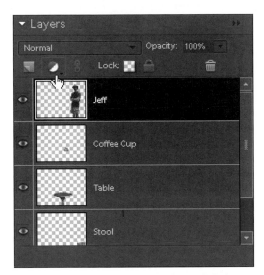

Figure 8.67 Once you've selected a layer, click the Create Adjustment Layer button at the top of the Layer menu.

About Fill Layers

The Create Adjustment Layer drop-down menu includes not only tonal correction options such as Levels, but a list of three layer fill options: Solid Color, Gradient, and Pattern. Follow my lead and ignore these options. They don't do anything that can't be accomplished by simply creating a new layer and applying a fill or pattern—except that they do it with more overhead, because adjustment layers require more processing power and create larger files than regular layers.

Making Color and Tonal Changes with Adjustment Layers

Adjustment layers let you make color and tonal adjustments to your image (much like the commands discussed in Chapter 7, "Changing and Adjusting Colors") without changing the actual pixels in your image. Adjustment layers work like filters, resting above the actual image layers and affecting any image layers below them. They can be especially useful when you want to experiment with different settings or compare the effects of one setting over another. Because you can apply opacity and blending mode changes to adjustment layers (just as you would to any other layer), they offer a level of creative freedom not available from their menu-command counterparts. For instance, you can create a Levels adjustment layer above an image, and then change the opacity of that adjustment layer to fine-tune the amount of tonal correction applied.

To create an adjustment layer:

1. On the Layers palette, identify the top-most layer to which you want the adjustment layer applied, and then select that layer.

   Remember that the adjustment layer affects all layers below it on the Layers palette, not just the one directly below it.

2. At the top of the Layers palette, click the Create Adjustment Layer button (**Figure 8.67**).

continues on next page

MAKING COLOR AND TONAL CHANGES

3. From the drop-down menu, choose from the list of adjustment layer options (**Figure 8.68**).

When you choose an adjustment layer option, its dialog opens, and a new adjustment layer is created above the selected layer (**Figure 8.69**).

4. Use the sliders to adjust the settings, and then click OK to close the dialog.

If you want to return to the adjustment layer dialog later, just double-click its layer thumbnail on the Layers palette.

By default, an adjustment layer affects all the layers below it in the Layers palette. But if you create a layer group, the effects of the adjustment layer will be limited to one specific layer.

To apply an adjustment layer to a single layer:

1. In the Layers palette, move the adjustment layer directly above the layer to which you want it applied.

2. With the adjustment layer still selected in the Layers palette, choose Group with Previous from the Layer menu, or press Ctrl+G.

The adjustment layer and the one directly below it are grouped, and the effects of the adjustment layer are applied only to that single layer (**Figure 8.70**).

✔ Tip

■ For a faster way to create a layer group, Alt-click the space between the two layers.

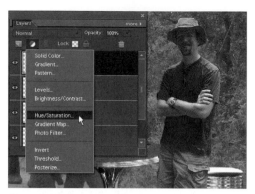

Figure 8.68 Choose an adjustment command from the drop-down menu.

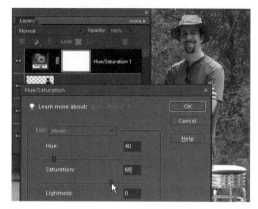

Figure 8.69 The edits you make in the adjustment dialog apply to all layers below the adustment layer, but do not change those layers' pixels.

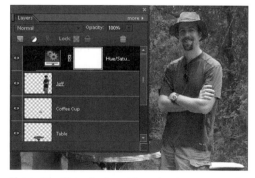

Figure 8.70 The adjustment layer has been grouped with the object layer directly below it.

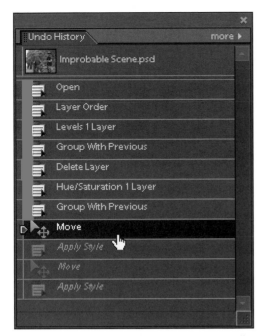

Figure 8.71 Use the palette slider to move to virtually any point in time in the creation of your project.

Using the Undo History Palette

The Undo History palette lets you move backward and forward through a work session, allowing you to make multiple undos to any editing changes you've made to your image. Photoshop Elements records every change and then lists each as a separate entry, or *state*, on the palette. With one click, you can navigate to any state and then choose to work forward from there, return again to the previous state, or select a different state from which to work forward.

To navigate through the Undo History palette:

1. To open the Undo History palette, *do one of the following:*
   - ▲ From the Window menu, choose Undo History.
   - ▲ From the palette bin, click the arrow on the Undo History palette tab.

2. To move to a different state in the Undo History palette, *do one of the following:*
   - ▲ Click the name of any state.
   - ▲ Drag the palette slider up or down to a different state (**Figure 8.71**).

✔ Tip

- The default number of states that the Undo History palette saves is 50. After 50, the first state is cleared from the list, and the palette continues to list just the 50 most recent states. The good news is you can bump the number of saved states up to 1000, provided that your computer has enough memory. From the Edit menu, choose Preferences > Performance; then in the History & Cache box enter a larger number in the History States field.

Save Some Memory

If memory is at a premium (and you'd rather Photoshop Elements not clog up your precious RAM by remembering your last 50 selections, brushstrokes, and filter effects), set the number in the Undo History States field to 1. You can still undo and redo your last action as you work along, but for all practical purposes, the Undo History palette is turned off.

To delete a state:

◆ Click the name of any state; then choose Delete from the palette menu (**Figure 8.72**).

The selected state and all states following it are deleted.

To clear the Undo History palette:

Do one of the following:

◆ From the palette menu, choose Clear Undo History (**Figure 8.73**).

This action can be undone, but it doesn't reduce the amount of memory used by Photoshop Elements.

◆ Hold down the Alt key, then choose Clear Undo History from the palette menu.

This action *cannot be undone*, but it does purge the list of states from the memory buffer. This can come in handy if a message appears telling you that Photoshop Elements is low on memory.

✔ Tips

■ Deletion of a state can be undone, but only if no changes are applied to the image in the interim. If you make a change to the image that creates a new state on the palette, all deleted states are permanently lost.

■ Sometimes—when you're working on an especially complex piece, for instance—the Undo History palette may become filled with states that you no longer need to manage or return to, or that begin to take their toll on your system's memory. At any time, you can clear the palette's list of states without changing the image.

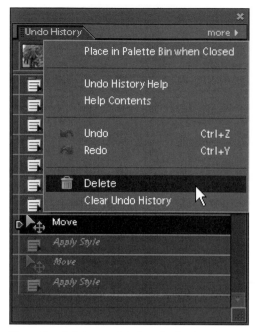

Figure 8.72 Delete any state by selecting it and choosing Delete from the palette menu.

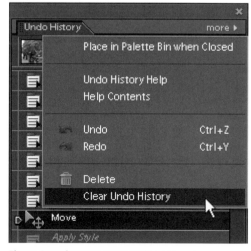

Figure 8.73 If system memory is a concern, you can periodically clear the palette of all states.

FILTERS AND EFFECTS

For decades, photographers have used lens filters to improve and alter the look of their photographs. Filters are frequently used to change the intensity of color values and to lighten certain tones and darken others. In addition to using filters, photographers also rely on darkroom and printing techniques to create wonderfully creative effects.

But thanks to the advancements of digital technology, you don't have to fiddle with chemicals or additional camera equipment to enhance your photographs. The filters and effects included in Photoshop Elements go far beyond what's been possible in traditional photography. Many of these filters (such as the Sharpen filters) allow you to make subtle corrections and improvements to your photos, whereas other filters, such as Artistic, Stylize, and Sketch, can transform an image into a completely new piece of artwork. Photoshop Elements also provides effects you can add to your photos, including striking image effects (lizard skin, anyone?) as well as type effects and unique textures.

In this chapter, I'll explore the many ways you can use filters and effects to take your work to a whole new level.

Using the Effects Palette

Photoshop Elements offers you almost unlimited possibilities for tweaking and enhancing your images. Most filters include a dialog where you can preview any changes and adjust the settings for either a subtle or dramatic effect. And some of the filters (such as the Liquify filter) are so comprehensive, they seem like separate little applications within Photoshop Elements.

Effects work a bit differently than filters. When you apply an effect, Elements actually runs through a series of automatic actions in which a number of filters and layer styles are applied to your image. Effects are a bit more complex than filters. If you want to add a drop shadow, picture frame, or brushed-metal type to a photo, browse through the Effects palette to see what's available.

Filters   *Photo Effects*   *Library drop-down menu*

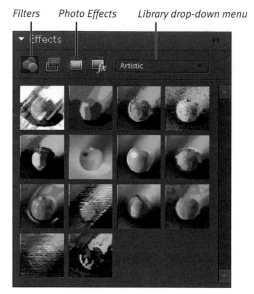

Figure 9.1 Access filters and photo effects from the Effects palette.

To view the Effects palette:

1. In the Editor, *do one of the following*:
   - ▲ From the Window menu, choose Effects.
   - ▲ Click the disclosure triangle on the Effects palette tab in the palette bin.

2. Choose either the Filters or Photo Effects icon at the top of the Effects palette (**Figure 9.1**).

Filter and Effect Plug-ins

Plug-ins provide a nifty way to extend your Photoshop Elements experience. Want to add some sophisticated 3D shadows or translucent effects to your photos? If you can't find the effect or filter you want in Photoshop Elements, chances are good that a plug-in might do the trick. Most of the plug-ins designed for Photoshop will work just as well in Photoshop Elements, since both applications use the same file format (PSD). Some plug-in packages, clearly meant for professionals and creative types, don't come cheap—they can cost a few hundred dollars. But many plug-ins are available free of charge. One of the best places to start looking for filter and effect plug-ins is at the Adobe Exchange site (www.adobestudioexchange.com), where you can download and share filters, effects, and other plug-in goodies with other Photoshop and Photoshop Elements users.

Show All

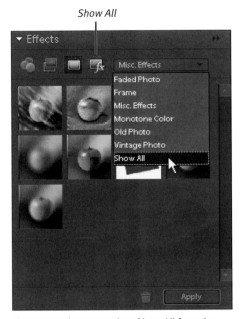

Figure 9.2 When you select Show All from the Library drop-down menu, all filters or effects in their respective libraries are displayed at once.

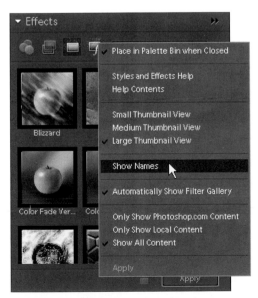

Figure 9.3 Select Show Names from the palette menu to display filters or effects with their names.

To change the number of filters or effects displayed in the palette:

Do one of the following:

◆ Click the Show All button to the right of the Photo Effects button.

◆ If it's not already selected, choose Show All from the Library drop-down menu at the top of the palette to see all filters or effects (**Figure 9.2**).

◆ Select a set of filters or effects from the Library drop-down menu to see just the ones in that set.

To change the palette view:

Do one of the following:

◆ From the More menu, choose Small, Medium, or Large Thumbnail View to change the size of the filters or effect previews. Medium is the default.

◆ From the More menu, choose Show Names to view the filters or effects with their identifying names (**Figure 9.3**).

✔ Tips

■ Filter plug-ins created by third-party developers usually appear at the bottom of the Filters palette menu.

■ If you've downloaded additional filters or effects from Photoshop.com (an option available to those who upgrade to the Plus membership), you can view just those options by choosing Only Show Photoshop.com Content on the More menu. Similarly, choose Only Show Local Content to list the items that shipped with Elements.

USING THE EFFECTS PALETTE

215

Applying Filters and Effects

Depending on the filter or effect you choose and the size of your image, your computer can take a while to apply and display these changes. Of course, computing power increases dramatically every year, along with the typical amount of RAM installed in most new machines. Both the speed of your processor and amount of RAM contribute to faster processing of these transformations. Fortunately, almost all of the filters include a preview window, which allows you to see the result before you decide to apply it.

Effects don't include a preview window, but you'll find useful examples of each effect on the Effects palette. For many filters and effects, a good approach is to select a small area of your image and apply the change to see the results—that way, you don't waste a lot of time waiting for your computer to process changes to the entire image. The exceptions are effects like Frames, where the effect is designed to be applied to your entire image. A few effects (such as the Cutout and Recessed frame effects) require you to make a selection before you can apply the effect.

To apply a filter:

1. To apply a filter to an entire layer, select the layer on the Layers palette to make the layer active. To apply a filter to just a portion of your image, select an area with one of the selection tools (**Figure 9.4**).

2. *Do one of the following*:
   - ▲ Double-click a filter on the Effects palette. The Filter Options dialog appears (**Figure 9.5**).
   - ▲ From the Filter menu, choose a filter from one of the filter submenus.
   - ▲ Drag any filter from the Effects palette onto your image in the image window.

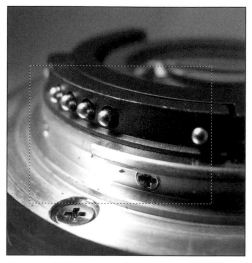

Figure 9.4 Filters and effects can be applied to an entire layer or to a selection.

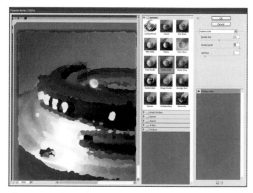

Figure 9.5 The Filter Options dialog includes a large preview window and sliders you can use to adjust a filter's settings.

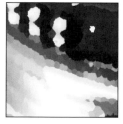 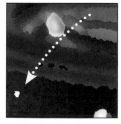

Figure 9.6 To move around (or pan) the preview image, just click and drag to move the image.

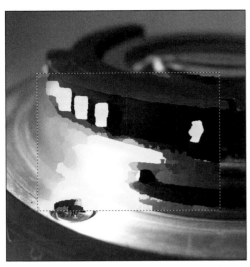

Figure 9.7 After you click OK, the filter is applied to your image.

The Filter Dialogs

Given the sheer number of filters in Photoshop Elements, there's no way to cover the specific steps for each filter in the space of this book. Fortunately, the vast majority of these filters work the same way. So once you've used a couple of them, you can figure out the rest pretty easily. Most filters use the same Filter Options dialog with a preview window and slider bars that allow you to control the level and intensity of the filter. When using a filter for the first time, you should preview the default filter setting and apply it by clicking OK. Not what you wanted? Just press Ctrl+Z to undo your changes and start over. When you're back in the filter's dialog, you can experiment by adjusting the sliders to preview more (or less) dramatic results in your photo.

3. When the Filter Options dialog opens, experiment with the available values and options until you get the look you want.

4. In the dialog preview window, you can change the view by *doing one of the following*:
   - ▲ To zoom in or out, click either the Zoom In (plus sign) or Zoom Out (minus sign) button.
   - ▲ To see a specific area of your image, click and drag within the preview window (**Figure 9.6**).

5. Click OK. The filter is applied to your image (**Figure 9.7**). If you're not happy with the result, choose Edit > Undo or select the previous state from the Undo History palette.

✔ Tips

- ■ Filters with additional options include ellipses (…) after their names.

- ■ The list in the lower-right corner of the Filter Options dialog lets you add multiple filters before applying them to your image. Click the New Filter Layer button (the document icon) and choose another filter to see how it affects the image.

- ■ As you add filters, you'll notice that you're presented with two different types of Option dialogs. The Add Noise filter, for instance, opens to a dialog specific to just that filter. But filters contained in the Artistic, Brush Strokes, Distort, Sketch, Stylize, and Texture groups open to an Option dialog where you can not only adjust the settings for the filter you've selected, but also choose a completely different filter from a filter sets menu in the center of the dialog. Just click any of the filter set names to open them, and then choose a new filter by clicking its thumbnail. A preview window changes to reflect the new filter you've selected.

APPLYING FILTERS AND EFFECTS

To apply effects:

1. To apply an effect to an entire layer, select the layer to make it active. To apply an effect to just a portion of the image, select an area using one of the selection tools.

2. In the Effects palette, double-click the chosen effect (**Figure 9.8**).

   If you prefer, you can also drag any effect from the Effects palette directly onto your image.

   When you apply an effect, it creates one or more new layers immediately above the selected layer (**Figure 9.9**).

✔ Tips

- To reduce the visible impact of an effect, change the opacity of the effect layer using the Opacity slider on the Layers palette.

- Sometimes the filter and effect names, and their thumbnails, don't represent the variety of results you might get by applying them to an image. Experiment by pushing the filter and effect options to extreme limits. You'll often be surprised by the results. Print a copy of your image for future reference and to use on other photos. It's also a good idea to rename the layer with a descriptive name related to the effect you used: for instance, Blizzard 30%.

- To change the look of an effect, experiment with the various blend modes on the Layers palette.

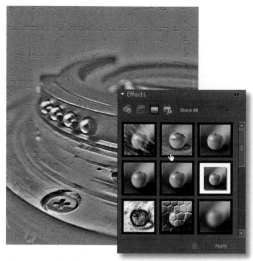

Figure 9.8 Double-click any effect in the Effects palette to apply it to an image or selection. You can also drag an effect or filter from the palette into the image window.

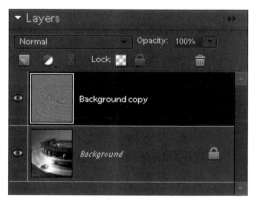

Figure 9.9 When you apply an effect, it generates one or more layers above the selected layers. The number of new layers depends on the series of actions required to create the specific effect.

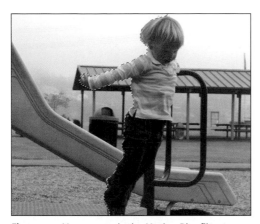

Figure 9.10 You can apply the Motion Blur filter to an entire layer or to a selection, as I'll do in this photo.

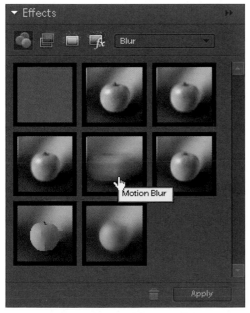

Figure 9.11 Once you've chosen a layer or selection, double-click the Motion Blur thumbnail.

Simulating Action with the Blur Filters

Photoshop Elements includes a few blur filters that can create a sense of motion where none exists. In many cases, you'll want to select a specific area in your photo when using these filters, so that the motion or movement is applied to one object, such as a person, your dog, or a pair of shoes.

The Motion Blur filter blurs a layer or selection in a specific direction and intensity. The result simulates the look of taking a picture of a moving object with a fixed exposure or of panning a camera across a still scene.

The Radial Blur filter creates the impression of a camera zoom or of an object moving toward or away from you. You can also create the impression of an object spinning at variable rates of speed. In either case, the Radial Blur filter lets you control the center of the effect and the amount of blurring or motion.

To add a motion blur to an image:

1. Select the desired layer to make it active. To create a feeling of motion in just a portion of your image, select an area with one of the selection tools (**Figure 9.10**).

2. *Do one of the following:*
   ▲ Choose Blur from the Library drop-down menu on the Effects palette, and double-click the Motion Blur filter (**Figure 9.11**).
   ▲ From the Filter menu, choose Blur > Motion Blur.
   The Motion Blur dialog appears with options for the motion angle and distance.

continues on next page

3. Set the Angle and Distance options to get the look you want (**Figure 9.12**). You can refer to the preview window in the dialog, and if the Preview option is checked, you can also see the results in the main image window.

By default, the Angle option is set to 0°, meaning that the pixels will be blurred along the horizontal axis as shown next to the Angle text box. So, the impression of motion will be right to left (or left to right) across your screen. You can change the angle by dragging the line on the Angle icon or by entering a number of degrees in the Angle text box.

The Distance option determines the number of pixels included in the linear blur, with the default set to 10 pixels (a moderate amount of blurring). When you reach the upper limits of this option (999 pixels), the objects in your photo may become barely recognizable.

4. When you are satisfied with the effect, click OK to apply it to your image (**Figure 9.13**).

✔ Tip

- It may look more realistic if you feather your selection before applying the blur (Select > Feather). See Chapter 5 for more on feathering selections.

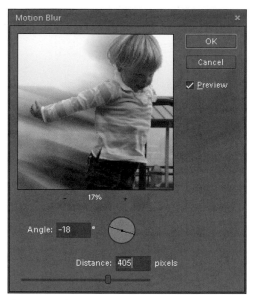

Figure 9.12 The Motion Blur dialog includes options for the angle and distance of the effect.

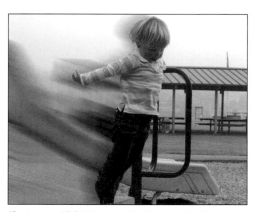

Figure 9.13 Click OK to see the Motion Blur filter applied to your image. If you want to back up and try again, just choose Edit > Undo and experiment with different settings.

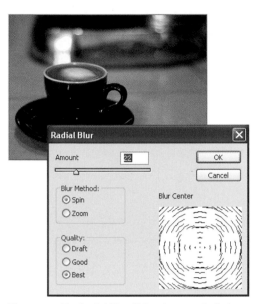

Figure 9.14 The Radial Blur dialog does not include a preview, but the Quality options include Draft, which you can use to quickly apply and view the effects of the filter on your image.

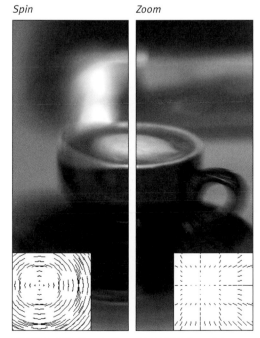

Spin   *Zoom*

Figure 9.15 To change the center point, drag the preview in the Blur Center window.

To add a circular blur to an image:

1. Select the desired layer to make it active. To create a feeling of radial motion in just a portion of your image, select an area with one of the selection tools.

   A circular (elliptical) selection works especially well when you want to create a circular effect.

2. Select the Radial Blur by *doing one of the following*:

   ▲ Double-click the Radial Blur filter on the Effects palette.

   ▲ Choose Filter > Blur > Radial Blur from the main menu.

   The Radial Blur dialog appears, with options for amount of blur, blur center, blur method, and quality (**Figure 9.14**).

3. Set the Amount and Blur Center values.

   The two Blur Method options are Spin and Zoom (**Figure 9.15**). Choose Spin to blur along circular lines or Zoom to blur along lines radiating from the center, as if you were zooming in or out of an image.

4. Select a Quality option for the filter.

   Draft quality produces a quicker rendering of the filter, but with slightly coarse results. The Good and Best options both take a bit longer to render, but provide a smoother look; there's not a big difference between the latter two options.

5. When you are satisfied with the effect, click OK to apply it to your image.

✔ Tip

■ The Radial Blur filter doesn't include a preview window, so if you aren't happy with your results and want to try different settings, just click the Edit Undo button (or press Ctrl+Z) to try again.

The Blur Filters

I've covered the steps for using a couple of my favorite blur filters, but the others can be just as effective. Here's a summary of how the blur filters work and when you might want to use them.

Blur softens the look of an image or selected area and is great for retouching photos where there's a harsh edge or transition. The results are similar to what you get with the Blur tool.

Blur More works like the Blur filter, but with much greater intensity—it's like using the Blur filter three times on the same image. The results are often too dramatic for minor photo retouching, but are great for blurring one particular area of an image (like the border), thereby emphasizing the untouched areas. Keep in mind that the Blur and Blur More filters don't include a dialog or preview window. Just select a layer or area and apply the filter to see the results.

Gaussian Blur allows you a greater amount of control over the blur effect, and you can use this filter to make anything from minor to major adjustments to your image. For most simple photo retouching, the Blur filter works well, but if you're not happy with your results and want to tweak a bit, try Gaussian Blur.

Motion Blur can be used to simulate a moving object or the panning of a camera.

Radial Blur results in either a zooming or spinning motion, depending on the option you choose.

Smart Blur lets you build customized blurs, with complete control over the blur radius (the area affected by the blur effect) and threshold (the number of pixels within a given area affected by the blur). Smart Blur is useful for softening an image or for times when you want a more subtle blur effect.

Surface Blur softens broad areas while keeping edges sharp. Surface Blur can be helpful on portraits where you want to minimize the appearance of wrinkles and minor imperfections. It's not the same as the retouching you'll find in any glossy magazine at the grocery store checkout stand, but it can smooth out common skin issues without resorting to touch-up tools such as the Healing Brush tool.

THE BLUR FILTERS

Distorting Images

The Distort filters include an amazing array of options that let you ripple, pinch, shear, and twist your images. Experiment with all of the Distort filters to get a feel for the different effects you can apply to your images. One filter in particular stands above the others in its power and flexibility: the Liquify filter.

The Liquify filter creates amazing effects by letting you warp, twirl, stretch, and twist pixels beyond the normal laws of physics. You've probably seen plenty of examples of this filter, where someone's face is wildly distorted with bulging eyes and a puckered mouth. However, you can also use the Liquify filter to create more subtle changes and achieve effects that would be impossible with any other tool.

The Liquify filter is unique in that it includes a dialog with its own complete set of image manipulation tools. And because the Liquify filter works within its own dialog box, you can't undo specific changes with the Edit > Undo command or Undo History palette. Fortunately, the Liquify filter offers its own Reconstruct tool to restore any area to its original (or less contorted) state. The Reconstruct tool allows you to "paint" over your image and gradually return to the original version, or stop at any state along the way. If you just want to go back and start over, clicking the Revert button is the quickest method.

The Liquify Tools

Warp lets you push pixels around as you drag with the mouse.

Turbulence works similar to the Warp tool, but it incorporates some actions of the other Liquify tools to create random variations, or turbulence. You can change the amount of turbulence with the Turbulence Jitter slider in the tool options.

Twirl Clockwise and **Twirl Counterclockwise** rotate pixels in either direction.

Pucker moves pixels toward the center of the brush area.

Bloat moves pixels away from the brush center and toward the edges of your brush.

Shift Pixels moves pixels perpendicular to the direction of your brush stroke.

Reflection copies pixels to the brush area, allowing you to create effects similar to a reflection in water.

Reconstruct restores distorted areas to their original state. As you brush over areas with this tool, your image gradually returns to its original state, undoing each change you've made with the Liquify tools. You can stop the reconstruction at any point and continue from there.

The **Zoom** and **Hand** tools work just like those on the Photoshop Elements toolbar.

To distort an image with the Liquify filter:

1. Select an entire layer, or make a selection of the area you want to change.

2. From the Filter menu, choose Distort > Liquify; or, on the Effects palette, choose Distort from the Library drop-down menu and double-click the Liquify filter.

   If your image includes a type layer, you will be prompted to simplify the type to continue. This means the type layer will be flattened into the rest of your image's layers. Be aware that if you click OK, the type will no longer be editable.

   The Liquify dialog appears, including a preview of the layer or selection area. The Warp tool is selected by default, with a brush size of 64 and a pressure of 50 (**Figure 9.16**).

   You'll probably want to change the brush size and pressure during the course of your work.

3. To change the brush settings, *do one of the following:*
   - ▲ To change the brush size, drag the slider or enter a value in the option box. The brush size ranges from 1 to 600 pixels.
   - ▲ To change the brush pressure, drag the slider or enter a value in the option box. The brush pressure ranges from 1 to 100 percent.

4. Distort your image with any of the Liquify tools located on the left side of the Liquify dialog (**Figure 9.17**) until you achieve the look you want. To use any tool, simply select it (just as you do tools on the main toolbar) and then move your pointer into the image (**Figure 9.18**).

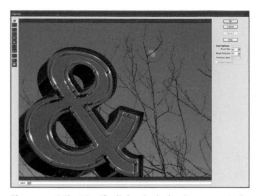

Figure 9.16 The Liquify dialog includes its own set of distortion tools as well as options for changing the brush size and pressure.

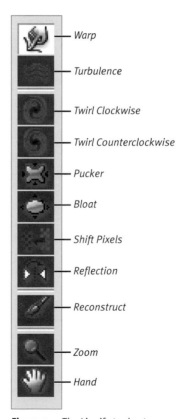

Warp

Turbulence

Twirl Clockwise

Twirl Counterclockwise

Pucker

Bloat

Shift Pixels

Reflection

Reconstruct

Zoom

Hand

Figure 9.17 The Liquify tool set.

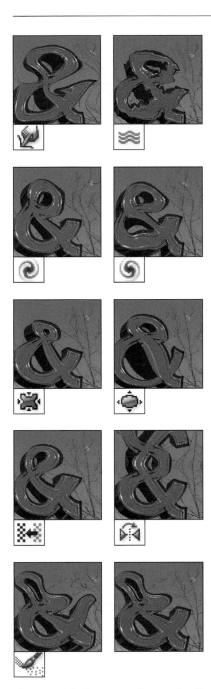

Figure 9.18 The best way to become familiar with the Liquify distortion tools is to experiment with them on a variety of images, as in this series of photos.

To undo changes:

◆ In the Liquify dialog, click the Reconstruct tool. Then, while holding down your mouse button, "brush" over your image to gradually undo each change you've made.

To undo all Liquify changes:

◆ In the Liquify dialog, click the Revert button to return the image to its original state.

✔ Tips

■ Here's another way to undo Liquify changes: In the Liquify dialog, hold down the Alt key. The Cancel button changes to Reset. Click the Reset button to undo any changes you've made with the Liquify tools. The Revert and Reset buttons work the same way, but the Reset button, true to its name, also resets the Liquify tools to their original settings.

■ The Reflection tool can be a little hard to get used to. You may find it works better if you use a large brush size and 100 percent pressure. Also, the direction of your stroke determines which way the image is reflected.

DISTORTING IMAGES

Correcting Camera Distortion

Most cameras may be digital these days, but it's still an optical medium, and every camera has tradeoffs; for example, some lenses offer incredible zoom, but at the expense of introducing barrel distortion around the edges. The Correct Camera Distortion filter provides tools to compensate.

To correct camera distortion:

1. Select a layer or make a selection to edit.

2. From the Filter menu, choose Correct Camera Distortion. The dialog of the same name appears (**Figure 9.19**).

3. Apply the following controls based on the distortion found in your image:

   ▲ **Remove Distortion.** Drag the slider to the left to bloat the image or to the right to pinch it (**Figure 9.20**).

   ▲ **Vignette.** To add or remove a vignette (such as found in old photographs), drag the Amount slider to match the vignette area. Use the Midpoint slider to adjust the vignette's size.

   ▲ **Perspective Control.** Drag the Vertical and Horizontal Perspective sliders to tilt the image. The Angle control rotates the image.

   ▲ **Edge Extension.** After using the controls above, you may want to scale the image with Edge Extension to crop unwanted blank areas caused by the adjustments.

4. Click OK to apply the changes.

✔ Tip

■ As with most adjustment dialogs, hold Alt and click the Cancel button if you want to reset the dialog's settings.

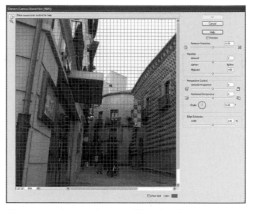

Figure 9.19 Correct Camera Distortion fixes many common photographic gaffes.

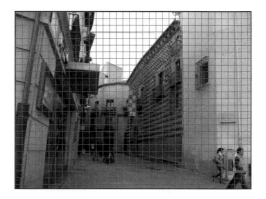

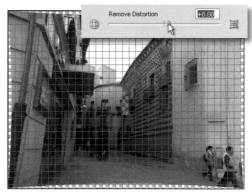

Figure 9.20 The corner of the building on the left curves due to lens distortion (top), so I've applied a small amount of Remove Distortion to pinch the image slightly and straighten the curve (bottom).

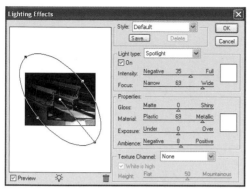

Figure 9.21 When you first open the Lighting Effects dialog, it may seem a bit intimidating. But it only takes a little experimentation with the settings to see the range of effects possible with this filter.

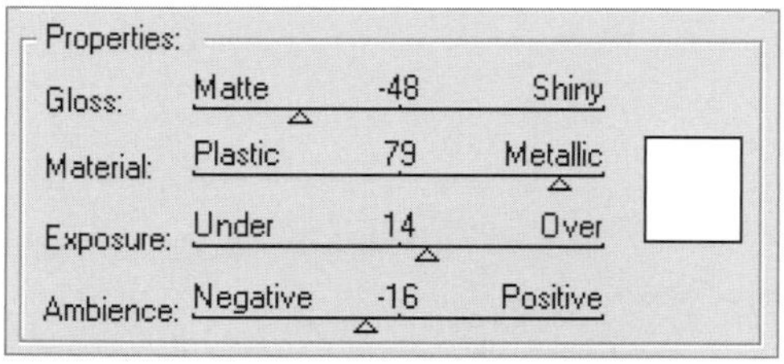

Figure 9.22 The Properties area offers an almost infinite combination of settings you can use to change the appearance and intensity of the lighting.

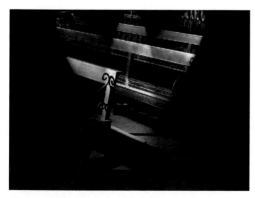

Figure 9.23 The Triple Spotlight filter has been applied to this image.

Creating Lights and Shadows

Lights and shadows add drama to almost any photograph. It's always best to plan your lighting before you take your picture, but there are times when you just can't control these factors. Elements includes some nifty filters to help you enhance the lighting after the fact. The Lighting Effects filter lets you create a seemingly infinite number of effects through a combination of light styles, properties, and even a texture channel. It's almost like having your own lighting studio.

To add lighting effects to an image:

1. Select the desired layer to make it active. To confine the lighting effect to just a portion of your image, select an area using one of the selection tools.

2. Select the Lighting Effects filter by *doing one of the following:*
   ▲ On the Effects palette, choose Render from the Library drop-down menu and double-click the Lighting Effects filter.
   ▲ From the Filter menu, choose Render > Lighting Effects.

   The Lighting Effects dialog appears (**Figure 9.21**).

3. Choose a predefined Style, or create your own using the following controls:
   ▲ Choose a Light Type. The Light Type drop-down menu includes Directional, Omni, and Spotlight options. Each lighting style is based on one of these three light types.
   ▲ Set light properties (**Figure 9.22**).

4. When you are satisfied with the effect, click OK to apply it to your image (**Figure 9.23**).

Light styles and types

The Lighting Effects dialog offers a mind-boggling number of properties, light types, and styles, making it more than a little difficult to figure out where to start. Here's a list of some of the most useful lighting styles and types, along with some pointers on how styles work with light types and properties.

Lighting styles

Flashlight focuses a direct spotlight on the center of the image, with the rest of the image darkened. It's set at a medium intensity with a slightly yellow cast.

Floodlight has a wider focus and casts a white light on your image.

Soft Omni and **Soft Spotlight** provide gentle lightbulb and spotlight effects respectively, and work well for many different kinds of images.

Blue Omni adds a blue overhead light to your image and offers insight into how lighting styles and types work together. If you select this light type, you'll see a blue color box in the Light Type area of the dialog. If you click on this box, the Color Picker appears (**Figure 9.24**), letting you change the color to anything you want. Once you've chosen a new color, click OK to apply your custom lighting style to your photo.

Most of the remaining lighting styles create more dramatic and specialized effects (for example, RGB Lights consists of red, yellow, and blue spotlights), but are worth exploring.

Light types

Directional creates an angled light that shines from one direction across your photo (**Figure 9.25**).

Omni produces a light that shines down on your image from above (**Figure 9.26**).

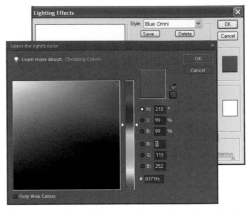

Figure 9.24 Some lighting styles, such as Blue Omni, include colored lights. Change the color by clicking the lighting color box, which opens the Color Picker.

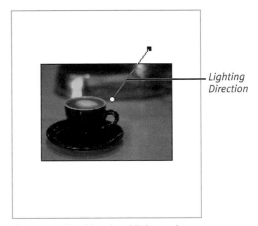

Figure 9.25 The Directional light produces a light source that shines in one direction across your photo, as indicated by the line in the image preview window.

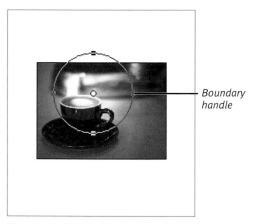

Boundary handle

Figure 9.26 The Omni light creates the impression of a light shining directly onto your photo. To change the size of the lit area, drag one of the boundary handles.

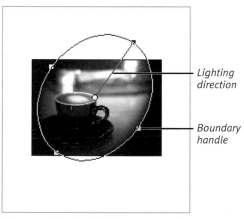

Lighting direction

Boundary handle

Figure 9.27 The Spotlight is represented by an elliptical boundary in the preview. Drag a handle to change the area being lit, and drag the lighting direction line to change the direction of the light source.

Spotlight creates a round spotlight in the center of your image. In preview mode, you'll see that the boundaries of the light look like an ellipse. You can change the size of the ellipse by dragging any of the handles. To change the direction of the light, just drag to move the line (**Figure 9.27**).

When you select a light style, it automatically defaults to whichever light type best supports that look—so, for example, the Floodlight style uses the Spotlight type.

Light properties

Once you've chosen a light style and type, you have complete control over four different lighting properties. To change these, just move the sliders to the left or right.

Gloss establishes how much light reflects off your image and can be set from Matte (less reflection) to Shiny (more reflection).

Material determines the surface properties of your image. It can be set from Plastic to Metallic. As you move the setting toward Plastic, the highlights scatter across the surface more; if you choose Metallic, the highlights are more contained.

Exposure increases or decreases the light. If you click through the light types, you'll notice that most of them leave this setting at, or very close to, 0. This is one setting you may just want to leave as is or make only subtle changes to since it has such a pronounced impact on the light.

Ambience refers to ambient lighting, or how much you combine the particular lighting effect with the existing light in your photo. Positive values allow in more ambient light, and negative values allow less.

To add a lens flare:

1. Select the desired layer to make it active. To confine the lighting effect to just a portion of your image, select an area using one of the selection tools.

2. Select the Lens Flare filter by *doing one of the following:*
   ▲ On the Effects palette, choose Render from the Library drop-down menu and double-click the Lens Flare filter.
   ▲ From the Filter menu, choose Render > Lens Flare.

   The Lens Flare dialog appears, with options for the brightness, flare center, and lens type (**Figure 9.28**).

3. Set the brightness option by dragging the slider to the right to increase or to the left to decrease the brightness.

4. To move the flare center, just click the image preview to move the crosshairs to another location.

5. Set the Lens Type options as desired, and when you're happy with what you see, click OK to apply the filter to your image (**Figure 9.29**).

   The options include settings for three common camera lenses (50–300mm Zoom, 35mm, and 105mm), plus Movie Prime, and the filter creates a look similar to the refraction or lens flare you'd get with each one (**Figure 9.30**).

Flare Center

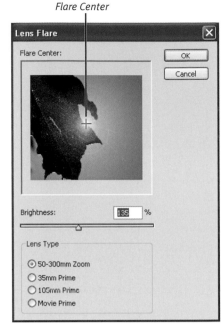

Figure 9.28 The Lens Flare dialog adjusts the brightness, flare center, and lens type.

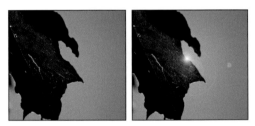

Figure 9.29 I applied the Lens Flare filter with the default brightness and lens type options.

35mm Prime   *105mm Prime*   *Movie Prime*

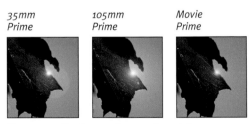

Figure 9.30 The lens options can be subtle.

PAINTING AND DRAWING | 10

A lifetime ago (in computer years, anyway) a little company just south of San Francisco introduced a small beige box with a tiny 9-inch keyhole of a monitor and a mouse resembling a bar of soap. It could display and print only in black and white, was incapable of reproducing even remotely convincing photographic images, and was strictly limited to a resolution of 72 pixels per inch. And yet, graphic artists smiled a collective smile, because bundled in its modest software suite, alongside its stunted little word processor, Apple's Macintosh gave the world MacPaint.

Painting and drawing programs have jumped by leaps and bounds since taking those first, early baby steps, but one feature remains the same: They're still so much fun to use!

In this chapter, you'll learn how to use Photoshop Elements' built-in drawing and painting tools to create original artwork or to enhance your digital photos—whether you're filling parts of your image with color, adding a decorative stroked border to a logo or design element, or "painting" a photo with Impressionist-style brushstrokes.

About Bitmap Images and Vector Graphics

Photoshop Elements' painting and drawing tools render artwork in two fundamentally different ways.

The painting tools, including all the varied fills, gradients, brushes, and erasers, work by making changes to pixels—adding them, removing them, or changing their colors. A bitmap image is composed entirely of tiny pixels; and digital photos, the mainstay of Photoshop Elements, are bitmap images. Although you can apply paintbrushes, color fills, special effects, and filters to bitmaps, they simply don't resize well. If you try to enlarge digital photo, for example, you'll see that its image quality suffers as the pixels get bigger, resulting in a blurry mess.

The drawing tools (shape creation tools, really) form images not by manipulating pixels but by constructing geometric paths based on precise mathematical coordinates, or vectors. Images created with these drawing tools, known as vector graphics, hold one decided advantage over their bitmap cousins: They can be scaled up or down, virtually infinitely, with no loss of detail or resolution (**Figure 10.1**). Elements' scalable fonts, for example, are based on vector shapes, so they can be stretched, warped, and resized to your heart's content. Vector graphics files also tend to be smaller than comparable bitmap image files, since a path shape requires less information for your computer to process and render than a similar shape constructed of pixels.

Although they're designed to work with different kinds of graphics, the painting and drawing tools are equally easy to use, and work well together if you want to combine vector and bitmap graphics—such as adding type or custom shapes to a favorite photo.

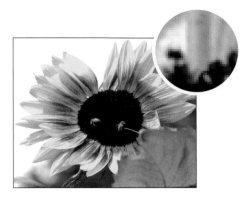

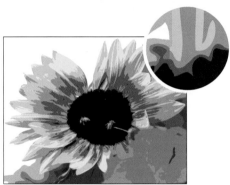

Figure 10.1 A photographic bitmap image (top) is constructed of pixels. Any attempt to zoom in on or enlarge a portion of the image can make the pixels more pronounced and the image more pixelated. A vector image (bottom) is drawn with a series of geometric paths rather than pixels. Vector graphics can be enlarged or reduced with no loss of detail or resolution.

Figure 10.2
Clicking the foreground or background color swatch in the toolbox opens the Color Picker.

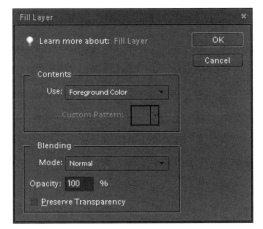

Figure 10.3 The Fill Layer dialog offers several options for filling a layer or selection with color.

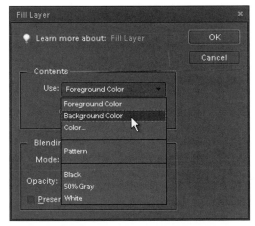

Figure 10.4 The Use drop-down menu contains various sources from which to choose a fill color. Choose the Foreground Color option to apply a specific color chosen from the Color Picker or Swatches palette.

Filling Areas with Color

You have two primary ways of filling areas with a solid color. With the Fill dialog, you can quickly blanket an entire layer or a selected area of a layer with color. The Paint Bucket tool operates in a more controlled manner, filling only portions of areas based on properties that you set on the options bar. Either method works especially well for those times when you want to cover large, expansive areas with a single color.

To fill a selection or layer with color:

1. Using any of the selection or marquee tools, select the area of your image you want to fill with color.

   If you want to fill an entire layer, it's not necessary to make a selection.

2. To select a fill color, *do one of the following*:

   ▲ Click either the current foreground or background color swatch at the bottom of the toolbox (**Figure 10.2**) to open the Color Picker; then select a color.

   ▲ From the Swatches palette, click any color to select it.

3. From the Edit menu, choose either Fill Selection or Fill Layer to open the Fill Layer dialog (**Figure 10.3**).

4. From the Use drop-down menu, choose a source for your fill color (**Figure 10.4**).

   In addition to the foreground and background colors, you can use the Fill command to fill a selection or area with a pattern or with black, white, or 50-percent gray. Or you can choose Color to open the Color Picker and select a different color altogether.

   continues on next page

5. From the Blending area of the dialog, select a blending mode and opacity for your fill. (For more information on blending modes, see "About Opacity and Blending Modes" in Chapter 8.)

6. Click the Preserve Transparency check box if you want to preserve a layer's transparency when you apply the fill.

7. Click OK to close the dialog.

The selection or layer is filled with the color and properties you specified (**Figure 10.5**).

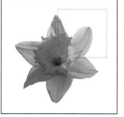 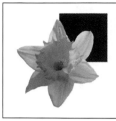

Figure 10.5 In this example, an area of the Background layer is selected (left), then filled with a color using the Fill dialog (right).

✔ Tips

■ To save time, use simple keyboard shortcuts to fill a selection or layer with either the current foreground or background color. Alt+Backspace will fill a selection or layer with the current foreground color, and Ctrl+Backspace applies the current background color.

■ To swap the foreground and background color swatches in the toolbox, press X.

■ To convert the foreground and background color to black and white (the defaults), press D.

About Preserving Transparency

The Preserve Transparency check box works just like the Lock Transparent Pixels button on the Layers palette. If the check box is highlighted and you fill a layer that has both opaque and transparent pixels, the transparent areas will be locked (or protected), and only the opaque areas of the layer will be filled (**Figure 10.6**). If you check Preserve Transparency and then try to fill an empty layer (one containing only transparent pixels), the layer will remain unfilled. That's because the whole layer, being transparent, is locked. If you fill a flattened layer, like Photoshop Elements' default background layer, the check box is dimmed and the option isn't available because a background layer contains no transparency.

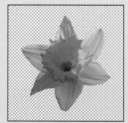 

Figure 10.6 When a layer (left) is filled using the Preserve Transparency option, the transparent areas of the layer remain protected and untouched, and only the layer object accepts the fill color (right).

Figure 10.7
The Paint Bucket tool.

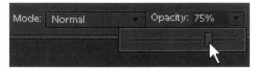

Figure 10.8 The Paint Bucket tool takes advantage of all of Photoshop Elements' blending modes and opacity options.

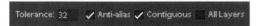

Figure 10.9 The options bar contains several settings that fine-tune the Paint Bucket's fill properties.

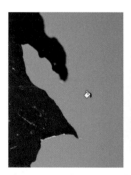 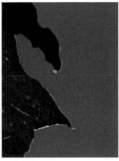

Figure 10.10 The Paint Bucket tool fills areas based on their tonal values. Here it automatically selects and fills just the light-colored background area.

To apply fill color with the Paint Bucket tool:

1. Select the Paint Bucket tool from the toolbox (K) (**Figure 10.7**).

2. Select a foreground color from either the Color Picker or the Swatches palette.

3. On the options bar, select a blending mode and opacity setting, if desired (**Figure 10.8**).

4. Still on the options bar, set a Tolerance value; then specify whether you want the colored fill to be anti-aliased, to fill only contiguous pixels, or to affect all layers (**Figure 10.9**).

   For more information on these options, see the sidebar "How Does that Paint Bucket Tool Work, Anyway?" on the next page.

5. Click the area of your image where you want to apply the colored fill.

   The selected color is painted into your image (**Figure 10.10**).

How Does that Paint Bucket Tool Work, Anyway?

If you're familiar with other painting and drawing programs, Photoshop Elements' Paint Bucket tool may leave you scratching your head. In many paint programs, the Paint Bucket tool does little more than indiscriminately dump color across large areas of an image. But Elements' Paint Bucket tool is much more intelligent and selective about where it applies color. Depending on the parameters you set in the options bar, it fills areas based on the tonal values of their pixels.

The **Tolerance** slider determines the range of pixels the Paint Bucket fills. The greater the value, the larger the range of pixels filled.

Click **Anti-alias** to add a smooth, soft transition to the edges of your color fill.

Click **Contiguous** to limit the fill to pixels similar in color or tonal value that touch, or are *contiguous* with, one another. If you're using the Paint Bucket tool to switch your car's color from green to blue, this ensures that only the *car's* green pixels are turned blue—not all the green pixels within the entire image.

If you select the **Use All Layers** check box, Photoshop Elements recognizes and considers pixel colors and values across all layers, but the fill is applied only to the active layer. This means if you click the Paint Bucket tool in an area of any *inactive* layer, the fill will be applied to the current *active* layer (**Figure 10.11**).

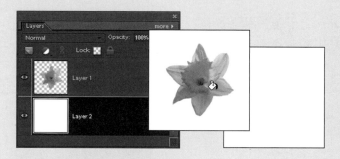

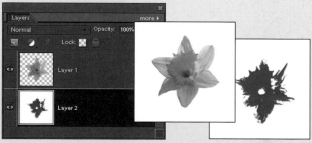

Figure 10.11 If the All Layers check box is selected and you click the Paint Bucket tool in an inactive layer (top), the fill for that specific area is applied to the active layer (bottom).

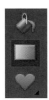

Figure 10.12
The Gradient tool.

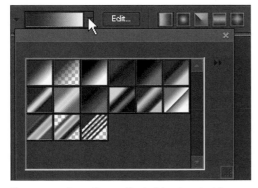

Figure 10.13 Open the gradient picker to select from sets of gradient thumbnails.

Filling Areas with a Gradient

The Gradient tool fills any selection or layer with smooth transitions of color, one blending gradually into the next. They can be rendered as opaque fills or seamlessly incorporated into a layered project using any of Elements' blending modes and opacity settings. Use a gradient to create an effective background image for a photo; to screen back a portion of an image; to create an area on which to place type; or apply it to any shape or object to simulate the surface texture of metal or glass.

To apply a gradient fill:

1. Using any of the selection or marquee tools, select the area of your image where you want to apply the gradient.

   If you want to fill an entire layer, you don't need to make a selection.

2. Select the Gradient tool from the toolbox (or press G) (**Figure 10.12**).

3. On the options bar, click to open the gradient picker (**Figure 10.13**).

4. Click to choose from the list of default gradients, or if you want to view additional gradient sets, click the More button (the triangles to the right of the thumbnail images) to open the gradient picker menu (**Figure 10.14**).

   Gradient sets are located in the bottom-most section of the menu. When you select a new gradient set, it replaces the set displayed in the gradient picker.

   continues on next page

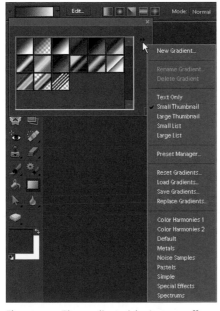

Figure 10.14 The gradient picker's menu offers several picker display options plus access to a variety of gradient sets.

5. On the options bar, click to choose a gradient style (**Figure 10.15**).

Choose from five gradient styles: Linear, Radial, Angle, Reflected, and Diamond.

6. In the image window, click and drag in the area where you want to apply the gradient (**Figure 10.16**).

The selection or layer is filled with the gradient.

✔ Tip

■ Hold down the Shift key to constrain a gradient horizontally, vertically, or at a 45-degree angle.

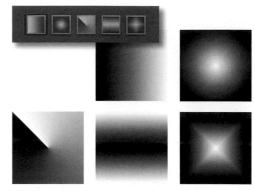

Figure 10.15 Click a gradient style button on the options bar to draw one of five gradient styles.

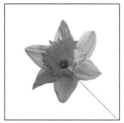 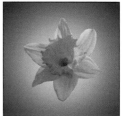

Figure 10.16 Drag from the center to the edge to create a halo effect with the Radial gradient.

Gradient Types

You can create two gradient types from the Gradient Editor: Solid and Noise.

Solid is the default gradient type. When creating or editing a gradient in Solid mode, you can add color and opacity stops and adjust the smoothness of the transition between colors with a percentage slider. You can also change the location of the Color and Opacity stops and their midpoints.

Noise is, well, largely useless. Noise creates random bands of color based on either the RGB or HSB color model, and although there must be some good application for it somewhere, I have yet to stumble on what it might be. Feel free to experiment with this gradient, but you probably won't end up using it much.

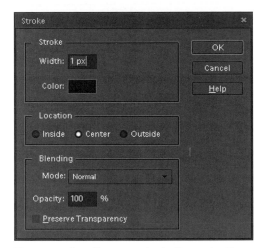

Figure 10.17 Draw lines around selections using the Stroke dialog.

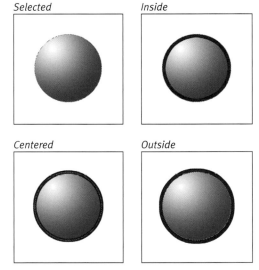

Figure 10.18 Once an object is selected, you can stroke it either inside, centered on, or outside of the selection.

Adding a Stroke to a Selection or Layer

Photoshop Elements' Stroke command adds a colored rule or border around any selected object or layer. With the Stroke command, you can easily trace around almost anything, from simple rectangle or ellipse selections to complex typographic characters. Because you can control both the stroke's thickness and where the stroke is drawn in relation to a selection (inside, outside, or centered), you can create everything from delicate, single-ruled outlines to decorative, multiple-stroked borders and frames.

To apply a stroke:

1. Using any of the selection or marquee tools, select the area of your image to which you want to add a stroke.

   If you're adding a stroke to an object on its own transparent layer, there's no need to make a selection. Instead, just check that the layer is active on the Layers palette.

2. From the Edit menu, choose Stroke (Outline) Selection to open the Stroke dialog (**Figure 10.17**).

3. In the Width text box, enter the stroke width, in pixels.

   There's no need to enter the pixel abbreviation (px) following the number value.

4. Change the stroke color by clicking the Color box and opening the Color Picker.

5. Select the location of the stroke. The location determines where the stroke is drawn: inside, outside, or centered directly on the selection (**Figure 10.18**).

continues on next page

6. Ignore the Blending portion of the dialog for now.

7. Click OK to apply the stroke to your selection or layer (**Figure 10.19**).

✔ Tip

■ Photoshop Elements uses the foreground color for the stroke color unless you change the color in the Stroke dialog. So if you want to pick a stroke color from the Swatches palette, click the Swatches palette to assign the foreground color before anything else; then choose Stroke from the Edit menu. The color you choose from the Swatches palette will appear as the stroke color in the dialog.

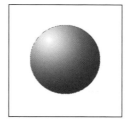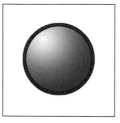

Figure 10.19 Select an object (left), and then choose the Stroke command to apply a stroke (right).

Creating a Stroke Layer

It's a good habit to create a new layer before applying strokes to your image. That way, you can control attributes such as opacity and blending modes right on the Layers palette. You can even turn strokes off and on by clicking the stroke layer's visibility icon. If you're adding a stroke to a selection, simply create a new layer and then follow the steps in the task "To apply a stroke." If you're stroking an object on a transparent layer and want its stroke on a separate layer, you need to perform a couple additional steps:

1. Identify the object to which you want to add a stroke; then press Ctrl and click once on the layer on the Layers palette. The object is automatically selected in the image window (**Figure 10.20**).

2. Create a new layer by clicking the New Layer button at the top of the Layers palette.

3. With the new layer selected on the Layers palette, choose Stroke (Outline) Selection from the Edit menu; then follow steps 3 through 7 of "To apply a stroke."

A stroke is created for the object, but placed on its own layer.

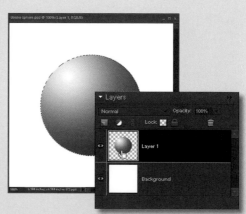

Figure 10.20 Ctrl+click the Layers palette to create a selection around a layer object.

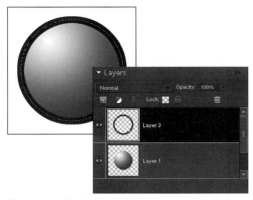

Figure 10.21 The first step in creating a multiruled border is to create a thick stroke. Here, I used a stroke of 15 pixels.

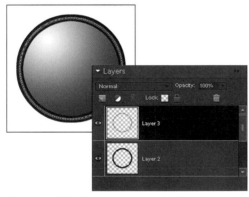

Figure 10.22 Placing a narrow stroke of a different color over the broad first stroke creates an attractive three-ruled border.

To create a decorative border:

1. Make a selection, either by using one of the selection or marquee tools, or by selecting an object on a transparent layer as described in the "Creating a Stroke Layer" sidebar.

2. Create a new layer; then apply a wide stroke to the selection (**Figure 10.21**). In this example, I used a stroke of 15 pixels.

3. With the selection still active, create a new layer above the first.

4. Apply a stroke narrower than the first and in a contrasting color or value (**Figure 10.22**).

5. Continue to add stroke layers until you achieve the desired result.

✔ Tip

■ You can create different effects by adding inside and outside strokes.

Using the Brush Tool

The Brush tool is a near limitless reservoir of hundreds of different and unique brushes. You can apply painted brushstrokes directly to the surface of any photograph, or open a new file to serve as a blank canvas upon which you can create an original work of fine art. The dozen preset brush libraries offer selections as varied as Calligraphic, Wet Media, and Special Effect, and any brush can be resized from 1 pixel to a staggering 2500 pixels in diameter. You can paint using any of Photoshop Elements' blending modes and opacity settings, and you can turn any brush into an airbrush with a single click of a button. So whether you're a budding Van Gogh, would like to add a color-tint effect to an antique black-and-white photograph, or just enjoy doodling while talking on the phone, Photoshop Elements' brushes can help to bring out your inner artist.

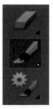

Figure 10.23 The Brush tool.

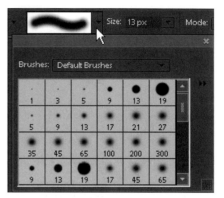

Figure 10.24 Open the Brush Presets palette to select from sets of different brushes.

To paint with the Brush tool:

1. To select a paint color, *do one of the following:*
   ▲ Click the current foreground color swatch at the bottom of the toolbox to open the Color Picker.
   ▲ Choose a color from the Swatches palette.

2. Select the Brush tool in the toolbox (or press B) (**Figure 10.23**).

3. On the options bar, click to open the Brush Presets palette (**Figure 10.24**).

4. Click to choose from the list of default brushes, or select a different brush set from the Brushes drop-down menu (**Figure 10.25**).

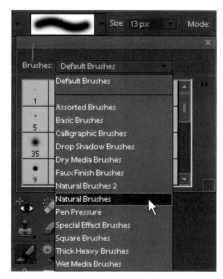

Figure 10.25 The Brushes drop-down menu gives you access to a variety of brush sets.

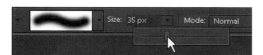

Figure 10.26 Use the brush Size slider to resize your brush.

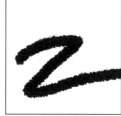

Figure 10.27 Create realistic brush effects simply by dragging through the image window.

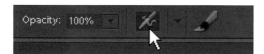

Figure 10.28 Click the Airbrush button on the options bar to give a brush the characteristics of an airbrush.

Once you've selected a brush, you can use it at its predefined size, or you can resize it using the brush Size slider on the options bar (**Figure 10.26**).

5. Again on the options bar, select a blend mode and opacity setting.

6. In the image window, drag to paint a brushstroke (**Figure 10.27**).

✔ Tips

■ You can easily resize brushes on the fly using simple keyboard shortcuts. Once a brush of any size is selected, press the] or [key to increase or decrease the current brush size to the nearest unit of 10 pixels. Thus, if you're painting with a brush size of 23 pixels and press the] key, the brush size increases to 30 pixels and then grows in increments of 10 each subsequent time you press]. Conversely, a brush size of 56 pixels is reduced to 50 pixels when you press the [key, and the brush continues to shrink by 10 pixels each time thereafter that you press [.

■ When any tool that uses a brush-type pointer is selected (the Eraser, Blur, Sharpen, and Clone tools, for instance), use the same keyboard shortcuts above.

■ Almost any brush can be made to behave like an airbrush by clicking the Airbrush button on the options bar (**Figure 10.28**). With the Airbrush activated, paint flows more slowly from the brush and gradually builds denser tones of color. The Airbrush option is most effective when applied to soft, round brushes or to brushes with scatter and spacing properties. (For more information on scatter and spacing properties, see the sidebar "Understanding the Brush Dynamics Palette" later in this chapter.)

USING THE BRUSH TOOL

Creating and Saving Custom Brushes

With so many different brushes and brush sets at your disposal, you may be surprised to discover you can change not only the *size* of brushes, but other characteristics such as flow, shape, and color. Photoshop Elements provides you with all the tools you need to modify existing brushes and create your own from photographs or scanned objects, such as leaves or flower petals. Once you've created a new brush, you can store it temporarily in an existing brush set or save and organize it into a new brush set of your own. Any new brush sets you create are then accessed and loaded from the Brushes dropdown menu on the Brush Presets palette.

To create a custom brush:

1. Select the Brush tool from the toolbox (B).

2. From the list of preset brushes on the options bar, click to select a brush you want to customize (**Figure 10.29**).

3. On the options bar, click the More Options button to open the Brush Dynamics palette (**Figure 10.30**).

4. Use the sliders on the palette to modify the Fade, Hue Jitter, Scatter, Spacing, and Hardness properties of the brush.

   For more information on these slider controls, see the "Understanding the Brush Dynamics Palette" sidebar later in this chapter.

5. You can also adjust the angle and roundness of the brush (**Figure 10.31**).

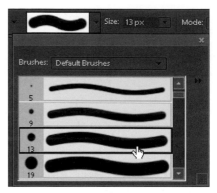

Figure 10.29 To create a new brush, select an existing brush and customize its properties.

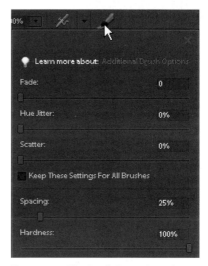

Figure 10.30 The Brush Dynamics palette contains slider controls to modify a brush shape.

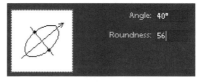

Figure 10.31 The lower portion of the Brush Dynamics palette offers controls for angle and roundness.

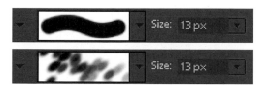

Figure 10.32 The Brush Presets preview area here shows an original brush (top) and the same brush customized on the Brush Dynamics palette (bottom).

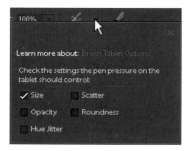

Figure 10.33 Tablet options give you control over how pen pressure affects certain brush settings.

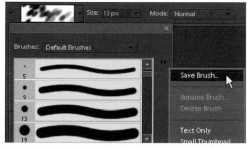

Figure 10.34 Save your customized brushes on the Brush Presets palette menu.

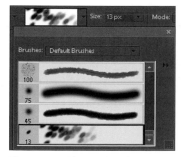

Figure 10.35 The new brush appears at the bottom of the palette list.

As you move the sliders, or enter angle and roundness values, refer to the brush presets preview on the options bar to see the effects of your changes. All but the Hue Jitter property will be reflected in the preview on the options bar (**Figure 10.32**).

6. If you have a pressure-sensitive digital tablet connected to your computer, you can control how the pen's pressure will affect your brush settings.

   On the options bar, click the Tablet Options button, then check the boxes for the brush settings you want the pen pressure to control (**Figure 10.33**).

7. When you're satisfied with your changes, click anywhere on the options bar to close the palette.

8. On the options bar, use the brush Size slider to size your brush.

9. Still on the options bar, open the Brush Presets palette; then select Save Brush from the palette options menu (**Figure 10.34**).

   The Brush Name dialog opens.

10. Type a name for your new brush and click OK.

    Your new brush appears at the bottom of the current brush presets list on the Brush Presets palette (**Figure 10.35**).

To create a brush from a photographic object:

1. Open an image that contains an object or area from which you want to create a new brush.

2. To select an object from the image, *do one of the following:*

   ▲ Using one of the selection tools, select the object or portion of a photograph you want to make into a brush. The Selection Brush and Magnetic Lasso tools both work well for this kind of selection (**Figure 10.36**).

   ▲ If you already have an object on its own transparent layer, hold down Ctrl and click on the layer thumbnail in the Layers palette.

3. From the Edit menu, choose Define Brush from Selection. The Brush Name dialog opens with a representation of your new brush in its preview box (**Figure 10.37**).

4. Enter a name for the brush and click OK to close the dialog.

5. Select the Brush tool from the toolbox; then from the options bar, open the Brush Presets palette. Your new brush appears at the bottom of the current brush presets list (**Figure 10.38**).

6. Click to select the new brush; then on the options bar, click the More Options button to open the Brush Dynamics palette.

7. Use the sliders on the palette to modify the brush attributes; then click anywhere on the options bar to close the palette.

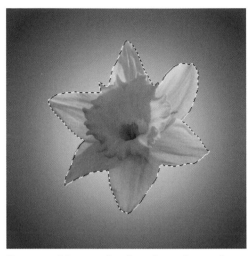

Figure 10.36 A custom brush can be made out of virtually any selected object. In this example, I've selected a large flower.

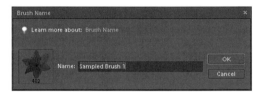

Figure 10.37 The selection appears in the brush preview of the Brush Name dialog.

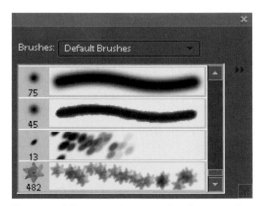

Figure 10.38 Once saved, your new brush appears in the brush presets list.

✔ Tips

- You can use these kinds of brushes to great effect as background textures, type borders, or homemade "rubber stamps" for greeting cards and invitations.

- Images with high contrast generally work best as brush shapes. Remember that you're not saving any color information—just the object's shape and its tonal values—so you'll want to use shapes with as much defined detail as possible.

- Don't be discouraged if you can't seem to duplicate the color and scatter effects of preset brushes such as Maple Leaves. A good number of the built-in brushes weren't created in Photoshop Elements at all, but in Adobe Photoshop. Photoshop offers a host of additional controls, including jitter properties for scatter, angle, hue, and size. For now, while you're working in Photoshop Elements, any blowing leaves or dune grass you create will all have to face the same direction.

CREATING AND SAVING CUSTOM BRUSHES

Understanding the Brush Dynamics Palette

With a bit of exploration, you'll find the Brush Dynamics palette to be a useful tool for creating new brushes and modifying existing ones.

The **Spacing** slider controls the spacing of the brush shape and is based on a percentage of the brush's current size (**Figure 10.39**). The default for most round brushes is 25 percent; 5 percent seems to be the optimum for most of the fine-art brushes such as Chalks, Pastels, and Loaded Watercolor.

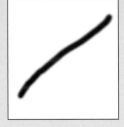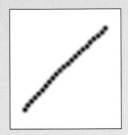

Figure 10.39 A brush spacing value of 25 percent (left) and 75 percent (right).

The **Fade** slider sets the number of steps a brush takes to fade to transparent and can simulate the effect of a brush running out of paint as it draws across a surface. One step is equal to a brush width, so the fade effect is dependent on Spacing (**Figure 10.40**).

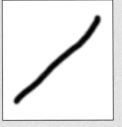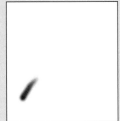

Figure 10.40 A brush fade value of 0 (left) and 15 (right).

The **Hue Jitter** slider determines how randomly the brush renders color, based on the foreground and background colors. The lower the jitter percentage, the more the foreground color is favored. If the percentage is set to the maximum of 100 percent, the foreground and background colors (and mixtures of the two colors combined) are represented in equal measure throughout the brushstroke.

The **Hardness** slider controls the hardness or softness of a brushstroke's edges. A Hardness value of 100 percent creates a solid brushstroke with no soft edges (**Figure 10.41**).

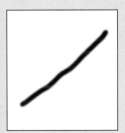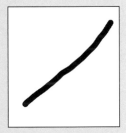

Figure 10.41 A brush hardness value of 0 percent (left) and 100 percent (right).

The **Scatter** slider determines how much a brush shape is spread around with each stroke. The higher the percentage, the more brush shapes are scattered and spread. Lower percentages create almost no scatter at all (**Figure 10.42**).

The **Angle** value allows you to rotate a brush shape to any angle, and the **Roundness** value can be used to flatten or squish a brush shape.

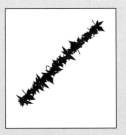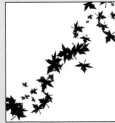

Figure 10.42 A brush scatter value of 0 percent (left) and 30 percent (right).

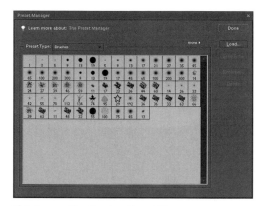

Figure 10.43 The Brushes Preset Manager.

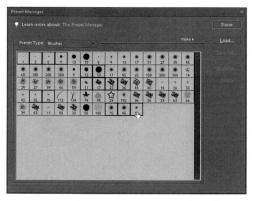

Figure 10.44 Select brushes you want included in your new brush set.

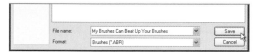

Figure 10.45 Name your new brush set in the Save dialog.

Managing brush sets

Managing brushes is no different than managing other presets (such as gradients and patterns). When you create a new brush, it's saved in the presets file. But once you reset the brushes on the Brush Presets palette or select a different brush set, any new brushes you've created will be lost. Use the Preset Manager to create and save new brush sets.

To create a new brush set:

1. Create as many new brushes as you like, as described in the previous procedures.

2. From the Brush Presets palette menu, choose Preset Manager.

   The Preset Manager dialog opens to the current brush set displayed on the Brush Presets palette (**Figure 10.43**).

3. Scroll through the thumbnail views until you find the brushes you want to include in your new set.

4. In the thumbnail area, Ctrl+click to select all of the brushes you want to include (**Figure 10.44**).

   If you select a brush by mistake, you can deselect it by holding down Ctrl and clicking the thumbnail a second time.

5. Click the Save Set button to open the Save dialog.

6. In the File name text box, enter a new name to describe your brush set and click Save (**Figure 10.45**).

   Your brush set is saved with the brushes you selected in step 4.

   Your new brush set is saved with the others, but it won't appear on either the More menu in the Preset Manager or the Brushes drop-down menu on the Brush Presets palette until after you quit and then restart Photoshop Elements.

CREATING AND SAVING CUSTOM BRUSHES

Creating Special Painting Effects

The Impressionist Brush tool adds a painterly look to any photographic image. Although similar in effect to some of the Artistic and Brush Stroke filters, the Impressionist Brush tool allows you to be much more selective about which areas of an image it's applied to. That's because it uses the same scaleable, editable brushes as the Brush tool. You can use the Impressionist Brush tool to create compelling works of art from even the most mundane of photographs.

To paint with the Impressionist Brush tool:

1. Open the image to which you want to apply the Impressionist Brush effect.

2. Select the Impressionist Brush tool from beneath the Brush tool in the toolbox (**Figure 10.46**).

   Alternatively, you can press B to select the Brush tool and then press B again to toggle to the Impressionist Brush tool.

3. On the options bar, select a brush from the Brush Presets palette.

   You can, of course, use any brush with the Impressionist Brush tool, but the round, soft-sided brush that Photoshop Elements picks as the default works especially well.

4. Again on the options bar, select a size with the brush Size slider (**Figure 10.47**).

   You can also select a mode and an opacity option, although in most cases the defaults of Normal and 100 percent are fine.

5. Still on the options bar, click the More Options button to open the Impressionist Brush Options palette (**Figure 10.48**).

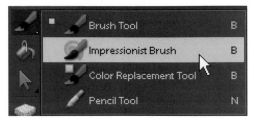

Figure 10.46 The Impressionist Brush tool.

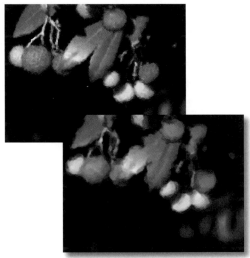

Figure 10.47 The brush size can have quite an impact on the way the Impressionist Brush tool affects your photograph. In the top photo, I painted with a brush-stroke of 10 pixels. In the bottom photo, I changed the brushstroke to 20 pixels.

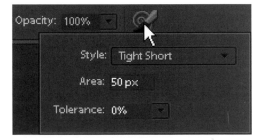

Figure 10.48 The Impressionist Brush Options palette has controls for different brush styles and the amount of image area they affect with each brushstroke.

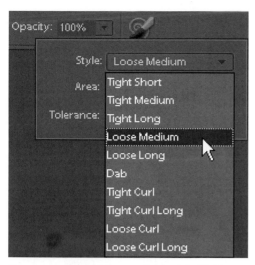

Figure 10.49 Brush styles vary from subtle (Dab) to extravagant (Loose Curl Long).

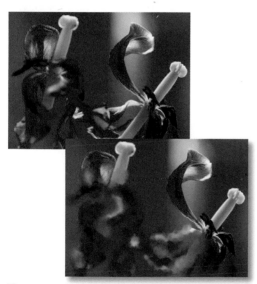

Figure 10.50 Simply drag the brush through your photo to create a work of art.

6. From the Style drop-down menu, select a brush style (**Figure 10.49**).

   I tend not to stray much beyond the top three Styles (Tight Short, Medium, and Long), although the Dab style also creates some pretty effects.

7. In the Area text box, enter a value, in pixels, for the amount of area you want to affect with each stroke of the brush.

   For example, let's say you start with a brush that makes a single brush mark 10 pixels wide, and then select an Area value of 80 pixels. As you move the brush through the image—and depending on the brush style you chose—it will swoosh around an area of 80 x 80 pixels, distributing the paint in 10-pixel dollops.

8. If desired, select a Tolerance setting to determine the range of pixels affected.

   You may want to keep the Tolerance slider set at 0 percent and leave it alone. In use with the Impressionist brush, this setting seems wildly erratic and not worth the trouble.

9. In the image window, drag the brush through your image. The image takes on a painterly look wherever the brush is drawn through it (**Figure 10.50**).

✔ Tips

- Images with resolutions of 150 pixels per inch and higher make the best candidates for the Impressionist Brush tool, because the higher resolution helps to preserve detail when the effect is applied.

- Stick to using smaller brush sizes, particularly on low-resolution images. Although any rules of thumb vary from image to image, a good starting place is a brush size between 6 and 10 pixels and an Area setting between 30 and 50.

Erasing with Customizable Brush Shapes

The images or brushstrokes you choose to remove from a photograph are often as important as those you decide to add or leave behind. The basic Eraser feature is a powerful tool for cleaning up and fine-tuning your images, taking full advantage of every brush style and size that Photoshop Elements has to offer. Not only can you perform routine erasing tasks such as rubbing away stray pixels, you can also customize an eraser's brush and opacity settings to create unique texture, color, and pattern effects. Three modes allow you to customize your erasers even further, so that you can erase with soft-edged brush shapes, hard-edged pencil shapes, or a simple hard-edged square block.

To use the Eraser tool:

1. Select the Eraser tool from the toolbox (or press E) (**Figure 10.51**).

2. On the options bar, select a brush from the Brush Presets palette (**Figure 10.52**).

3. Again on the options bar, select a size using the brush Size slider.

4. From the Mode drop-down menu, select one of the three eraser modes (Brush, Pencil, or Block).

   If you select a soft, anti-aliased brush and then choose Pencil from the mode menu, the eraser will become coarse and aliased (**Figure 10.53**).

5. Still on the options bar, select an opacity using the Opacity slider.

6. In the image window, drag the eraser through your image.

   The image is erased according to the attributes you've applied to the eraser.

Figure 10.51 The Eraser tool.

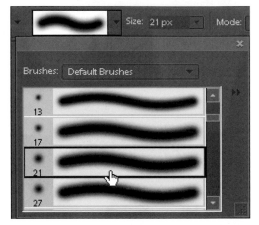

Figure 10.52 The same brush presets are available for the Eraser tool as for the Brush tool.

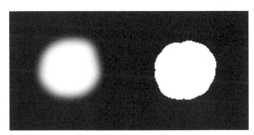

Figure 10.53 An eraser in Brush mode (left) and in Pencil mode (right).

Erasing on Flattened vs. Layered Images

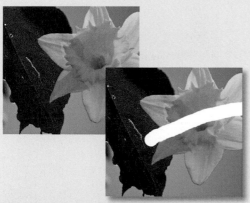

Figure 10.54 On a flattened image layer, the Eraser tool paints with the current background color wherever the eraser is dragged.

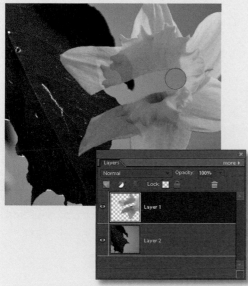

Figure 10.55 When erasing on a layer with transparency, the Eraser tool actually removes image pixels (here, the center of the flower layer) and exposes the image on the layer below (the leaf).

The Eraser tool functions in a fundamentally different way, depending on whether it's erasing on a flattened image, such as Photoshop Elements' default background, or on a layer of a multilayered file. When erasing on a flattened image, the Eraser tool doesn't really erase at all. Instead, it replaces the image with the current background color displayed in the toolbox. In other words, it simply paints over the image with the background color (**Figure 10.54**).

On the other hand, when erasing a portion of an image from a layer, the Eraser tool actually removes the pixels from the layer, creating a transparent hole and exposing the image on the layer directly below it (**Figure 10.55**).

✔ Tip

- You're not limited to round or square brush shapes for your erasers. Any brush, even pictorial ones (for instance, Maple Leaves and Dune Grass) or photographic ones (like Scattered Leaves) can be used as erasers. Try experimenting with different brush shapes and opacity settings to create unusual textures and patterns in your photographs.

Understanding Shapes

In Photoshop Elements, you create shapes not by rendering them with pixels, but by constructing them from vector paths, which are actually vector *masks*. I'll use some simple circle and square shapes to illustrate what that means.

Each time you draw a shape with one of the shape tools, Photoshop Elements is performing a little behind-the-scenes sleight of hand. Although it may appear that you're drawing a solid, filled circle, for instance, what you're really creating is a new layer containing both a colored fill and a mask with a circle-shaped cutout (**Figure 10.56**). When you move, reshape, or resize a shape, you're actually just moving or reshaping the cutout and revealing a different area of the colored fill below it (**Figure 10.57**). When you add to or subtract from a shape by drawing additional shapes, you're simply revealing or hiding more of the same colored layer (**Figure 10.58**).

Every time you create a new shape, a new shape *layer* is added to the Layers palette. A shape layer is represented in the palette thumbnails by a gray background (the mask) and a white shape (the mask cutout, or path). Since a shape's outline isn't always visible in the image window—if you deselect it, for instance—the Layers palette provides a handy, visual reference for every shape in your project (**Figure 10.59**). And as with any other layered image, you can use the Layers palette to hide a shape's visibility and even change its opacity and its blending mode.

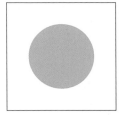
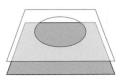

Figure 10.56 When you draw a shape, you're actually drawing a shape mask.

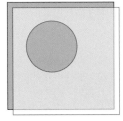
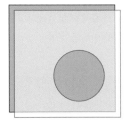

Figure 10.57 Moving a shape really means moving the cutout portion of the mask.

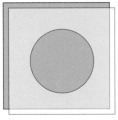
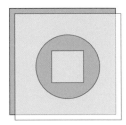

Figure 10.58 Adding a shape to a layer masks off another portion of the colored fill below it, in this case giving the illusion that the circle has a square hole in its center.

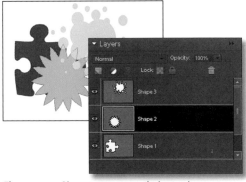

Figure 10.59 Shapes appear on their own layers.

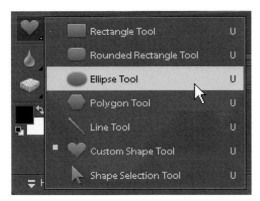

Figure 10.60 The Ellipse shape tool.

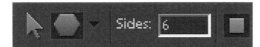

Figure 10.61 Some shape tools, such as the Polygon tool, have properties you can set on the options bar.

Drawing Basic Shapes

In Photoshop Elements, you can draw five basic geometric shapes (a shape selection tool and a tool for creating custom shapes are discussed in detail later in this chapter). Shapes can be drawn freely by clicking and dragging, or they can be constrained according to your specification of size, proportion, and special characteristics. You can use the shape tools to create logos or geometric designs; or, because a new layer is created with every shape you draw, you can draw shapes directly over any photograph or scanned image without fear of damaging the image.

To draw a shape:

1. Select a shape tool from the toolbox (U) (**Figure 10.60**).

    To cycle through the shape tools, press U again until you arrive at the shape you want.

2. To select a shape color, *do one of the following:*

    ▲ Click the current foreground color swatch at the bottom of the toolbox, or click the color box on the options bar to open the Color Picker.

    ▲ Choose a color from the Swatches palette.

3. If they're available for the tool you've selected, you can set special properties for your shape before you draw. On the options bar, enter values specific to the shape you've chosen (**Figure 10.61**).

continues on next page

For the Rounded Rectangle tool, you can enter a corner radius. For the Polygon tool, you can enter the number of sides. For the Line tool, you can enter a pixel weight.

4. On the options bar, click the arrow next to the shape buttons to open the Geometry Options palette (**Figure 10.62**).

   In the Geometry Options palette, select from the available options for that particular shape or leave the options set to the default of Unconstrained.

5. In the image window, click and drag to draw the shape (**Figure 10.63**).

   If you like, you can add a style to your shape from the Shape tool's built-in style picker.

6. On the options bar, click the icon or arrow to open the style picker (**Figure 10.64**).

7. Choose from the list of available styles or click the arrows to the right of the thumbnail images to open the Style palette menu.

   The style picker displays the new style set.

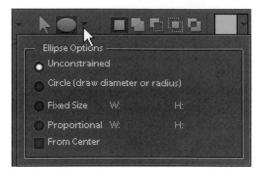

Figure 10.62 Every shape tool has its own particular set of geometry options.

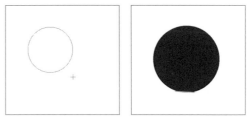

Figure 10.63 Drawing a shape is as simple as clicking and dragging.

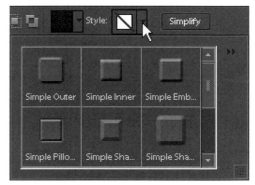

Figure 10.64 Whenever any of the shape tools are selected, the shape tool style picker appears on the options bar.

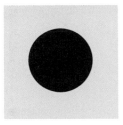 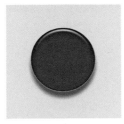

Figure 10.65 A simple circle drawn with the ellipse shape tool (left) is transformed into a glossy button (right) using just one of the many styles from the style picker.

8. Click a style in the style picker to apply it to your shape (**Figure 10.65**).

9. To deselect the shape and hide the path outline, press Enter.

✔ Tip

- If you decide to remove a style from a shape, you have two options. With the shape layer selected in the Layers palette, either open the Style palette menu in the style picker and then choose Remove Style; or, right-click the Layer Style icon on the desired layer in the Layers palette and choose Clear Layer Style.

About the Shape Geometry Options Palettes

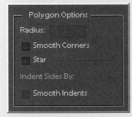 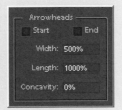

Figure 10.66 The Polygon tool's geometry options and the Line tool's arrowhead options.

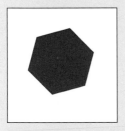 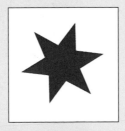

Figure 10.67 Using the Polygon tool's Star option, a six-sided polygon (left) can be changed into a six-point star (right).

Each shape tool (with the exception of the Shape Selection tool) has its own unique Geometry Options palette. The two rectangle tools and the Ellipse and Custom Shape tools all offer similar options for defining size, proportions, and constraint properties; and the Polygon and Line tools each have their own unique sets of options (**Figure 10.66**). The Polygon tool's most distinctive option is the Star check box. When Star is selected, you're presented with a couple of indent properties that fold the polygon in on itself, so that the points of its angles become the tips of a star shape (**Figure 10.67**). When the Line tool is selected, you can choose from a small set of Arrowheads options based on the pixel weight of the line.

✔ Tip

- To constrain the proportions of any shape (to make a rectangle a perfect square or an ellipse a perfect circle, for example) without the aid of the Geometry Options palette, hold down the Shift key as you drag.

DRAWING BASIC SHAPES

Transforming Shapes

You're not limited to just creating shapes in Photoshop Elements. You can also scale (resize), rotate, and distort them to your liking. Shapes can be altered either numerically, by entering specific values on the options bar, or manually, by dragging their control handles in the image window. Constrain options, such as proportional scaling, are available for most transformations, and a set of keyboard shortcuts helps to simplify the process of adding distortion and perspective.

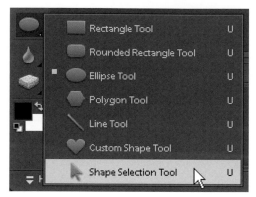

Figure 10.68 The Shape Selection tool.

To scale a shape:

1. Select the Shape Selection tool by *doing any of the following*:

   ▲ Choose the Shape Selection tool from beneath the current shape tool in the toolbox (**Figure 10.68**).

   ▲ Press U to select any shape tool and then press U again until you toggle to the Shape Selection tool.

   ▲ Select any shape tool in the toolbox, and then choose the Shape Selection tool from the options bar (it looks like an arrow).

2. In the image window, select the shape with the Shape Selection tool.

3. From the Image menu, choose Transform Shape > Free Transform Shape, or press Ctrl+T.

   The options bar changes to show the scale and rotation text boxes, and the reference point locator (**Figure 10.69**).

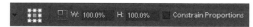

Figure 10.69 Precise scale and rotation values can be entered for any shape.

TRANSFORMING SHAPES

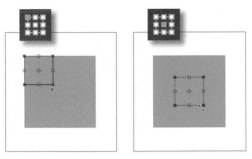

Figure 10.70 These squares are both being reduced in size by about half. The one on the left is scaled toward its upper-left corner, and the one on the right is scaled toward its center.

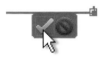

Figure 10.71 The Commit Transform button scales the shape to the size you define.

4. On the options bar, click to set a reference point location.

   The reference point determines what point your shape will be scaled to: toward the center, toward a corner, and so on (**Figure 10.70**).

5. If you want to scale your shape proportionately, click the Constrain Proportions check box.

6. Enter a value in either the height or width text box.

   The shape is scaled accordingly.

7. Click the Commit Transform button (**Figure 10.71**), or press Enter.

✔ Tips

- You can scale a shape manually by selecting it with the Shape Selection tool and then dragging any one of the eight handles on the selection border. Constrain the scaling by holding down the Shift key while dragging one of the four corner handles.

- If you want to simply reposition a shape in the image window, click anywhere inside the shape with the Shape Selection tool and then drag the shape to its new position.

To rotate a shape:

1. Select the Shape Selection tool from the toolbox or options bar.

2. In the image window, select the shape with the Shape Selection tool.

3. From the Image menu, choose Rotate > Free Rotate Layer (**Figure 10.72**).

   The options bar changes to show the scale and rotation text boxes, and the reference point locator.

4. On the options bar, click to set a reference point location.

   The reference point determines the point around which your shape will be rotated (**Figure 10.73**).

5. Enter a value in the rotate text box.

   The shape will rotate accordingly.

6. Click the Commit Transform button, or press Enter.

✔ Tips

- To rotate your shape in 90- or 180-degree increments or to flip it horizontally or vertically, choose Image > Rotate; then choose from the list of five menu commands below the Free Rotate Layer command.

- You can rotate a shape manually by selecting it with the Shape Selection tool and then moving the pointer outside of the selection border until it becomes a rotation cursor (**Figure 10.74**). Drag around the outside of the selection border to rotate the shape. In addition, you can constrain the rotation to 15-degree increments by holding down the Shift key while dragging the rotation cursor.

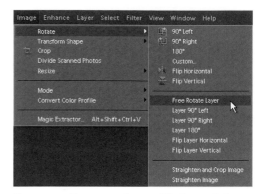

Figure 10.72 You can apply any of the layer rotation menu commands to your shapes.

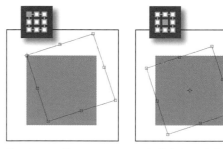

Figure 10.73 These squares are both being rotated about 20 degrees. The one on the left is rotated around its upper-left corner, and the one on the right is rotated around its center.

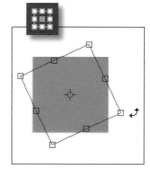

Figure 10.74 Rotate any shape manually by dragging it around its reference point with the rotation pointer.

TRANSFORMING SHAPES

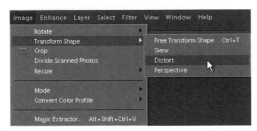

Figure 10.75 Choose one of the three specific transformation commands.

Figure 10.76 The same square shape transformed using Skew (left), Distort (center), and Perspective (right).

To distort a shape:

1. Select the Shape Selection tool from the toolbox.

2. In the image window, select the shape with the Shape Selection tool.

3. From the Image menu, choose Transform Shape; then choose Skew, Distort, or Perspective (**Figure 10.75**).

4. On the options bar, check that the reference point location is set to the center.

   The reference point can, of course, be set to any location, but the center seems to work best when applying any of the three distortions.

5. Drag any of the shape's control handles to distort the shape.

   Dragging the control handles will yield different results depending on the distort option you choose (**Figure 10.76**).

6. Click the Commit Transform button, or press Enter.

Distortion Shortcuts

With a few keyboard shortcuts, you can avoid having to return to the Image menu each time you want to apply a different distortion.

From the Image menu, choose Transform Shape > Free Transform Shape; then use the following shortcuts while dragging the shape handles in the image window:

To Distort: Ctrl

To Skew: Ctrl+Alt

To create Perspective: Ctrl+Alt+Shift

TRANSFORMING SHAPES

Creating Custom Shapes

Once you've gained a basic understanding of working with Elements' geometric shapes, you can begin adding those shapes together to create even more interesting and intricate shapes. Shape option buttons allow you to perform a little vector path magic by creating brand-new shapes out of the intersections and overlapping portions of the rectangle, ellipse, and polygon shapes.

The Custom Shape tool is in a world unto itself, working from a library of nearly 400 complex vector graphics grouped into categories as diverse as ornaments, music, fruit, symbols, and nature—far beyond the relatively simple icons and graphics you can build with the basic geometric shape tools.

To add a shape to an existing shape:

1. Follow steps 1 through 5 in the task "To draw a shape" earlier in this chapter.

   Make sure that this first shape's path remains selected (**Figure 10.77**).

2. From the toolbox, select the shape tool for the next shape you want to add.

   You can use the same shape more than once, if you wish.

3. On the options bar, set color, value, and geometry options as desired.

4. Still on the options bar, click to select one of the shape area options (**Figure 10.78**).

5. In the image window, click and drag to draw the new shape (**Figure 10.79**).

6. To deselect the shapes and hide their path outlines, press Enter.

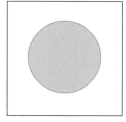

Figure 10.77 When a shape is selected, its path outline is visible (left). The path disappears when the shape is deselected (right).

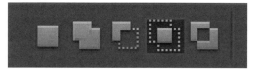

Figure 10.78 The shape area options define how one shape reacts with another.

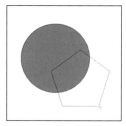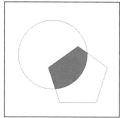

Figure 10.79 As the new shape is drawn, only its outline is visible (left). When the new shape is completed, it's filled according to the preset shape area option (right). In this case, the option was set to Intersect Shape.

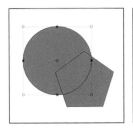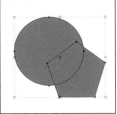

Figure 10.80 Shift+click to select the shapes you want to combine.

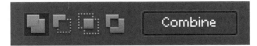

Figure 10.81 The Combine button groups multiple shapes together.

To combine multiple shapes:

1. Select the Shape Selection tool from the toolbox.

2. In the image window, click to select the first shape; then Shift+click to select the additional shapes you want to group (**Figure 10.80**).

3. On the options bar, click the Combine button (**Figure 10.81**). The shapes are combined into one complex shape.

✔ Tip

■ The Layers palette can be a useful tool when working with the shape tools. Its layer thumbnails provide good visual feedback, particularly when you're building complex shapes and want to verify that the new shapes you create are being placed on the correct layers.

About the Shape Area Options Buttons

Photoshop Elements gives you five options to choose from when creating a new shape or modifying an existing one (**Figure 10.82**).

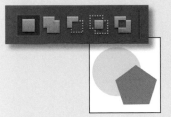

Figure 10.82 On the options bar, click to select one of five shape area options.

Create New Shape Layer does just that; it draws a new shape on its own, separate layer.

Add to Shape Area draws a new shape on the same layer as the existing shape.

Subtract from Shape Area adds a shape to the same layer as the existing shape, creating a cutout or hole.

Intersect Shape Areas adds a shape to the same layer as the existing shape and causes only those areas where the two shapes overlap to be visible.

Exclude Overlapping Shape Areas does just the opposite of Intersect Shape Areas, creating a cutout or hole where the two shapes overlap.

✔ Tips

■ You can only combine shapes that appear on the same layer on the Layers palette; like those I created in the previous procedure. However, if you've created shapes on separate layers and then decide you want to combine them, all is not lost. With the Shape Selection tool, select one of the shapes. Then from the Edit menu, choose Cut (Ctrl+X). In the Layers palette, click to select the shape layer you want to combine the "cut" shape with, and then from the Edit menu, choose Paste (Ctrl+V). The shape will be pasted into the selected layer along with the other shape. From there, just follow the steps to combine multiple shapes.

■ When selecting multiple shapes, work from the inside out. In other words, if you have a large shape with a smaller cutout or intersecting shape inside it, select the smaller, inside shape first. Photoshop Elements doesn't assign any stacking order per se to multiple shapes on a layer, but if a larger, outside shape is selected first, the selection sort of covers up any smaller shapes inside, making them next to impossible to select.

■ Up until the moment multiple shapes are grouped together with the Combine button, they can be selected individually and then scaled, rotated, distorted, and even duplicated with the Copy and Paste commands.

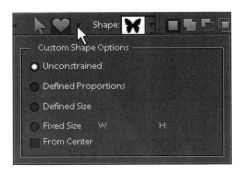

Figure 10.83 The Custom Shape tool offers geometry options similar to those for the Ellipse and Rectangle tools.

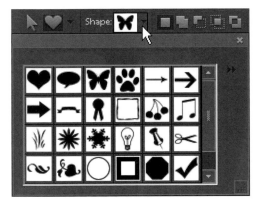

Figure 10.84 Open the custom shape picker to select from sets of complex shape thumbnails.

Figure 10.85 You draw a custom shape just as you would any other shape: simply by clicking and dragging. Here, I clicked to apply the butterfly shape (left) and then dragged with the mouse to enlarge it (right).

To draw a custom shape:

1. Select the Custom Shape tool by *doing one of the following:*
   - ▲ Select the Custom Shape tool from beneath the current shape tool in the toolbox.
   - ▲ Press U to select any shape tool; then press U again to toggle to the Custom Shape tool.

2. To select a shape color, *do one of the following:*
   - ▲ Click the current foreground color swatch at the bottom of the toolbox, or click the color box on the options bar to open the Color Picker.
   - ▲ Choose a color from the Swatches palette.

3. On the options bar, click the arrow next to the Custom Shape button to open the Custom Shape Options palette (**Figure 10.83**). Select from the available options or leave the options set to Unconstrained.

4. Still on the options bar, click to open the custom shape picker (**Figure 10.84**).

5. Click to choose from the list of default shapes, or select a different shape set from the Custom Shapes drop-down menu.

6. In the image window, click and drag to draw the selected shape (**Figure 10.85**).

7. Press Enter to deselect the shape.

✔ Tip

- ■ Custom shapes can be used in combination with other shapes and with the shape area options just like any of the basic geometric shapes.

If you ever want to paint on a shape or apply any filter effects to it, you'll first need to convert the shape from a vector path to a bitmap.

To convert a vector shape to a bitmap:

1. To open the Layers palette, *do one of the following:*

   ▲ From the Window menu, choose Layers.

   ▲ Click the arrow on the Layers palette tab in the palette bin.

2. On the Layers palette, click to select the layer containing the shape (or shapes) you want to convert to bitmaps (**Figure 10.86**).

3. From the More menu on the Layers palette, select Simplify Layer (**Figure 10.87**).

   The vector shape is converted to a bitmap, and instead of showing the shape's path, the layer thumbnail displays the shape's image on a transparent background (**Figure 10.88**).

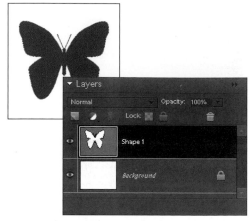

Figure 10.86 Use the Layers palette to select a custom shape's layer.

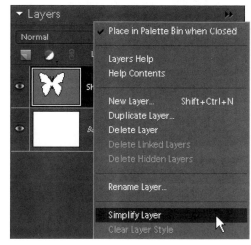

Figure 10.87 The Simplify Layer command converts a custom shape's vector path to a bitmap graphic.

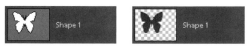

Figure 10.88 The vector path layer thumbnail (left) and the converted bitmap thumbnail (right).

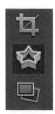

Figure 10.89
The Cookie Cutter tool.

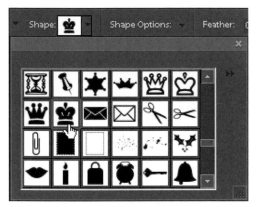

Figure 10.90 The Cookie Cutter tool uses the same shape libraries as the Custom Shape tool.

Using the Cookie Cutter Tool

The Cookie Cutter tool isn't exactly a painting *or* drawing tool, although right up to the moment you press the Commit Transform button, it behaves in exactly the same way as the Custom Shape tool. The Cookie Cutter tool uses the Custom Shape tool's libraries of shapes to create distinctive masked versions of image layers. The difference between the two (and it's a biggie) is that whereas the Custom Shape tool creates *vector shapes*, the Cookie Cutter tool creates a *raster image*. So, although you can initially scale, rotate, and otherwise distort a Cookie Cutter shape just like a vector graphic, once you commit the shape to your image, the final result is still a raster (or bitmap) image layer. Once you understand the Cookie Cutter's limitations, it can still be a fun and useful tool.

To mask an image with the Cookie Cutter tool:

1. From the toolbox, click to select the Cookie Cutter tool, or press Q (**Figure 10.89**).

2. On the options bar, click the Shape Options button to open the Cookie Cutter Options palette.

   Select from the available options or leave the options set to Unconstrained.

3. Still on the options bar, click to open the Cookie Cutter shape picker (**Figure 10.90**).

4. Click to choose from the list of default shapes, or select a different shape set from the Custom Shapes drop-down menu.

continues on next page

USING THE COOKIE CUTTER TOOL

5. In the image window, click and drag over an image layer to draw the selected shape.

The image now appears only within the Cookie Cutter shape, leaving the rest of the layer transparent (**Figure 10.91**).

If you apply the Cookie Cutter tool to a flattened, background layer, it automatically converts the layer to a working layer with transparency.

6. To reposition the shape in the image window, place the cursor anywhere inside the shape bounding box, and then click and drag.

Notice that as you drag the shape, different areas of the original image are revealed, as if you were moving a window around on a solid wall (**Figure 10.92**).

7. To scale, rotate, or otherwise transform the shape, refer to the section "Transforming Shapes," earlier in this chapter.

8. When you're satisfied with the size and position of your masked shape, click the Commit Transform button, or press Enter (**Figure 10.93**).

Once you commit the shape to the image layer, you can apply blending modes, opacity changes, and filters just as you would on any other raster image layer.

✔ Tip

■ For a similar effect that affords you more flexibility (namely, the ability to transform your layer mask indefinitely), create a shape with the Custom Shape tool, and then follow the steps in the section "Creating Masking Effects with Layer Groups," in Chapter 8.

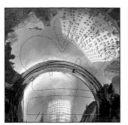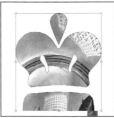

Figure 10.91 When you draw a shape with the Cookie Cutter tool, any underlying images are visible only within the shape.

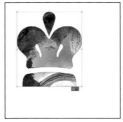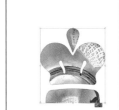

Figure 10.92 You can position, scale, rotate, and otherwise transform a Cookie Cutter shape right up to the moment you commit the shape to the image layer.

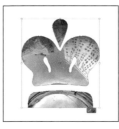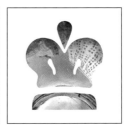

Figure 10.93 Once you commit the shape, its bounding box disappears.

WORKING WITH TYPE

When you think about all of the sophisticated photo retouching, painting, and drawing you can do in Photoshop Elements, manipulating type may not be a priority on your to-do list. However, you can create some amazing projects with the type tools, including greeting cards, posters, announcements, and invitations—and you don't even have to fire up another software application.

This chapter covers the text formatting options and special type effects you can create with Photoshop Elements. If you've had any experience with word processing programs, the basic text formatting options will be familiar to you. Unlike a word processor, however, Photoshop Elements lets you create myriad special effects, using the type warping and masking tools and layer styles.

Creating and Editing Text

When you use the type tools, your text is automatically placed on a new, unique layer. Since the text exists on its own layer, you can do all the modifications to your text that layers allow, including moving, applying blending modes, and changing the opacity. Also, having text on its own layer allows you to go back and edit it whenever you want.

You'll likely want to adjust the position of your text, and this is done just as easily as moving an object on any other layer. If you want to paint on your text or apply filters or effects to it, you'll need to simplify the layer by converting it to a standard bitmap. But remember: After a type layer has been simplified, it becomes part of the image, which means you can no longer edit the text. Fortunately, as long as you don't close the file, the Undo History palette will let you go back to the state your type was in before it was simplified. And you can always save a separate version of your file prior to simplifying the type layer.

To add text to an image:

1. With an image open, click to select the Horizontal Type or Vertical Type tool on the toolbar (or press T) (**Figure 11.1**).

    Your pointer changes to an I-beam, as in many other text editing programs (**Figure 11.2**).

2. In the image window, move the pointer to the area where you want to insert your text, and then *do one of the following:*

    ▲ Click to create a text insertion point. This method is perfect if you're setting just a single line of text, or a simple two- or three-line title or heading.

    ▲ If you want to set a long text paragraph, click and drag to create a paragraph text box (**Figure 11.3**).

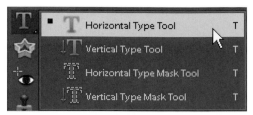

Figure 11.1 Click the type tool icon to choose from four different type tools.

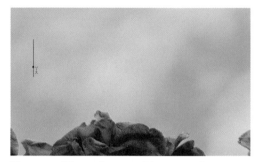

Figure 11.2 When using one of the type tools, your pointer changes appearance to look like an I-beam. The text entry point is indicated by a vertical line whose height is based on the type size.

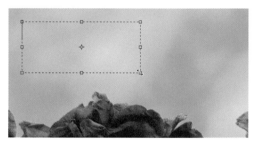

Figure 11.3 Alternatively, drag the I-beam to create a paragraph text box.

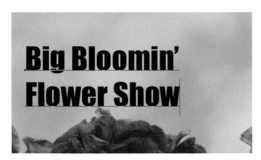

Figure 11.4 After you click once to establish the insertion point of your type, just start entering text. Press the Enter key to move to a new line.

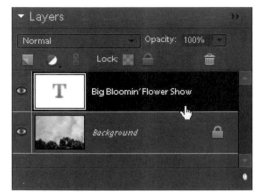

Figure 11.5 To make changes to existing text, click the appropriate layer on the Layers palette.

3. Type your text (**Figure 11.4**). If you want to start a new line, press Enter.

   If you've created a paragraph text box, the text automatically flows to a new line when it bumps up against the border of the text box.

4. To confirm the text you've entered, *do one of the following:*

   ▲ Press the Enter key on the numeric keypad.

   ▲ Click anywhere in your image, click a palette, or click a tool on the toolbar.

   A new type layer is created and is visible on the Layers palette. The layer name is the text you entered.

To edit text:

1. Click a type layer on the Layers palette to make it active (**Figure 11.5**).

2. In the image window, click in the text and edit as you would in any basic word processor.

3. Confirm your edits by clicking anywhere in your image.

✔ Tips

■ Consider changing the font size before you begin typing (which I describe shortly); 12-point text is easily lost in a high-resolution photo.

■ If you want to add more text to a different part of your image, simply click elsewhere in the image and start typing. The new text is added to its own separate layer.

■ Your image must be in grayscale or RGB mode if you want to add type to it. Elements' two other image modes, bitmap and index, don't support type layers.

To move text:

1. On the Layers palette, click the type layer you want to move.

2. Click the Move tool on the toolbar.

   When you click the Move tool, your type is surrounded by a selection bounding box, allowing you to move the type as a single object anywhere on your image.

3. In the image window, drag your text to a new location (**Figure 11.6**).

To simplify a type layer:

1. Choose a type layer on the Layers palette by clicking on it.

2. From the Layer menu or from the Layers palette menu, choose Simplify Layer.

   The layer ceases to be a type layer and the text is treated as pixels instead.

✔ Tips

- You can also move a type layer with the Type tool selected: Hold Ctrl and click the layer; then drag it into position.

- When you simplify a type layer, does its icon in the Layers palette look empty? The tiny thumbnail may not appear to display your text if the type is small in relation to the full image size. Try this: Click the More drop-down menu (which appears as two right-facing triangles when the palette is docked in the Palette Bin) and choose Palette Options. In the dialog that appears, click Layer Bounds in the Thumbnail Contents section, and then click OK. The layer's thumbnail icon displays only the text, not the entire image.

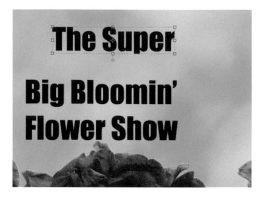

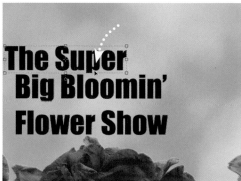

Figure 11.6 Because text exists on its own separate layer, you can move it to different areas in the image by using the Move tool.

Point and Click vs. Paragraph Type

Photoshop Elements allows you to enter text using both the *point and click* and the *paragraph* type methods. When you enter text with the *point and click* method, you simply click a point in the image window and then begin to type. The line of text you enter will continue until you press Enter to create a new line. When you enter *paragraph* type, you drag to create a text area (or text box), and the type you enter will automatically wrap to a new line when you reach the edge of the type's bounding box.

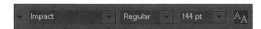

Figure 11.7 The type formatting tools are all available on the text options bar.

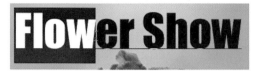

Figure 11.8 To select your text, drag across it with the text pointer.

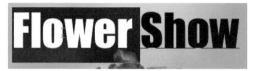

Figure 11.9 Double-click within a word to select it.

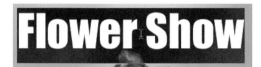

Figure 11.10 Triple-click anywhere in a line of type to select the entire line.

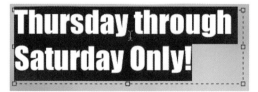

Figure 11.11 Quadruple-click anywhere in a paragraph to select the entire paragraph.

Changing the Look of Your Type

You should be comfortable using the type formatting tools—font family, font style, and font size—because they're very similar to those found in most word processing programs. You can also change the text alignment and text color. All of these options are available on the text options bar (**Figure 11.7**).

To change any of these attributes, you first need to select the text characters you want to change. Most of the time, you'll want to select and apply changes to an entire line of text, but you can also select individual words or even individual characters.

To select text:

1. Click the type layer you want to edit on the Layers palette, or click on the type itself with the Move tool.

2. Select a type tool.

3. To select the text, drag across the characters to highlight them (**Figure 11.8**), or *do one of the following:*
   ▲ Double-click within a word to select it (**Figure 11.9**).
   ▲ Triple-click to select an entire line of text (**Figure 11.10**).
   ▲ Quadruple-click to select an entire paragraph of text (**Figure 11.11**).

✔ Tip

■ You can select all the text on a layer without even touching the text with your pointer. Just select the type layer on the Layers palette and double-click the T icon.

To choose the font family and style:

1. Select the text you want to change.

2. From the options bar, choose a font from the font family menu (**Figure 11.12**).

3. Still on the options bar, choose a style from the font style menu (**Figure 11.13**). If the font family you selected doesn't include a particular style, you can click the Faux Bold or Faux Italic button to change the look of your text (**Figure 11.14**).

✔ Tip

- If you haven't memorized the look of each and every font on your computer (and who has?), Photoshop Elements' font family menu displays an example of each font next to its font name. You can change the size of font samples or turn the display of the samples off by choosing Edit > Preferences > Type and then using the drop-down menu in the Type Options section of the Type Preferences dialog (**Figure 11.15**).

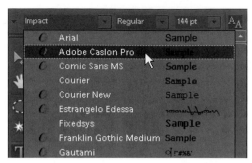

Figure 11.12 All available fonts are listed on the font family menu.

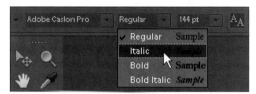

Figure 11.13 Many fonts allow you to select a style from the font style menu.

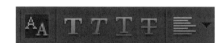

Figure 11.14 If a font doesn't include style options, you can apply a bold or italic format with the icons on the options bar.

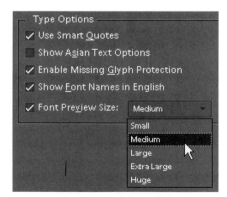

Figure 11.15 Options in the Type Preferences dialog let you control the display of font previews in the font family menu.

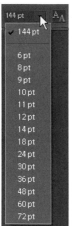

Figure 11.16
Use the type size menu to adjust the size of your type. To use a size not listed, just enter it in the text box.

To change the font size:

1. Select the text you want to change.

2. Choose a size from the type size menu on the options bar (**Figure 11.16**).

   To change to a type size not listed on the menu, just enter a new value in the type size text box.

✔ Tips

- You can quickly adjust the type size up and down using keyboard shortcuts. Just select your text and then press Ctrl+Shift+. (period) to increase the size in 2-point increments. To reduce the size of the text, press Ctrl+ Shift+, (comma).

- You can also adjust the type size up and down in 1- or 10-point increments. Select your text and then select the type size in the type size menu on the options bar. Next, use the up and down keys on your keypad to size the type up and down in 1-point increments. If you hold down the Shift key while pressing the up or down keys, the type will adjust in 10-point increments (**Figure 11.17**).

- To change the default measurement unit for type, select Edit > Preferences > Units and Rulers. Here you can select among pixels, points, and millimeters (mm).

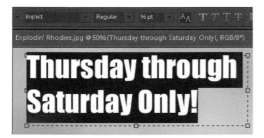

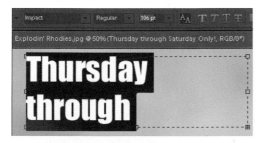

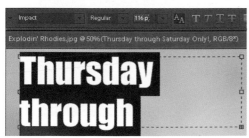

Figure 11.17 Hold down the Shift key to quickly increase your type size in 10-point increments.

CHANGING THE LOOK OF YOUR TYPE

To change the line spacing:

1. Select the lines of text you want to change.

2. Choose a value from the line space menu on the options bar (**Figure 11.18**).

   To change to a line spacing value not listed on the menu, enter a new value in the line space text box.

To apply underline or strikethrough:

1. Select the text you want to change.

2. Click either the Underline or Strike-through icon on the options bar to apply that style to your text (**Figure 11.19**).

✔ Tips

■ The default line spacing value for any type size (Auto) serves as a good starting point, but it's surprising that something as simple as increasing or decreasing line spacing can have a dramatic visual impact (**Figure 11.20**).

■ If your type layer is set to a vertical orientation, the underline appears on the left side of the type.

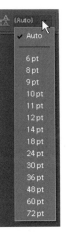

Figure 11.18 Use the line space menu to select line spacing for your type. You can also enter a line spacing value in the menu text box.

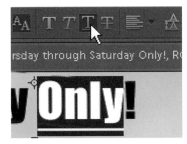

Figure 11.19 Apply underline and strikethrough from the options bar.

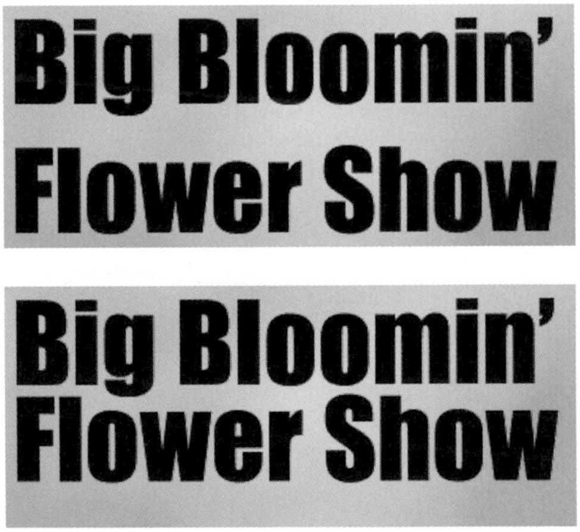

![Big Bloomin' Flower Show shown twice with different line spacing]

Figure 11.20 Default line spacing (top), and the same type size but with smaller line spacing (bottom).

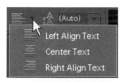

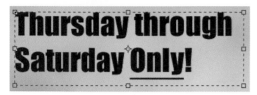

Figure 11.21 Aligning text within a paragraph box: Left Align (top); Center (middle); Right Align (bottom).

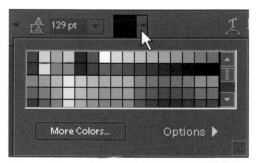

Figure 11.22 Change the text color by clicking the color selection drop-down menu.

To change the alignment:

1. Select the text you want to change.

2. From the options bar, choose an alignment option (**Figure 11.21**).

   The type shifts in relation to the origin of the line of text, or in the case of paragraph text, in relation to one side of the text box or the other. For *point and click type*, the origin is the place in your image where you first clicked before entering the type.

   ▲ **Left Align** positions the left edge of each line of type at the origin, or on the left edge of the paragraph text box.

   ▲ **Center Align** positions the center of each line of type at the origin, or in the center of the paragraph text box.

   ▲ **Right Align** positions the right edge of each line of type at the origin, or on the right edge of the paragraph text box.

To change the text color:

1. Select the text you want to change.

2. Click the color selection drop-down menu on the options bar and choose a color from the palette (**Figure 11.22**). Or, click inside the box to open the Color Picker.

3. Click OK to apply the new color to your text.

✔ Tip

■ You can also change the color of all the text on a text layer without selecting the text in the image window. With the Text tool selected in the toolbox, click to select a text layer in the Layers palette to make it the active layer, then follow the procedure to change the text color.

Working with Vertical Text

Most of the time, you'll use the standard Horizontal Type tool. But you can also change your type to a vertical orientation whenever you want. One of the reasons Elements includes both horizontal and vertical type is to accommodate the needs of the Asian-language versions of the product, such as Korean, Japanese, and Chinese.

To create vertical text:

1. With the image window open, click the Vertical Type tool on the toolbar (**Figure 11.23**).

   The pointer changes to an I-beam.

2. Move the pointer to the area where you want to insert your text, and then *do one of the following:*

   ▲ Click to create a text insertion point.

   ▲ Click and drag to create a paragraph text box.

3. Type your text on the image (**Figure 11.24**). The characters appear in descending order on your image.

4. To start a new line that will appear to the left of the first line, press Enter (**Figure 11.25**).

   If you've created a paragraph text box, the text automatically flows to a new line when it bumps up against the bottom of the text box.

   To create and control the position of another line of vertical text, reselect the Vertical Type tool and create a separate, independent vertical type layer.

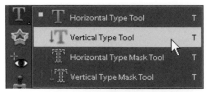

Figure 11.23 The Vertical Type tool is located directly under the Horizontal Type tool.

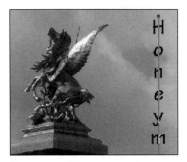

Figure 11.24 When you use the Vertical Type tool, your text appears in descending order (from the top down) on your image.

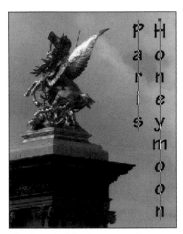

Figure 11.25 When you press Enter, another line of vertical type is added to the left of the first line.

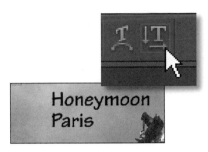

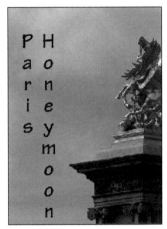

Figure 11.26 Switch between horizontal and vertical type by clicking the Change text orientation icon on the options bar.

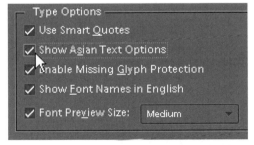

Figure 11.27 If your system supports Asian text options, you can work with them by selecting this feature in the Preferences > Type dialog.

To change the orientation of the text:

1. Select a type layer on the Layers palette.

2. Select the Type tool on the toolbar and then click the Change text orientation icon on the options bar (**Figure 11.26**).

   The text changes to the opposite orientation: If your text is horizontal, it flips to vertical orientation—and vice versa.

✔ Tip

- If you have Asian language fonts installed on your computer and you want to use the Asian type formatting options, choose Edit > Preferences > Type and select Show Asian Text Options (**Figure 11.27**).

Anti-aliasing Type

You can choose to smooth the edges of, or *anti-alias*, your type, just as you can with image selections as discussed in Chapter 5, "Making Selections." In most cases, you'll use Photoshop Elements to create fairly large, display-size text. For this reason, you'll normally want to anti-alias your text so it doesn't appear to be jagged (**Figure 11.28**).

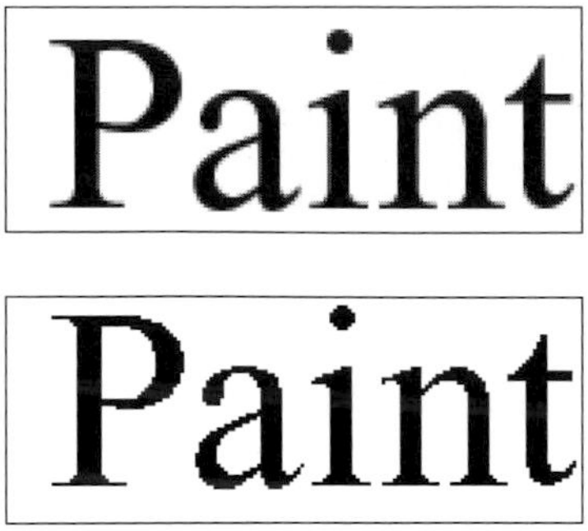

The exception is in cases where you are using smaller font sizes, such as 14 points or less, and are planning to use the image for onscreen viewing on the Web. At smaller sizes, anti-aliasing actually makes your text less readable, and the smoothing effect looks more like blurring (**Figure 11.29**). Also, in the process of anti-aliasing, many more colors are generated, and not all Web browsers support all of these colors, so some unwanted color artifacts may appear around the edges of your type. By default, anti-aliasing is turned on.

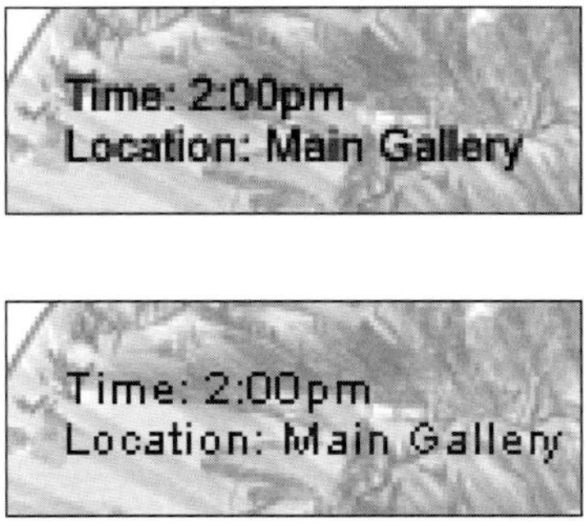

To turn anti-aliasing off and on:

1. Select a type layer on the Layers palette.

2. *Do one of the following*:

   ▲ Click the Anti-aliasing icon on the options bar. To reselect anti-aliasing, click the icon again (**Figure 11.30**).

   ▲ From the main menu, choose Layer > Type > Anti-Alias Off, or Layer > Type > Anti-Alias On.

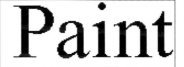

Figure 11.28 You'll usually want to anti-alias your type, especially when using larger type sizes. This example shows 60-point type viewed at 200 percent.

Figure 11.29 When using type sizes of about 14 points or less, you may want to turn off anti-aliasing so your text doesn't become blurry. This example shows 10-point type viewed at 200 percent.

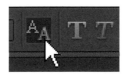

Figure 11.30 Turn anti-aliasing off and on with this icon on the options bar.

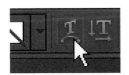

Figure 11.31
Click the Create Warped Text icon on the options bar to experiment with various type distortions.

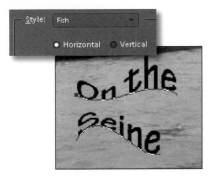

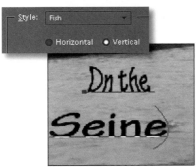

Figure 11.32 The Horizontal and Vertical orientation options create radically different results.

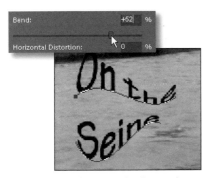

Figure 11.33 In this example, the Bend slider helps to dramatically exaggerate the fish shape.

Warping Text

Photoshop Elements lets you distort text easily using the Warp tool. You can choose from 15 different warping options in the Warp Text dialog. In this dialog, you can adjust the amount of the bend in the type, as well as the horizontal and vertical distortion.

Even after you've warped your text, it's still completely editable, and you can make additional formatting changes to it at any time. But because the warp effect is applied to the entire type layer, you can't warp individual characters—it's all or nothing.

To warp text:

1. Select a type layer on the Layers palette.

2. From the toolbar, select a type tool (so that the type options appear on the options bar) and click the Create Warped Text icon (**Figure 11.31**).
   The Warp Text dialog appears.

3. Choose a warp style from the drop-down menu.

4. Choose either Horizontal or Vertical orientation for the effect (**Figure 11.32**).

5. You can also modify the amount of Bend and Horizontal or Vertical distortion using the sliders (**Figure 11.33**).

6. Click OK to apply the effect.

To remove text warp:

1. On the Layers palette, select a type layer that's been warped.

2. Select a type tool and click the Create Warped Text icon on the options bar.

3. Choose None from the Style drop-down menu (**Figure 11.34**).

4. Click OK to remove the effect.

✔ Tip

■ As you experiment with the various warping options, your text can undergo some pretty dramatic changes. For this reason, you might want to move your text around to see how it looks in different parts of your image. Luckily, you can do this without closing the Warp Text dialog. If you move your pointer into the image area, you'll see that it automatically changes to the Move tool so you can move your text around while adjusting the warping effect.

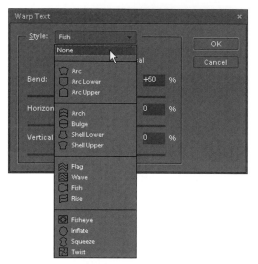

Figure 11.34 To remove text warp, select None from the Style drop-down menu.

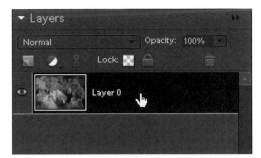

Figure 11.35 To create a type mask, first select the layer on which you want it to appear.

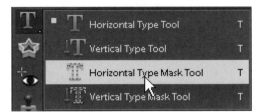

Figure 11.36 You can choose either the Horizontal or Vertical Type Mask tool.

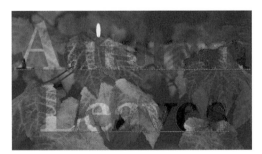

Figure 11.37 Your type appears reversed out of the colored mask.

Creating Text Effects Using Type Masks

Sometimes the text effects you want to create are better done with a type *selection*, not the actual, editable type. The Horizontal and Vertical Type Mask tools let you enter text, which is automatically converted to a selection in the *shape* of type. Since it's a selection, you can do everything you can do to any other selection—you can paint or fill the type or transform its geometry by skewing it or applying perspective. Unlike the previous type tools discussed, the type mask tools do not create a unique layer. The type selection appears on whichever layer is active at the time you use the tool. The bottom line: A type selection is just like any other selection, but in the shape of text.

To create a selection with the type mask tools:

1. Make sure your active layer is the one where you want the text selection to appear (**Figure 11.35**).

2. Select either the Horizontal or Vertical Type Mask tool (**Figure 11.36**).

3. Set the type options (such as font, style, or size) on the options bar.

4. Enter text on the image by either clicking or clicking and dragging and then typing your text.

   The text appears reversed out of the colored mask overlay (**Figure 11.37**).

continues on next page

5. Commit your text selection by clicking outside the selection or pressing Enter.

Your text area is selected (**Figure 11.38**).

You can now apply additional changes to the selection.

To fill a text selection with an image:

1. Create a text selection following the steps in the preceding task.

Be sure to position the selection over the image you want to show through the text.

2. Copy the selection to the clipboard by choosing Copy from the Edit menu, or by pressing Ctrl+C.

3. From the File menu, choose New > Image from Clipboard (**Figure 11.39**).

Your text selection appears in its own file, with the image peeking through (**Figure 11.40**).

✔ Tips

■ Up until the moment you commit the text, you can edit your type masks (change their font, size, line spacing, and alignment) just as you would any other line or paragraph of type.

■ You can move a text selection around in the image window as if it were any other selection. Once you click the Commit icon, select any of the marquee selection tools from the toolbox. Move the cursor over your text selection until it becomes the Move Selection icon. Then you can click and drag to reposition your text selection.

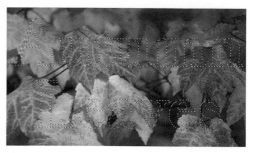

Figure 11.38 After you commit the type, it appears as a selection with the typical selection border.

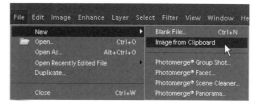

Figure 11.39 When you select File > New > Image from Clipboard, a new file is created that contains your text selection.

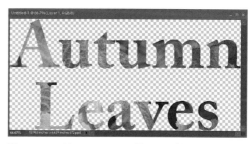

Figure 11.40 You can create all sorts of interesting text effects by filling type with images.

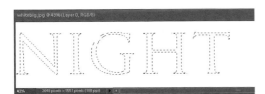

Figure 11.41 To fill text with a gradient, start by making a type selection.

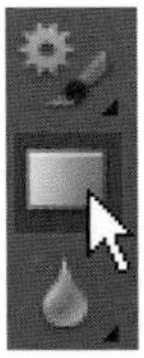

Figure 11.42
Click the Gradient tool on the toolbar and then choose a gradient.

To apply a gradient to a text selection:

1. Create a text selection following the steps in the task "To create a selection with the type mask tools" (**Figure 11.41**).

2. Click the Gradient tool on the toolbar and choose any gradient style on the options bar (**Figure 11.42**).

3. Drag across your text selection to establish the direction of the gradient (**Figure 11.43**).

4. Deselect the text selection.
   Your text appears with the gradient fill (**Figure 11.44**).

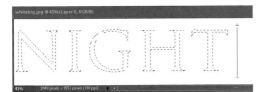

Figure 11.43 Drag in the direction you want the gradient to appear inside your type.

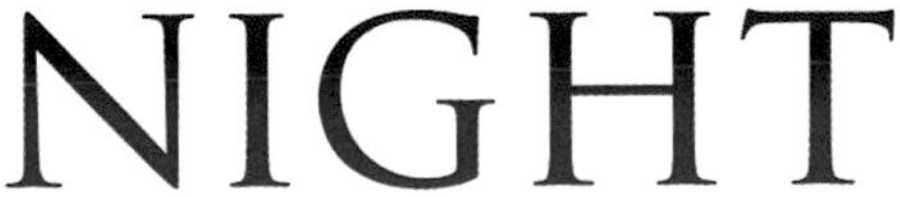

NIGHT

Figure 11.44 This example uses the Linear gradient.

CREATING TEXT EFFECTS USING TYPE MASKS

Applying Layer Styles to Type

Since the Horizontal and Vertical Type tools create a unique text layer, you can use layer styles to make all sorts of unusual and interesting changes to your type. The significant advantage of using layer styles with your text (as opposed to using type masks) is that your text remains editable.

When choosing a font, it's a good idea to go with bolder sans-serif typefaces. This way, your type is more likely to remain readable after you've applied the style. Take a look at the Text Layer Style Gallery to see just a few examples of the different styles available.

To apply a layer style to type:

1. Enter text in your image using either the Horizontal or Vertical Type tool (**Figure 11.45**).

2. Make sure the appropriate type layer is selected on the Layers palette; then, on the Effects palette, choose a style from the Layer Styles palette list (**Figure 11.46**).

3. Click the Apply button to apply the style to your text (**Figure 11.47**).

✔ Tip

- If you're not quite getting the look you want, remember that you can set lighting angle, shadow distance, and other options by selecting Layer Style > Style Settings from the Layer menu, or by double-clicking the Layer Style icon to the right of the layer name in the Layers palette.

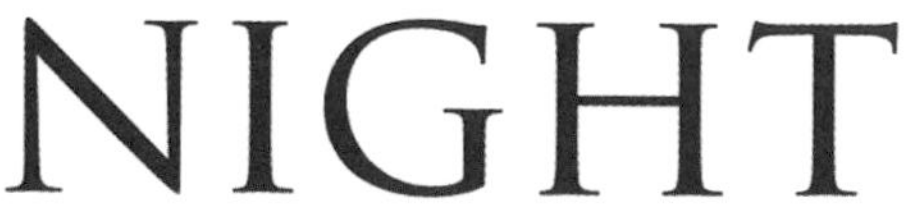

NIGHT

Figure 11.45 To use layer styles with your type, first enter text with one of the type tools.

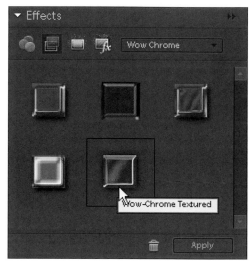

Figure 11.46 You can use any of Photoshop Elements' dozens of layer styles on your type.

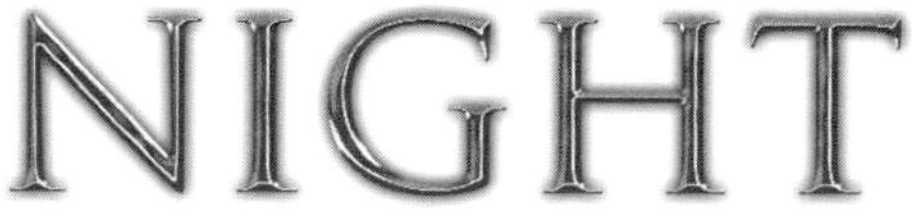

NIGHT

Figure 11.47 Sophisticated effects that would be difficult to create manually are easily applied to text.

PREPARING IMAGES FOR THE WEB

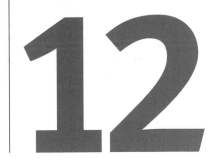

If you take digital photos, you may want to post them to a Web page or a social-networking site like MySpace or Facebook. (Elements 7 can now upload directly to Flickr and other photo-sharing sites; see Chapter 14, "Sharing Your Images," for more information.) Whether you decide to post a snapshot of an old push mower to eBay or just want to share vacation photos with your Aunt Ruth, the considerations are much the same.

Size and speed influence most decisions regarding image preparation for the Web, and they are the central themes of this chapter. While broadband is now widely available worldwide, it's still a good idea to *optimize* the size of your digital images: the smaller the image file size, the more quickly it appears, even with the fastest Internet connection.

That's not to say I'm abandoning aesthetics—after all, there's little purpose in uploading a photograph that's too fuzzy or distorted to be seen clearly. This chapter's focus is also about creating compact files that look *good*.

If you're looking to post a gallery of photos instead of optimizing and saving images one at a time, see Chapter 14.

Understanding Image Requirements for the Web

Preparing images for the Web presents a set of challenges distinct from commercial and ink-jet printing. Even with abundant broadband worldwide, a significant percentage of Web users have dial-up or relatively slow broadband connections. This means your images need to be small enough to download quickly while retaining color and clarity comparable to your original image.

Photoshop Elements offers some digital sleight-of-hand through a process called *optimization*. Optimization pares down and streamlines an image's display information based on settings you can choose among and preview to determine the best combination of values.

By limiting the number of colors in an image, or by selectively discarding pixels that are less critical than others, Elements removes information from an image and reduces the associated file size. Once an image has been streamlined in this way, it is *optimized* (**Figure 12.1**).

Photoshop Elements offers four file format options for optimizing an image: JPEG, GIF, PNG-8, and PNG-24. Generally speaking, JPEG and PNG-24 are most appropriate for images that contain subtle transitions of tone and color (like photographs), while GIF and PNG-8 are best for graphics or illustrations containing a lot of flat color or typography (**Figure 12.2**).

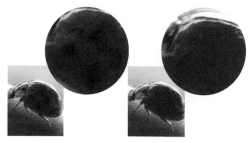

Figure 12.1 The original illustration of the ladybird beetle (left) contains a great deal of detail and subtle gradations of tone and color. The over-optimized version (right) is greatly simplified and contains far less color and image information.

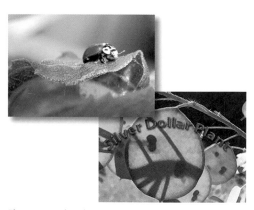

Figure 12.2 The photograph on the left, with its subtle and varied tones and color, is a good candidate for JPEG optimization, whereas the flat, bold colors and use of typography in the illustration on the right make it more appropriate for GIF optimization.

About the Save for Web Dialog

The Save for Web dialog might be more appropriately called the "Prepare Web Images" or "Optimization" dialog. Within it, you'll find all the tools, drop-down menus, and text fields necessary to transform any digital photograph, painting, or illustration into a graphic that will work well in a Web browser.

The original and optimized image previews, the heart of this dialog, provide instant visual feedback whenever setting adjustments are made. Information fields below the image previews constantly update to reflect the current optimization format, file size, and download times. And at any time in the optimization process, you can preview and verify exactly how your image will appear in any Web browser loaded on your computer.

Choosing File Formats

JPEG: JPEG is the most common file format for images on the Web. Because it supports 24-bit color (which translates to over 16 million colors), it's the ideal format for optimizing photos without sacrificing too much image quality. However, because it's a *lossy* format—meaning that it doesn't provide as much fidelity as the original information by selectively reducing quality to reduce image file size—it's not the best choice for images where detail and sharpness are critical, such as scanned line art, vector graphics, or images containing a lot of type.

GIF: If you want to keep the detail in your images as sharp as possible, try using the GIF format. The GIF format sacrifices subtle gradations of tone and color, but retains the sharpness and image detail that can be lost with the JPEG format, making it a good choice for animations, images with transparency, vector graphics, and images with type.

PNG: PNG comes in two main flavors, both supported by Elements: PNG-8, which is similar to GIF, and PNG-24, which is similar to JPEG. PNG is a newer image format than both GIF or JPEG, and it wasn't until 2002 or 2003 that you could rely on browsers to display PNG images correctly.

Versions of Internet Explorer earlier than IE 7 still may have problems with features like transparency. If you're creating images that will mostly be viewed by people who have newer browsers, PNG is a reasonable choice; if your audience is mostly using old computers and browsers, it's not so good.

Although in some cases PNG-8 images can be slightly smaller than comparable GIF images, PNG formats (particularly PNG-24) tend to produce images markedly larger than their GIF and JPEG counterparts. Keeping with the goal of controlling file size, stick with GIF and JPEG formats for optimizing your images.

Optimizing an Image for the Web

With the Save for Web command, Photoshop Elements provides a simple, automated method that not only saves an optimized copy of your original image, but also preserves the original high-resolution image, untouched and intact. Simply choose from a list of predefined settings, and your image is instantly optimized for the Web. You may want to experiment with the custom optimization settings, but the predefined settings should satisfy the requirements of most of your optimization tasks.

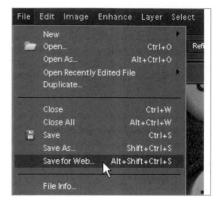

Figure 12.3 Open the Save for Web dialog from the File menu.

To save an image for the Web:

1. Open the image you want to optimize.

2. From the File menu, choose Save for Web (**Figure 12.3**), or press Alt+Shift+Ctrl+S. The Save for Web dialog opens on top of the active image window, displaying the image in side-by-side original and optimized previews (**Figure 12.4**).

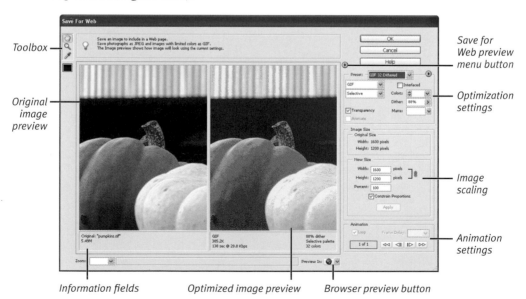

Figure 12.4 The Save for Web dialog. The image on the left shows the original image. The image on the right shows a preview of what the same image will look like after it's been optimized.

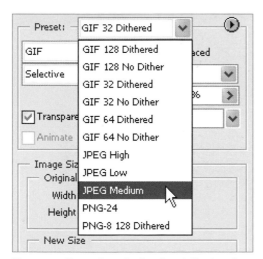

Figure 12.5 Choose from the list of predefined settings for JPEG, GIF, or PNG optimization formats.

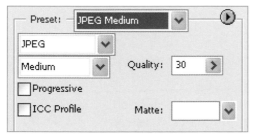

Figure 12.6 Once you've chosen a predefined optimization setting, the rest of the options change accordingly. Here, the options have automatically changed to reflect the Medium JPEG optimization format.

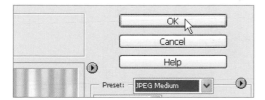

Figure 12.7 Click OK to save your optimized image.

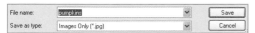

Figure 12.8 Enter a name and destination for your optimized file in the Save Optimized As dialog.

3. From the Preset drop-down menu, choose a predefined optimization setting (**Figure 12.5**).

   The various drop-down menus within the Preset portion of the dialog change to reflect the setting you've selected (**Figure 12.6**), as does the optimized preview in the center of the dialog.

4. Click the OK button (**Figure 12.7**).

5. In the Save Optimized As dialog, type a new name for your file and verify that the file type matches the optimization format you chose in the Save for Web dialog (**Figure 12.8**).

6. Choose a location for your file and then click Save.

   The Save Optimized As and Save for Web dialogs automatically close, and your optimized image is saved to the location you specified.

OPTIMIZING AN IMAGE FOR THE WEB

The Save for Web Preview Menu

The Preview menu (**Figure 12.9**), which you can find by clicking the triangle button to the right of the optimized image in the Save for Web dialog, is one of those easy-to-overlook tools in a space already packed with check boxes, palettes, and drop-down menus.

As its name implies, the Preview menu works with the image preview (the optimized side of the image preview, to be exact) and establishes parameters for the way that the image preview is displayed. Depending on the color space you select in the top portion of the Preview menu, you can view your image as it would appear in a browser on your own monitor or on a standard Macintosh or PC monitor; or, you can see a preview of how it would appear if it were saved with its color profile.

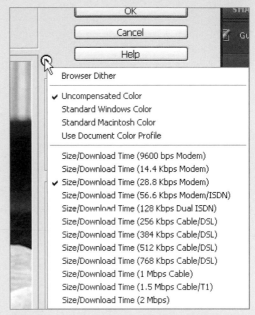

The bottom portion of the menu offers a variety of standard dial-up and high-speed Internet connection settings. Whichever connection speed you choose here determines the estimated connection speed value displayed in the information box below the optimized preview image (**Figure 12.10**). So, by doing nothing more than selecting from a handful of menu options, you can get a good idea of how much time it will take anyone, with any number of connection speeds, to download and display your image.

Figure 12.9 It's a little hard to find, but the Preview menu controls the appearance of the optimization preview and the information displayed below it.

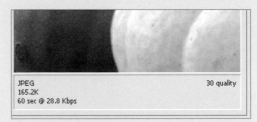

None of the settings you choose from the Preview menu affect the actual image file in any way. They're for the purpose of previewing only and are completely independent of the attributes you actually apply to an image in the Settings portion of the dialog. There's no way to include a setting for connection speed with an image, since connection speed depends on the type of Internet service each individual uses.

Figure 12.10 After you've chosen a connection speed from the preview menu, the Save for Web dialog uses that input, along with the optimization format you've selected, to estimate the size the file will be when optimized and the time it will take to download. That information is displayed below the optimized preview.

About Color Models and Color Lookup Tables

Although you certainly don't have to be proficient in Web color theory to save images for the Web that look good, a little background information on the different color models will help you make more informed decisions as you choose colors for your Web images. When you optimize an image using the GIF format, Photoshop Elements asks you to pick a *color model* from the Color Reduction Algorithm drop-down menu. Since GIF images are limited to just 256 colors, color models help to define which colors—from the vast spectrum of *millions* of colors—will be used in any individual optimized image. Sets of colors are given priority over others depending on the color model chosen, as follows:

Perceptual color leans toward colors to which the human eye is most sensitive.

Selective color draws from the largest possible range of colors, incorporating colors from the Web-safe palette as much as possible. Selective is the default option.

Adaptive color favors those colors that appear most often in a particular image. For instance, a seascape may contain colors primarily from the blue spectrum.

Restrictive (Web) is limited to the standard 216 Web colors and typically produces color the least true to the original image. Virtually all browsers and personal computer monitors are capable of displaying in thousands and millions of colors; Web colors are an artifact of a time in which 8-bit (256-color) video cards were common, nearly a decade ago.

After you've selected a color model and chosen a maximum number of colors from the Colors drop-down menu, Photoshop Elements builds a *color lookup table* specific to the image you're optimizing.

A color lookup table can be thought of as a palette of color swatches. If an original image contains more colors than you specify for its GIF version's color lookup table, any missing colors will be re-created as best they can, using the existing number of colors in the color palette. If the original image contains *fewer* colors than you've specified, the color lookup table will shrink and will contain only the colors in the image.

Either way, no unnecessary color information is included in the color lookup table, meaning that your image's file size is kept to a minimum.

ABOUT COLOR MODELS AND LOOKUP TABLES

Adjusting Optimization Settings

You're not limited to using predefined settings to optimize your images. You can fine-tune these settings further by using the collection of drop-down menus, check boxes, and sliders available in the Settings portion of the Save for Web dialog. For example, if you want your JPEGs to retain a little more image quality as they're compressed for the Web, you can change the default quality setting for a Medium JPEG image from 30 to 45, improving its sharpness and detail without much increasing its download time. As you make adjustments, refer to the optimized image preview to the left of the Settings column where you can see how your changes affect the image, as well as view its current potential file size and download time.

To apply custom JPEG optimization settings to an image:

1. Open the image you want to optimize, then choose File > Save for Web to open the Save for Web dialog.

2. From the Preset drop-down menu, choose one of the predefined JPEG settings (**Figure 12.11**).

   You don't have to choose one of the presets, but they can serve as a good jumping-off point for building your own settings. For instance, if you decide small file size and quick download time are priorities, you might want to start with the predefined JPEG Low setting and then customize the settings from there.

3. Verify that JPEG is selected from the Optimized file format drop-down menu, or if you've decided to skip step 2, choose JPEG from the Optimized drop-down menu (**Figure 12.12**).

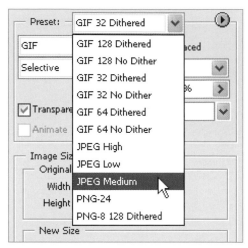

Figure 12.11 If you like, choose one of the predefined JPEG settings to use as a baseline for your own custom settings.

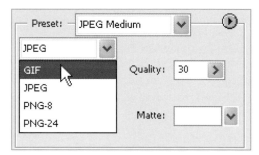

Figure 12.12 Optimization formats can be changed at any time from the drop-down menu.

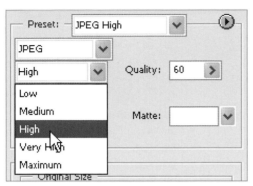

Figure 12.13 Choose from five basic quality options for JPEG images.

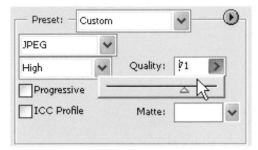

Figure 12.14 Once a quality option has been selected, use the slider control to fine-tune it.

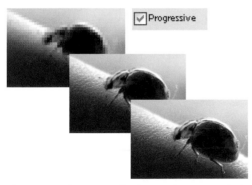

Figure 12.15 The Progressive feature draws your JPEG image incrementally on a Web page as it downloads, eventually displaying the image in its final state.

4. To set the image quality, *do one of the following:*

▲ From the compression quality drop-down menu, select a quality option (**Figure 12.13**).

▲ Drag the Quality slider while referring to the optimized preview (**Figure 12.14**).

The Quality slider has a direct impact on the Quality drop-down menu, and vice versa. When the slider is set between 0 and 29, the level in the Quality drop-down menu will be Low. A setting of 30 through 59 registers as Medium, 60 through 79 as High, 80 through 99 as Very High, and 100 as Maximum. Remember that a setting in the Very High or Maximum range will create a file six to eight times larger than one saved in the Low range.

5. Select the Progressive check box if you want your image to build from a low-resolution version to its final saved version as it downloads in a Web browser (**Figure 12.15**).

This option is more critical for large, high-quality images with download times in the tens of seconds. Rather than leaving a blank space, the low-resolution image appears almost immediately, giving your Web page visitors *something* to look at until the complete file is downloaded.

6. Select the ICC Profile check box if you've previously saved a color profile with your image and want that information preserved in your optimized image.

Unless your photo or art contains some *critical* color (a logo with a very specific corporate color, for instance), you should leave this box unchecked. Not all Web browsers support color profiles, and the inclusion of the profile information can increase a file's size significantly.

continues on next page

7. If your original image contains transparency, see "Making a Web Image Transparent" later in this chapter.

8. Click the OK button in the Save for Web dialog to rename and save your optimized image.

To apply custom GIF optimization settings to an image:

1. Open the image you want to optimize, then choose File > Save for Web to open the Save for Web dialog.

2. From the Preset drop-down menu, choose one of the predefined GIF settings, or choose GIF from the Optimized file format drop-down menu (**Figure 12.16**).

3. From the Color Reduction Algorithm drop-down menu, choose a color lookup table to apply to your image (**Figure 12.17**). (For more information, see the sidebar "About Color Models and Color Lookup Tables" earlier in this chapter.)

4. From the Colors drop-down menu, choose the maximum number of colors that will be displayed in your image by specifying the number of colors the image's palette will contain (**Figure 12.18**).

   You can choose from the list of eight standard color palette values, use the arrows to the left of the text box to change the values in increments of one, or simply enter a value in the text box and press Enter.

   When formatting GIF images, the number of colors you specify will have a larger impact on final file size and download time than any other attribute you set. Naturally, the fewer colors you select, the smaller the image file size will be, so experiment with different values, gradually reducing the number of colors, until

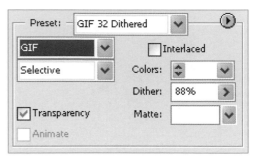

Figure 12.16 Choose the GIF setting to optimize illustrations, vector art, or type.

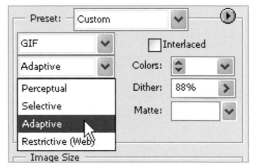

Figure 12.17 The GIF format offers several schemes for interpreting and displaying the color in your image.

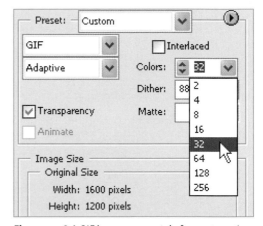

Figure 12.18 A GIF image can contain from 2 to 256 colors.

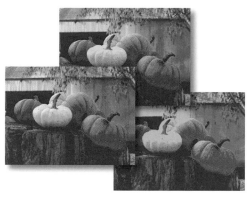

Figure 12.19 This illustration was optimized with three GIF color palettes containing progressively fewer colors. From left to right, the illustrations were saved with palettes of 16, 8, and 4 colors, creating file sizes of roughly 88K, 72K, and 50K, respectively.

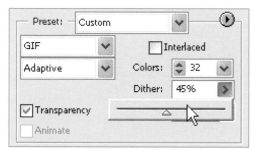

Figure 12.20 Since diffusion is the default dither option for any GIF image you create in the Save for Web dialog, you can control the amount of dithering that occurs: from 0 to 100 percent.

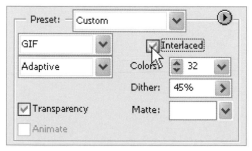

Figure 12.21 The Interlaced feature works like JPEG's Progressive option to draw your image incrementally on a Web page as it downloads.

you arrive at a setting you find acceptable (**Figure 12.19**).

5. Use the Dither slider to specify a percentage for the dither (**Figure 12.20**).

   Higher percentages create finer dither patterns, which tend to preserve more detail in images where limited color palettes have been specified.

   Although not accessible from the Save for Web dialog, Photoshop Elements gives you the option to save a GIF image with one of three different Dither options. (For more information, see the sidebar "Choosing Dithering Options.")

6. If you want your image to build from a low-resolution version to its final saved version as it downloads in a browser, select the Interlaced check box (**Figure 12.21**).

   Interlacing a GIF image works in much the same way as applying the Progressive option to a JPEG image. If you choose not to select the interlace option, your image won't display on a Web page until it's completely downloaded.

7. If your original image contains transparency, see "Making a Web Image Transparent" later in this chapter.

8. Click the OK button to rename and save your optimized image.

✔ Tip

■ If you want to save an image in the PNG-8 format, you'll notice it uses all the same options as for GIF, and the procedures for applying custom PNG-8 settings will be exactly the same as those for GIF. The only options available for PNG-24 are transparency and interlacing.

Choosing Dithering Options

Because a GIF image works with a limited color palette, it's impossible to reproduce most of the millions of colors visible to the human eye, much less subtle gradations of tone and color. GIF optimization employs a little visual trick called *dithering* to fool the eye into perceiving more colors and softer transitions than are actually there. By reorganizing pixels of different hues and values, dithering can do a surprisingly good job of simulating thousands of colors with a palette of a hundred colors or less (**Figure 12.22**). Dithering involves placing colors adjacent to one another in a small checkerboard pattern of pixels to create the illusion of another color. Blue and yellow pixels mixed together will blend to create green. Black and white pixels mixed in varying proportions will simulate a graduated fill or soft-edged drop shadow. (Dithering is related to *halftoning*, which uses dots of different sizes to show varying shades of gray or colors.)

Dithered GIFs created via Save for Web use a *diffusion* dither. But if you save an image from the Save As dialog (File > Save As) and select CompuServe GIF from the Format drop-down menu, Photoshop Elements offers you a choice of three dithering options.

Diffusion is the default scheme for any of the predefined GIF settings; it creates a random pattern that usually yields the most natural-looking results. Diffusion is the only option that allows you to control the percentage of dither present in your image.

Pattern, as its name implies, lays down pixels in a uniform grid pattern. It can have the effect of a very coarse halftone screen such as you might see in low-resolution newspaper photography.

Noise creates a random pattern similar to Diffusion, but attempts to blend color transitions further by allowing color from one area to spill over slightly into an adjoining area. It occasionally produces an interesting effect, but will rarely be your first choice.

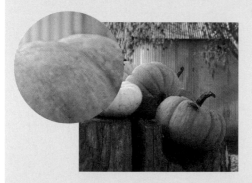 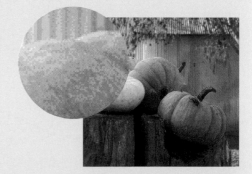

Figure 12.22 The original image (left) relies on thousands of subtle tonal and value changes to define shapes, shadows, and highlights. The GIF-optimized version (right) shows the close-up results of dithering. Since GIF optimization uses a limited palette of colors, it gathers together pixels of whatever colors are available to reproduce an approximation of the original image.

Optimizing Images to Specific File Sizes

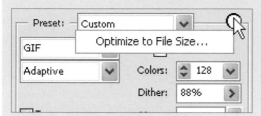

Figure 12.23 Choose Optimize to File Size for additional optimization control.

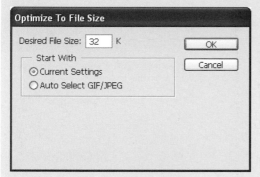

Figure 12.24 In the Optimize to File Size dialog, you can choose to have file size take priority over image quality.

Photoshop Elements has yet one more little optimizing trick. There may be times when image quality isn't as critical as the data size of your files. Perhaps you want to e-mail a weekend's trip worth of photos to some friends, but don't want to clog up their mailboxes with megabytes of image files. You can send a batch of mediocre-quality images, and then let them pick out the ones they'd like you to create high-resolution copies or prints of. On the right side of the Save for Web dialog, just next to the main optimization settings drop-down menu, is the Optimize to File Size arrow button. Click the button, and then select Optimize to File Size (**Figure 12.23**). In the Optimize to File Size dialog, type in the size you want your file to be (**Figure 12.24**). In the Start With area of the dialog, you can also choose from Current Settings, which tells Elements to do its best with your Save for Web settings; or Auto Select, which allows Elements to choose the format that will work best for your image, given the file size constraints.

Making a Web Image Transparent

In just a few simple steps, you can preserve the transparency of any image using options available in the GIF formatting settings. Once transparency has been set, an image of any shape (even one with a transparent cutout) can be placed on a Web page and made to blend seamlessly—*matted*—with its background.

To apply transparency to an image:

1. Open the image you want to make transparent.

2. By default, Elements creates a single layer for an image called Background (**Figure 12.25**). In the Layers palette, double-click the Background layer, change its name in the Name field to something like "Regular Layer" (**Figure 12.26**), and then click OK.

3. Using any combination of selection tools you choose, select the part of the image that you want to be transparent. (See Chapter 5, "Making Selections.")

4. Choose Edit > Delete to remove those selected parts of the image. A checkerboard pattern fills those areas, indicating they're now transparent (**Figure 12.27**).

5. Choose File > Save for Web to open the Save for Web dialog.

6. Select any one of the GIF formats from the Preset drop-down menu.

7. If it's not already selected, click to select the Transparency check box.

   The image in the optimized preview area will be displayed against a transparency grid pattern (**Figure 12.28**).

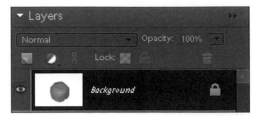

Figure 12.25 The Background layer is created by default when an image is opened, but it doesn't allow transparency.

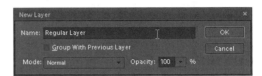

Figure 12.26 Rename the background layer so you can create transparency in the image.

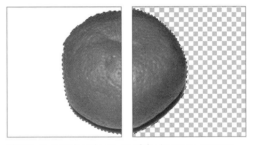

Figure 12.27 Select the parts of the image to remove, and use Delete to create a transparent background.

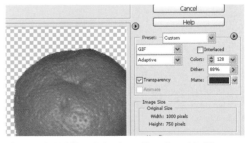

Figure 12.28 GIF optimization offers the added bonus of preserving transparency in your Web-bound images.

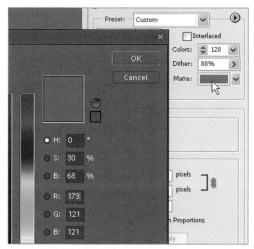

Figure 12.29 Choose a matte color from the Color Picker to match your intended Web page background.

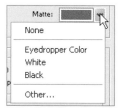

Figure 12.30 Choose an option from the drop-down menu to use a preset color.

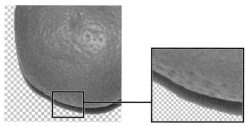

Figure 12.31 The color you select from the Matte drop-down menu or color box fills in the semitransparent pixels around your image, helping to maintain a smooth edge and creating a seamless transition when the image is placed on a Web page of the same color.

8. To select the color that will be used to blend, or *matte*, your image with the Web page background color, *choose one of these two options:*

   ▲ Click the Matte color box to open the Color Picker; then select a color from the main color window or enter color values in either the HSB, RGB, or Web color space text boxes (**Figure 12.29**).

   ▲ From the Matte drop-down menu, choose a color option (**Figure 12.30**).

   Only the semitransparent pixels around the edges of the image are filled with the matte color. If the matte color matches the color of the Web page background, the transition between the transparent image and its background will be seamless (**Figure 12.31**).

✔ Tips

- JPEG doesn't support true transparency, but you can set transparent areas in your source image with the background of the Web page for which the JPEG image is intended. Follow the steps in the earlier task, "To apply custom JPEG optimization settings to an image," and then click the Matte color box to open the Color Picker. Select a color; then click OK. The transparent areas fill with the matte color.

- If your Web page will use a patterned background, set the matte color to None; otherwise, you'll get a distracting halo of color around the image.

- The Eyedropper Color option is helpful only if the color of your Web page background also happens to be present in your image. The Other option simply opens the Color Picker. You're better off using the Matte drop-down menu only when selecting the White, Black, or None options.

Identifying Web Page Background Colors

You'll need to do a little homework to identify the color of your Web page background if you didn't choose that value yourself (or haven't made a note of it) before you can precisely assign a matte color to your transparent GIF images in Photoshop Elements.

The most accurate method of determining the color of the Web page is to identify the color values in the Web page's source code. This isn't nearly as intimidating as it sounds. Open any Web page, then from the browser's menu, find the command to view the source code. (In Internet Explorer, you simply choose View > Source; in Mozilla Firefox, View > Page Source.) A window will open, with code describing everything from the location of graphics and text to the background color.

Once you have the source code window open, scan down the entries for the one that begins with <body> near the top of the page. In the same line, directly to the right, it will say, bgcolor= followed by either a 6-digit Web color code (something like #663300) or RGB color values (**Figure 12.32**). The "bgcolor" stands for background color with the number corresponding to that color. Simply jot down the color values from the Web page source code, and then return to Photoshop Elements and enter those same values in the bottom field of the Color Picker to assign the matte color.

If the site uses Cascading Style Sheets (CSS) to define a background color, look for an area near the top of the page that reads body { color: #number, and use the code that appears instead of number.

Sometimes CSS styles are linked to another file. Look for a line near the top of the source code that reads in part, <link href="stylesheet.css". Open that file via your browser (enter the filename after the domain name), and look for the body { color: information there.

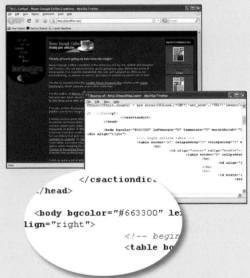

Figure 12.32 In this example, I'm viewing the source code for a page from a Web site. On the <body> line is the color code for the Web page background— bgcolor="#669900"—which translates to brown.

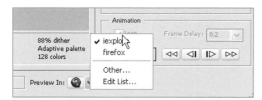

Figure 12.33 You can open your optimized image directly in a browser for previewing.

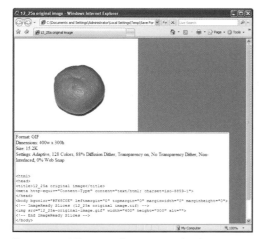

Figure 12.34 When your image opens in a browser, it's accompanied by all of the settings you specified in the Save for Web dialog.

Previewing an Image

Before you commit to saving your optimized image, you should see exactly how the image will appear in a Web browser window. Although the Save for Web optimized preview gives you a good approximation of how the final image will look, there's no substitute for seeing the image displayed in its natural environment.

Additionally, you can remain within the Save for Web dialog to preview your image as if it were viewed on an older, lower-end system, limited to just 256 colors. This can be helpful, because it allows you to design primarily for most current computer systems while giving you the opportunity to fine-tune your settings to accommodate the limited display capabilities of older systems. Note that this is only a preview and has no affect on your actual image file and its settings.

To preview an image in a Web browser:

1. Open the image you want to preview, then choose File > Save for Web to open the Save for Web dialog.

2. At the bottom of the Save for Web dialog, choose a Web browser or click the current browser icon on the Preview In drop-down menu (**Figure 12.33**).

   The browser opens displaying the optimized image plus its dimensions and the settings you specified (**Figure 12.34**).

3. Close the browser window to return to the Save for Web dialog.

To preview an image as it would display on older monitors:

1. From the preview menu in the Save for Web dialog, choose Browser Dither (**Figure 12.35**).

   The image in the optimized preview window appears just as it would on an 8-bit (256-color) monitor, allowing you to anticipate what this image will look like on older computer systems (**Figure 12.36**).

2. To turn off the browser dither preview, choose Browser Dither again from the preview menu.

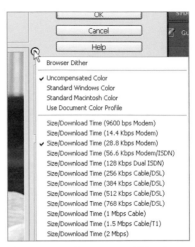

Figure 12.35 Select Browser Dither from the preview menu if you want to view your image using a limited Web-safe palette.

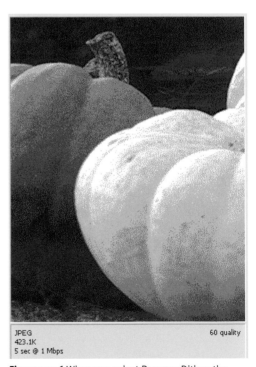

JPEG
423.1K
5 sec @ 1 Mbps
60 quality

Figure 12.36 When you select Browser Dither, the optimized preview changes to display your image as it would appear on an older, 256-color monitor.

SAVING AND PRINTING IMAGES

With Photoshop Elements, you can save images in a number of file formats, each with its own set of specialized uses and limitations. In this chapter, I'll begin with a discussion of formatting options and then move on to other considerations for saving your image files and preparing them for printing. I'll look at how to format and save multiple images (known as *batch processing*) and then look at tools you can use to lay out, organize, and catalog your image files. In addition, I'll look closely at the steps necessary to get the best prints from your digital images, whether you're printing them at home or uploading your files to an online photo service.

Understanding File Formats

Photoshop Elements lets you save an image in any of 16 different file formats, from the native, information-rich Photoshop format to optimized formats for the Web, such as GIF and JPEG. Among these is an extremely specialized collection of formats (PCX, PICT Resource, Pixar, PNG, Raw, Scitex CT, and Targa) you'll rarely need to use and won't be discussed here. What follows are descriptions of the most common file formats, presented in the order they appear in the Format drop-down menu in the Save As dialog.

Photoshop

Photoshop (PSD) is the native file format of Photoshop Elements, meaning that the saved file will include information for any and all of Elements' features, including layers, styles, effects, typography, and filters. As its name implies, any file saved in the PSD format can be opened not only in Photoshop Elements, but also in Adobe Photoshop. Conversely, any Photoshop file saved in its native format can be opened in Photoshop Elements. However, Photoshop Elements doesn't support all the features available in Photoshop, so although you can open any file saved in the PSD format, some of Photoshop's more advanced features (such as layer sets) won't be accessible to you within Photoshop Elements.

A good approach is to save every photo you're working on in the native Photoshop format and then, when you've finished editing, save a copy in whatever format is appropriate for that image's intended use or destination. That way, you always have the original, full-featured image file to return to if you want to make changes or just save in a different format.

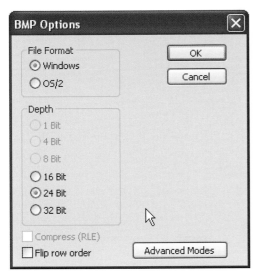

Figure 13.1 The choices available in the BMP Options dialog vary depending on the color or tonal content of the particular image.

BMP

As a Windows user, you may recognize the .bmp file extension, which identifies a bitmap file. BMP has long been Windows' standard graphics format, and it's the one you'll want to use if you're creating images for screen savers or computer wallpaper.

Radio buttons in the BMP Options dialog (**Figure 13.1**) offer bit-depth options you can use to set the maximum number of colors or values, but Photoshop Elements does a pretty good job of selecting the appropriate settings for any particular image. So, unless you know you have a special requirement (like keeping file size to a minimum to conserve disk space, for instance) you can leave these options alone.

A *compression* (or optimization) scheme is available when certain combinations of file format and bit depth are selected. However, if you plan to use this format to save an image for wallpaper or a screen saver, *don't* select this compression. If you do, Windows won't recognize your file.

Photoshop EPS

Photoshop EPS is actually a format you'll probably *not* want to save to. Although EPS (Encapsulated PostScript) files are compatible with a host of graphics and page layout programs, they're not the best choice for saving bitmap images, which are what Photoshop Elements creates. The EPS format adds layers of PostScript code to describe everything from the way an image appears in preview to the way it is color managed, which translates into overhead in the form of bloated file size and slower display time. Any advantage this format holds for displaying and printing vector art and typography is lost on Photoshop Elements' raster art.

Photoshop PDF

Portable Document Format (PDF) is the perfect vehicle for sharing images across platforms or for importing them into a variety of graphics and page layout programs. PDF is also one of only three file formats (native Photoshop and TIFF are the other two) that support an image file's layers; layer qualities (like transparency) are preserved when you place a PDF into another application like Adobe Illustrator or InDesign. The real beauty of this file format is that any document saved as a PDF file can be opened and viewed by anyone using Adobe's free Acrobat Reader software, which Adobe bundles with its applications and makes available as a free download from its Web site.

PDF offers two compression schemes for controlling file size: ZIP and JPEG (**Figure 13.2**). ZIP removes whatever extraneous file information it can without the loss of any image quality and so is referred to as *lossless* compression. Since some degree of image fidelity is lost in the JPEG compression process, it's known as a *lossy* compression. JPEG compression also offers you image quality options from Low to Maximum.

TIFF

Tagged Image File Format (TIFF) is the one true workhorse among the file formats. The TIFF format was designed to be platform independent, so TIFF files display and print equally well from both Windows and Macintosh machines. Additionally, any TIFF file created on one platform can be transferred to the other and placed in almost any graphics or page layout program.

You can optimize TIFF files to save room on your hard drive using one of three compression schemes, or you can save them with

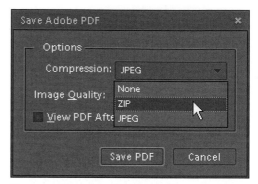

Figure 13.2 When you save your work as a PDF file, you can apply JPEG or ZIP compression.

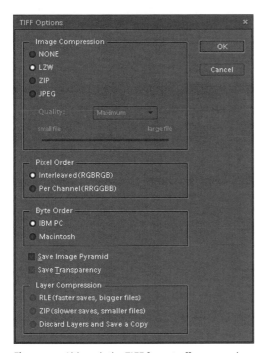

Figure 13.3 Although the TIFF format offers several compression schemes, LZW is usually the most reliable.

no compression at all (**Figure 13.3**). Of the three compression options, LZW is the one supported by the largest number of applications and programs.

The Pixel Order option should be left at the default of Interleaved, because that is the option supported by Photoshop Elements' Organizer.

The Byte Order option encodes information in the file to determine whether it will be used on a Windows or Macintosh platform. On rare occasions, TIFF files saved with the Macintosh option don't transfer cleanly to Windows machines. But since the Mac has no problem with files saved with the IBM PC byte order, I recommend you stick with this option.

Checking the Save Image Pyramid check box saves your image in different tiers of resolution, so you can choose to use the full-resolution image or a lower-resolution version. However, not many applications (Photoshop Elements included) support the Image Pyramid format as yet, so you should leave this box unchecked.

Checking the Save Transparency check box ensures transparency will be maintained if you place your image into another application like Illustrator or InDesign.

If your image contains layers, you can choose from two Layer Compression schemes, or choose to discard the layers altogether and save a copy of your image file.

JPEG and GIF

The two major Web file formats (JPEG and GIF) are covered in detail in Chapter 12, "Preparing Images for the Web," so I'll look at them just briefly here. Of particular note is the fact that you can indeed use the Save As command to save an image as a GIF or JPEG file, with virtually all of the same file options as in the Save for Web dialog—so the obvious question is: Why use one saving method over the other when saving for the Web?

The Save for Web dialog offers several features the individual GIF and JPEG Save As command dialogs don't. For one, Save for Web provides a wonderful before-and-after preview area, displaying side-by-side comparisons of your original and optimized images while an information area displays the optimized version's file size and projected download time.

No less valuable is the flexibility you have to change and view different optimization formats on the fly. An image just doesn't appear the way you expected in GIF? Try JPEG. Additionally, with the click of a button, you can open and preview your optimized image in any browser present on your system.

Choosing Compression Options

As you save images in the various formats available, you're presented with a variety of format-specific dialogs, each containing its own set of options. One of those options is a choice of compression settings. Compression (or optimization) makes an image's file size smaller; the file downloads faster when you post it to a Web page, for example. Following is a brief rundown of the compression schemes.

JPEG: JPEG works best with continuous-tone images like photographs. It compresses by throwing away image information and slightly degrading the image, and is therefore a lossy compression.

LZW: This is the standard compression format for most TIFF images. Although it works best on images with large areas of a single color, LZW helps reduce file sizes at least a little for nearly any image to which it's applied. Since it works behind the scenes, throwing out code rather than image information (and so doesn't degrade the image), LZW is a lossless compression.

RLE: This is a lossless compression similar to LZW, but it's specific (in Elements) to BMP compressed files. It's particularly effective at compressing images containing transparency.

ZIP: This compression scheme is also similar to LZW, but it has the advantage of adding a layer of protection to files that makes them less susceptible to corruption if they're copied between systems or sent via e-mail. Zip files are common on the Windows platform, and Mac OS X can open them; however, some older Macintosh systems can open them only if Stuffit Expander is installed.

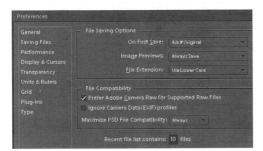

Figure 13.4 The Saving Files window of the Preferences dialog.

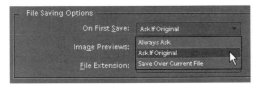

Figure 13.5 The On First Save drop-down menu lets you control when the Save As dialog appears.

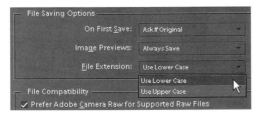

Figure 13.6 Use the File Extension drop-down menu to determine how you want filename extensions displayed.

Setting Preferences for Saving Files

The Saving Files portion of the Preferences dialog provides a number of ways to control how Elements manages your saved files.

To set the Saving Files preferences:

1. From the Edit menu, choose Preferences > Saving Files. The Preferences dialog opens with the Saving Files window active (**Figure 13.4**).

2. From the On First Save drop-down menu, you can choose when you want to be prompted with the Save As dialog (**Figure 13.5**).

3. From the Image Previews drop-down menu, choose an option to either save or not save a preview with the file.

4. From the File Extension drop-down menu, choose whether you want your file extensions in uppercase or lowercase characters (**Figure 13.6**).

5. In the File Compatibility portion of the dialog, set the Maximize PSD File Compatibility drop-down menu to Always. This gives you the maximum number of compatibility options.

6. If you're pre-processing RAW files in another program, deselect the Prefer Adobe Camera Raw for Supported Raw Files option.

7. Digital cameras assign their own color profiles (EXIF profiles) to your digital photos. If you'd prefer to assign your own profiles in Elements, select the Ignore Camera Data (EXIF) profiles check box.

8. In the text box labeled Recent file list contains, enter a number from 1 to 30.

9. Click OK to close the dialog and apply your preferences settings.

Adding Personalized File Information in the Editor

With any Photoshop Elements file open, choose File Info from the File menu to open the File Info dialog (**Figure 13.7**). Within this simple dialog, you can add personalized information specific to any file, including title, author, caption, and copyright information. Although most of the information entered here is accessible only by opening the dialog from within Photoshop Elements, some of it does have practical uses both inside and outside the application. Entries from the Title, Author, Caption, and Copyright Notice text fields can be included when you create a Picture Package.

Also, the Caption field can be included with any saved image (see "Setting additional printing options" later in this chapter). And if you select Copyrighted from the Copyright Status drop-down menu, a copyright symbol appears in the Image Window title bar, alerting anyone who receives a copy of your file that it's copyright protected (**Figure 13.8**).

The File Info dialog is useful for retrieving information, too. Many digital cameras include EXIF annotations (such as date and time, resolution, exposure time, and f-stop settings) for each digital photo. To access this information, click the Camera Data 1 or Camera Data 2 head in the left column of the dialog. Any EXIF information imported with the photo from your digital camera will be displayed in the File Info dialog (**Figure 13.9**). You can use this information to record settings from your more successful photos—a handy reference for future outings. You can also view EXIF annotations in the Information area of the File Browser, or in the Properties pane in the Organizer.

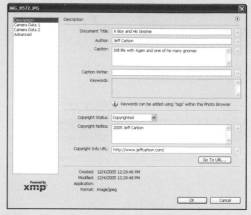

Figure 13.7 Use the File Info dialog to add title, copyright, and other information to any specific file.

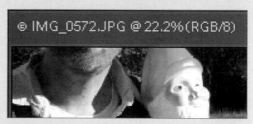

Figure 13.8 When a file is assigned copyright status in the File Info dialog, a copyright symbol appears next to the filename at the top of the image window.

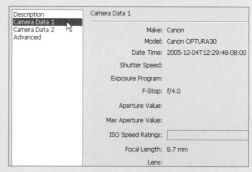

Figure 13.9 The File Info dialog displays EXIF information included with photos imported from digital cameras.

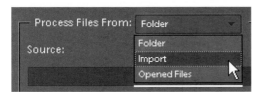

Figure 13.10 You can save groups of files from a number of different sources.

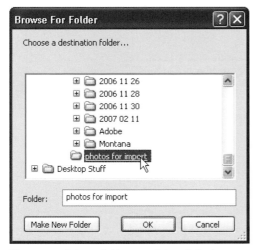

Figure 13.11 Select a folder containing all the images you want to save at one time.

Formatting and Saving Multiple Images

You've just finished a prolific day of shooting pictures, and as a first step to sorting through all those images, you'd like to convert them to Elements' native Photoshop format and then change their resolution to 150 dpi. You could, of course, convert them individually, but the Batch Processing command can do all that tedious, repetitive work for you.

To batch process multiple files:

1. From the File menu, choose Process Multiple Files to open the Process Multiple Files dialog.

2. From the Process Files From drop-down menu (**Figure 13.10**), *do one of the following*:

   ▲ To select images within a folder on your hard drive, choose Folder, click the Browse button, and then locate and select the folder containing the images you want to convert (**Figure 13.11**). If you spot folders within the folder you select that *also* contain files you want to convert, click the Include All Subfolders check box in the Process Multiple Files dialog.

   ▲ To select images stored in a digital camera, scanner, or PDF, choose Import; then select the appropriate source from the From drop-down menu. The choices in the From drop-down menu will vary depending on the hardware connected to your computer.

   ▲ To select files that are currently open within Photoshop Elements, choose Opened Files.

   continues on next page

3. Click the Destination Browse button; then locate and select a folder to save your converted files.

In the Browse for Folder dialog that appears, you're also offered the option of creating a new folder for your converted files.

4. If you want to add a file naming structure to your collection of converted images, select the Rename Files check box; then select naming options from the two drop-down menus (**Figure 13.12**).

Refer to the Example text (located below the Rename Files check box) to see how the renaming changes will affect your filenames.

5. Select the Compatibility check boxes for whichever platforms you want your filenames to be compatible with.

A good approach is to select all three of these, just to be on the safe side. Notice that the Windows platform is preselected for you and dimmed.

6. If you want to change either the physical dimensions of your image or its resolution, click the Resize Images check box, then *do one or both of the following:*

▲ To convert all of your images to a specific size, first select a unit of measure from the Units drop-down menu, then enter the width *or* height in the appropriate text box, making sure that the Constrain Proportions check box is selected (**Figure 13.13**).

▲ From the Resolution drop-down menu, choose a resolution in dots per inch (dpi) to change the resolution of all your images (**Figure 13.14**).

The resolution setting in this dialog is in dots per inch (print resolution) rather than pixels per inch (screen resolution), so changing just the resolution here will

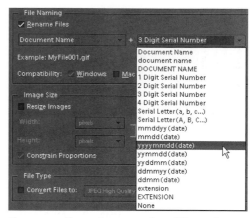

Figure 13.12 Choose from a number of file naming options to arrange your images in consecutive order.

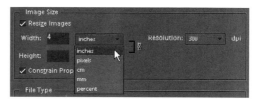

Figure 13.13 You can resize entire groups of images to the same width or height dimensions.

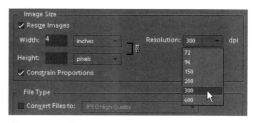

Figure 13.14 Choose a resolution to apply to all of the files in your selected group.

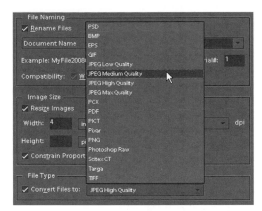

Figure 13.15 Choose a formatting option to apply to all the files in your selected group.

do nothing to alter your image, or change its file size. It changes only the dimensions of the final printed image and has no effect on the size it displays onscreen. (For more information on image resizing, see "Changing Image Size and Resolution" in Chapter 3.)

7. From the Convert Files to drop-down menu, choose the desired format type (**Figure 13.15**).

8. Click OK to close the dialog and start the batch process. The selected files are opened, converted in turn, and then saved to the folder you've chosen.

If you've chosen one of the import options, an additional series of dialogs will appear, guiding you through the selection of images you want to import.

✔ Tips

■ The import options in the Process Multiple Files dialog are also accessible by choosing Import from the File menu. But the Import command offers no options for image sizing, resolution, or file naming (not to mention the ability to save to specified destination folders). So even if you're importing just one image at a time (as would normally be the case when importing from a scanner, for instance) you may find that the Batch dialog still holds a decided advantage over the File menu's Import command.

■ Using a little simple math can help you to convert pixel dimensions to inches. Just multiply the resolution you've selected by the number of inches (of either height or width) that you want your final image to be. For example, if you've selected a resolution of 72 dpi, and you want the width of your images to be 4 inches; simply multiply 72 by 4, then enter the total (288) in the width text box.

Choosing Paper

A wide range of papers is available for your inkjet printer. For most photos, you'll want to print on either photo paper or glossy photo paper (glossy photo paper is thicker, and a little more durable). Quality matte paper is often preferred for high-resolution photographs, and you can even find archival-quality paper that won't fade for 100 years. If you just want to print a quick proof, your regular inkjet printer paper will do in a pinch.

Before you start buying paper, it's a good idea to review the documentation that came with your printer (or check out your printer manufacturer's Web site) to see a list of recommended paper choices.

Creating a Contact Sheet

You may have lots of photos downloaded from your digital camera, but with unhelpful filenames like 102-0246_IMG.JPG, organizing and sorting them can be a difficult task. And although the Organizer lets you view and sort through your images, sometimes it's nice to have a printed hard copy to study and mark up. In traditional photography, contact sheets are created from film negatives and provide a photographer or designer with a collection of convenient thumbnail images organized neatly on a single sheet of film or paper. The Contact Sheet feature works in much the same way. Taking advantage of the Organizer, you can select photos from groups and collections you define ahead of time.

To make a contact sheet:

1. Open one or more photos you would like to include in your contact sheet; then from the File menu, choose Print Multiple Photos. Elements automatically launches the Organizer, and the Print Photos dialog appears (**Figure 13.16**).

   If you're already in the Organizer, simply select one or more images and choose Print from the File menu.

2. From the Select Printer drop-down menu, choose a printer.

3. From the Select Type of Print drop-down menu, choose Contact Sheet (**Figure 13.17**).

   The preview window in the center of the dialog changes to reflect your print type selection (**Figure 13.18**).

   Now you can add more photos to your contact sheet.

4. In the lower-left corner of the Print Photos dialog, click the Add button (**Figure 13.19**).

   The Add Photos dialog opens.

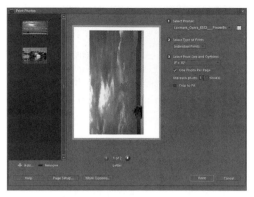

Figure 13.16 In the Print Photos dialog, Elements has rotated the image to fit best on a sheet of paper.

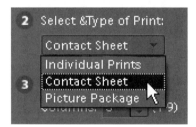

Figure 13.17 Choose Contact Sheet from the list of available print options.

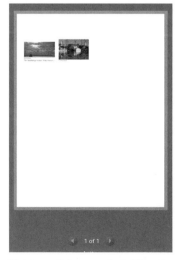

Figure 13.18 As you select different print options, the preview window will change.

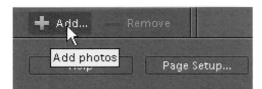

Figure 13.19 The Add button sends you to the Add Photos dialog, where you select the photos you want included in your contact sheet.

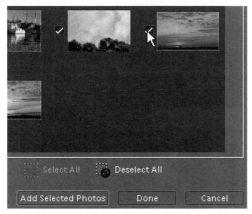

Figure 13.20 In the Add Photos dialog, select the photos to include in your contact sheet.

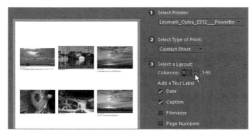

Figure 13.21 You can control the number of thumbnails that appear on each page of your contact sheet.

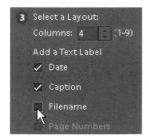

Figure 13.22 You can include labeling information with each photo on your contact sheet.

5. In the Add Photos From area of the Add Photos dialog, select from one of five options:

   ▲ Photos Currently in Browser displays all of the photos currently visible in the Organizer's Browser window.

   ▲ Entire Catalog displays every photo you've imported into the Organizer.

   ▲ Album displays photos that you've organized into a single photo album.

   ▲ Keyword Tag displays photos to which you've assigned a specific attribute tag, like Favorites, People, or Places.

6. If you choose the Album or Tag option, choose a photo group from the Select drop-down menu.

   The Add Photos dialog is populated with all of the photos from the option you selected in the Add Photos From area.

7. Click to select the photos you want to include on your contact sheet, and then click Done (**Figure 13.20**).

   The preview window in the center of the Print Photos dialog now includes all of the photos you have selected.

8. Click on the arrows to the right of the Columns text box to designate the number of columns per page your photo thumbnails will occupy (**Figure 13.21**).

9. Click to select the type of text information you would like to have appear below each photo thumbnail (**Figure 13.22**).

10. Click Print to send your completed contact sheet to your printer.

CREATING A CONTACT SHEET

Creating a Photographer's Picture Package

Photoshop Elements' Picture Package creates a page with multiple copies of the same image, just like the kind you'd receive from a professional photographer's studio. Photos can be arranged in a number of layouts and sizes, from a sheet made up only of wallet-sized images to a variety pack of different sizes and quantities. Printing images this way is also more economical, because you waste less photo paper.

To make a picture package:

1. Open the photo you would like to include in your picture package; then from the File menu, choose Print Multiple Photos. Elements automatically launches the Organizer, and the Print Photos dialog appears.

2. From the Select Printer drop-down menu, choose a printer.

3. From the Select Type of Print drop-down menu, choose Picture Package (**Figure 13.23**). The preview window changes to reflect your print type selection. If the file you intend to print is at too low a resolution to yield a good quality image, a Printing Warning dialog appears, including information on the final print resolution you should expect to see.

4. From the Select a Layout drop-down menu, choose the layout and dimensions for your picture package (**Figure 13.24**).

5. Click the Fill Page With First Photo check box to include as many copies of the image as will fit (**Figure 13.25**).

6. If you like, select a frame from the bottom-most drop-down menu, and then click Print to send your completed picture package to the printer.

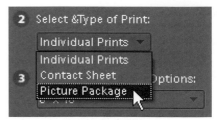

Figure 13.23 Choose Picture Package from the list of available print options.

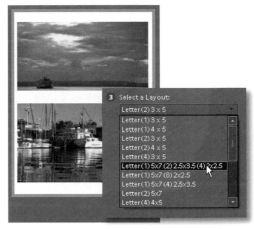

Figure 13.24 Layout templates let you display and print a variety of image sizes and orientations.

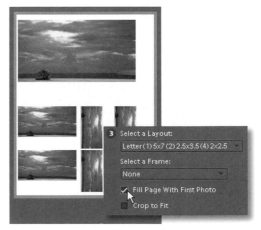

Figure 13.25 Mark the Fill Page With First Photo option to group the prints onto the page.

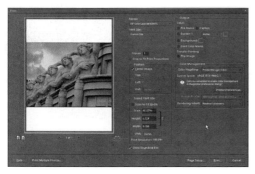

Figure 13.26 The Photoshop Elements Print dialog.

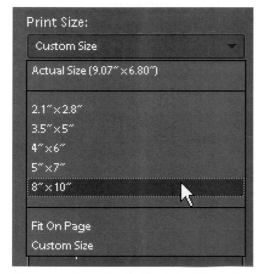

Figure 13.27 Choose the size the photo will be on the printed page.

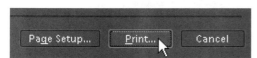

Figure 13.28 After you've applied print settings to your image, click the Print button in the Print Preview dialog.

Printing an Image

Many photographers create their own prints instead of sending files to a print service, which you can do easily from within Elements.

Confusingly, the Editor and the Organizer use different print dialogs; printing from the Organizer takes you to the Print Photos dialog described on the preceding pages. Printing from the Editor, however, gives you a more flexible Print dialog, where you can position your image on the page, scale it, and even make some last-minute modifications. That's the approach I'll cover here.

To print an image from the Editor:

1. From the File menu, choose Print to open the Print dialog (**Figure 13.26**).

2. Click the Print Size drop-down menu and choose the size at which the image will print (**Figure 13.27**). The page preview reflects the page size in proportion to the image you want to print. (I'll cover how to manually resize shortly.)

   Note that Print Size refers only to the size of the image on the page. If you want to print to a different paper size, click the Page Setup button and choose the applicable paper size.

3. To customize the appearance of the image on the printed page, perform the instructions on the following pages.

4. Click the Print button (**Figure 13.28**) to open the Windows Print dialog.

5. In the Print dialog, set the desired options. Print dialogs vary from one printer to another, so you should refer to your printer's documentation if you have any questions regarding options.

6. Click OK to close the Print dialog and send your image file to the printer.

PRINTING AN IMAGE

To position an image on a page:

1. If you want your image printed in the center of the page, confirm that the Center Image check box is selected (**Figure 13.29**).

2. If you want to move your image to a different area of the page, first uncheck Center Image; then, make sure the Show Bounding Box check box is selected below the Scaled Print Size section (**Figure 13.30**).

3. To move the image to a new area on the page, *do one of the following:*

   ▲ Move the pointer onto the image until it becomes a crossed-arrow cursor; then drag the image to a new spot on the page (**Figure 13.31**).

   ▲ Enter new values in the Top and Left text boxes. You can change the measurement system from the default of inches by selecting a different unit from the drop-down menu (**Figure 13.32**).

   Note that in either case, the position displayed in the text boxes is measured from the upper-left corner of the page to the upper-left corner of the image. In other words, if you enter 0 in both the Top and Left text boxes, your image will be positioned in the upper-left corner, directly on the top and left margins of the page.

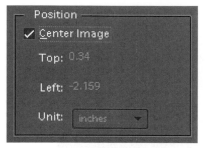

Figure 13.29 Enabling the Center Image check box centers your image on the page.

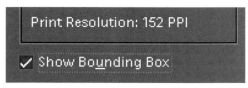

Figure 13.30 The Show Bounding Box check box must be selected before you can reposition your image.

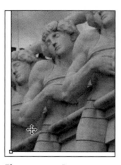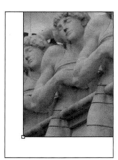

Figure 13.31 Drag to manually move your image to a new location on the page.

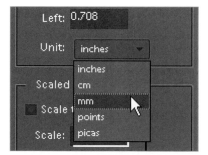

Figure 13.32 To reposition your image on the page, choose a measurement value for your document.

PRINTING AN IMAGE

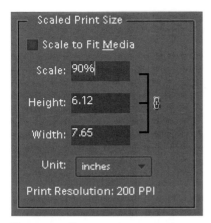

Figure 13.33 Choose a measurement system, and then enter either a Scale or a Height or Width value to resize an image numerically.

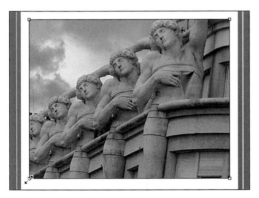

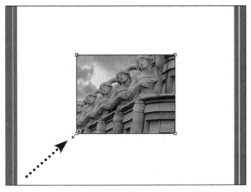

Figure 13.34 Drag to manually resize your image.

To resize an image:

To resize, *do one of the following*:

◆ From the Print Size drop-down menu, choose Fit On Page. The image is sized proportionally to most efficiently fill the page.

The Fit On Page option is best used if the original image is too large to fit on the page and needs to be reduced. Remember when rescaling an image, it's best to avoid scaling up (upsampling) when possible.

◆ With Scale to Fit Media unchecked, enter a new percentage in the Scale text box (**Figure 13.33**).

◆ Enter either a new Height or Width value in the respective text box.

Note that the Scale, Height, and Width text boxes are linked together, and that a change to any one of the boxes will be reflected in the other two.

◆ See that the Show Bounding Box check box is selected; then, in the image preview, drag any of the four bounding box handles (**Figure 13.34**).

The image is resized, and its new scale and dimension values are displayed in the Scaled Print Size text boxes.

✔ Tip

■ Remember that the changes you make to an image from within the Print Preview dialog have no effect on the actual image itself—that is, the image's file size and physical dimensions don't actually change. Any repositioning, scaling, or other modifications you perform in the Print Preview dialog affect only the way the image appears on the printed page.

Setting additional printing options

At the top of the Print dialog, you'll find a set of features you can use to modify the printed output of your image. The Border option can be particularly handy if you want to experiment with adding a colored stroke to your image without the risk of harming the actual image files.

To add a stroked border:

1. Click the Border check box to select the Border option. Then, click Show Bounding Box to disable that option. The border can be difficult to see in the page preview if the Bounding Box is also visible.

2. Click the small color swatch to open the Color Picker, where you can select a color for your border (**Figure 13.35**).

3. From the Units drop-down menu, select a measurement unit, and then in the Border text box, enter a border size (**Figure 13.36**).

    A stroke is applied to the image in the page preview.

    To resize the border, enter a new value in the Border text box.

4. To delete the border, click the Border check box to deselect the border option.

To add crop marks:

◆ Select the Print Crop Marks check box (**Figure 13.37**).

    Crop marks appear outside the corners of the image in the page preview (**Figure 13.38**).

✔ Tip

■ You can also assign a background color by clicking its swatch and selecting a color from the Color Picker.

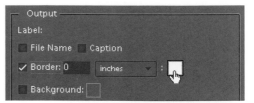

Figure 13.35 Click the color swatch to open the Color Picker, where you can choose the color to apply to your border.

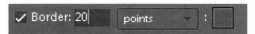

Figure 13.36 Select a measurement unit and size for your stroked border.

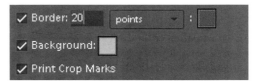

Figure 13.37 Click to add crop marks around your printed image.

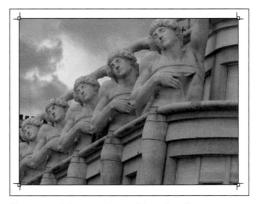

Figure 13.38 Crop marks positioned at the corners.

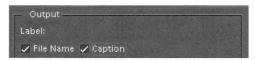

Figure 13.39 Additional print options appear if you click the Show More Options check box.

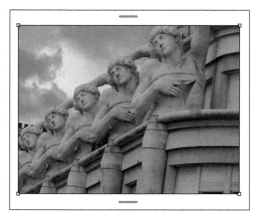

Figure 13.40 Labeling information appears as simple gray bars in the preview window.

To add a label:

◆ In the Output section under the Label heading, click to select the File Name and/or the Caption check box (**Figure 13.39**).

   If a document title or description has been entered for the image in the File Info dialog, it will be represented in the page preview as gray bars. The document title (File Name) appears at the top, and the description (Caption) appears at the bottom (**Figure 13.40**). (See the sidebar "Adding Personalized File Information" earlier in this chapter.)

   When the image is printed, the labels will appear in the locations indicated in the page preview.

✔ Tips

■ Clicking the Print Multiple Photos button sends you back to the Organizer's Print Photos dialog, from which you can select additional photos for this print run.

■ Click the Flip Image check box under Transfer Printing to invert the image horizontally (great if you're making t-shirt transfers!). If your printer's driver has an invert image option, make sure that's not selected—otherwise, the image will flip back to its original orientation when printed.

PRINTING AN IMAGE

Ordering Prints

In the past, you'd shoot a roll of film, take it to a photo developer, and after a few days (or a few hours) you'd have prints of all your images. Now, you can order prints directly from within Photoshop Elements—and order just the images you want. The photos are printed by Kodak on photo paper and mailed within a few days.

To make things easy, it's best to set up a few contacts: yourself and anyone you might want to send prints to (grandparents, for example). Once that's done, you can drag photos to the Quick Share palette.

To set up contacts:

1. Open the Organizer, and then expand the Quick Share palette, which is found in both the Organize and Share tabs. If it's not visible, select it from the Window menu.

2. Click the Create New Order Prints Recipient button (**Figure 13.41**). You can also drag one or more photos to the entry marked *Drag photos here to create an order*.

3. In the New Order Prints Recipient dialog that appears, fill out the contact information. If you're shipping to yourself, click the This Is My Home Address check box.

4. Click OK.

5. Repeat these steps for as many contacts as you wish (or don't; you can add new contacts the next time you order prints).

✔ Tip

■ When in the Editor, clicking the Order Prints button from the Share tab sends you back to the Organizer and opens a dialog with options similar to the Review Order dialog.

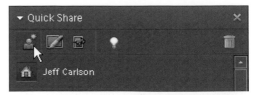

Figure 13.41 The Order Prints palette makes it easy to order prints for multiple people.

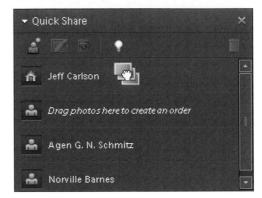

Figure 13.42 Drag images from the gallery to the Order Prints palette.

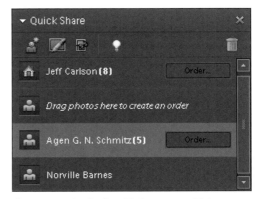

Figure 13.43 Gradually add photos to multiple contacts until you're ready to place an order.

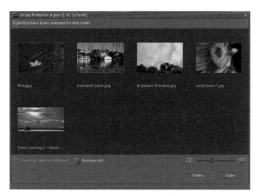

Figure 13.44 Review your selections and remove any photos before ordering prints.

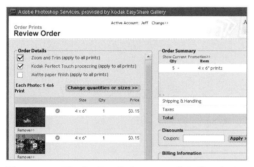

Figure 13.45 The Review Order screen lists the photos you've chosen along with other ordering options.

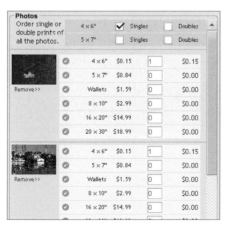

Figure 13.46 You can order prints in various sizes and quantities.

To order prints:

1. Select one or more photos to print.

2. Drag the image(s) to a contact name in the Quick Share palette (**Figure 13.42**).

   The benefit of using the Quick Share palette is that you can add photos to orders before placing them (**Figure 13.43**).

3. To view the photos in an order, double-click the contact name or click the View Photos button. In the Order Prints dialog that appears, you can remove selected photos or all photos (**Figure 13.44**).

4. Click the Order button (in either the Quick Share palette or the Order Prints dialog) to bring up the Review Order dialog (**Figure 13.45**).

5. You may enable the following options:
   ▲ **Zoom and Trim.** This option enlarges the image slightly to fill the paper size. To avoid this, crop your images before ordering prints; see Chapter 6.

   ▲ **Kodak Perfect Touch processing.** Kodak applies some color correction; if you've worked hard to perfect your image, deselect this option.

   ▲ **Matte paper finish.** Choose matte paper instead of a glossy stock.

6. A single 4 x 6 print is selected for each image. Click the Change quantities or sizes button if you want other sizes, multiple prints, etc. (**Figure 13.46**). If you make changes, click the Back button to return to the Review Order dialog.

7. When you're ready to place the order, click the Checkout button.

8. Enter your credit card information and billing address, and then click the Place Order button.

ORDERING PRINTS

SHARING
YOUR IMAGES

If you're shooting photographs and making
your own compositions within Photoshop
Elements, it's a safe bet that you want to
share them with others. In the past, you'd
make prints and either carry them every-
where or send them through the mail. Now,
you can make your own slideshow (without
the cumbersome projector), put images on
a Web site for family to view, e-mail photos,
and much more.

Making Your Own Slide Show

With Photoshop Elements, you can create a self-contained, portable slide show—a useful and elegant way to share your photos and images with friends and family.

Although Elements can output a slide show as a movie (.wmv) or even burn it to a DVD, in this exercise I'll focus on creating a slide show as an Adobe Acrobat PDF (Portable Document Format) file. The operative word here is portable. You can view a PDF file on nearly any Windows or Macintosh computer, as long as Adobe's Acrobat Reader is installed.

When you open the PDF file in Acrobat Reader, the slide show automatically opens in full-screen mode. Slides can change with a transition you select when creating the PDF (**Figure 14.1**). In an automatic slide show, the slides change at preset intervals you set when you generate the file. Alternatively, if you prefer to advance each slide manually, you can create a slide show that changes slides with keyboard commands.

To create a PDF slide show:

1. In the Organizer, select one or more photos that will appear in the slide show.

2. In the Task Pane, click the Create tab. A list of items you can create appears.

3. Click Slide Show (**Figure 14.2**). The Slide Show Preferences dialog opens, where you select the different options for your slide show. Here you can apply transition effects, change the background color, crop photos to fit a landscape or portrait format, and set quality options (**Figure 14.3**).

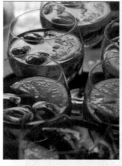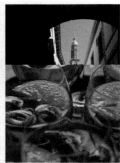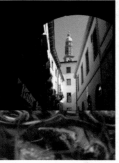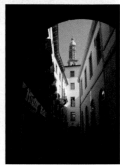

Figure 14.1 When you create a slide show, you can specify how your slide show transitions from one image to the next. This slide show displays the Wipe Down transition, where a new image rolls down over the previous image's slide.

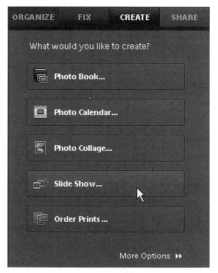

Figure 14.2 The Create tab leads to a variety of creations.

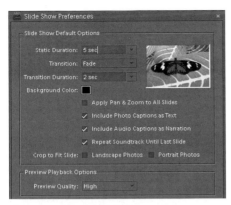

Figure 14.3 Set options before you create your slide show in the Slide Show Preferences dialog.

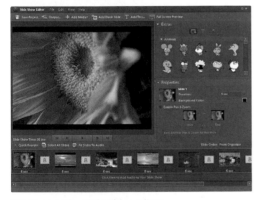

Figure 14.4 The Slide Show Editor.

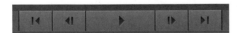

Figure 14.5 The Slide Show Editor features a set of controls to help you play and navigate through your slide show during its creation.

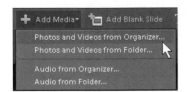

Figure 14.6 Add photos, video, and even audio to a slide show from the Organizer or from a folder.

4. Select the options you would like to apply to your slide show, then click OK to close the dialog. The Slide Show Editor window opens (**Figure 14.4**).

5. To preview your slide show, first click the Rewind and then the Play button below the Slide Show preview (**Figure 14.5**).

To add photos to the slide show:

1. Click the Add Media button above the preview window, and then choose a source for your photos from the menu (**Figure 14.6**).

   Note that not only can you add photos to a slide show, but you can also add video and audio files.

2. Click to select the photos you want to include in your slide show, and then click Done (or click Open, if your source was a folder). The Slide Show Bin at the bottom of the Slide Show Editor is populated with all of the photos and video you selected, complete with the transitions you chose from the Slide Show Preferences dialog.

✔ Tips

- You can return to the Slide Show Preferences dialog at any time during the creation of your slide show by choosing Slide Show Preferences from the Edit menu.

- A variation of a slide show is a flipbook, which creates a movie out of images; click the Create tab and choose Flipbook from the More Options menu.

To reorder slides:

1. In the Slide Show Bin, click to select the slide you want to move (**Figure 14.7**).

2. Hold down the mouse button and drag the slide to a different location in the Slide Show Bin.

   When you release the mouse button, the slide and its transition snap into place in the new location (**Figure 14.8**).

   Alternately, you can click the Quick Reorder button above the Slide Show Bin so that you can see all of the slides in your slide show at once. Click and drag to move slides in the Quick Reorder window just as you do in the Slide Show Bin.

To edit slide transitions:

1. In the Slide Show Bin, click the transition between the two slides you would like to change (**Figure 14.9**).

2. From the Transition drop-down menu, select a new transition (**Figure 14.10**).

   If you'd like, you can also change the duration of the transition—the amount of time it takes to transition from one slide to the next.

3. From the Duration drop-down menu, select a time, in seconds.

✔ Tip

■ You can apply new transition effects to more than one slide at a time by selecting multiple transitions at once. Click to select the first transition you want to change, and then Ctrl-click to select subsequent transitions. Alternately, if you want to select every transition in your slide show, choose Select All Transitions from the Slide Show Editor Edit menu.

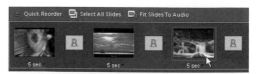

Figure 14.7 Select slides and transitions in the Slide Show Bin.

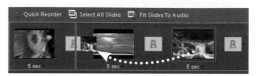
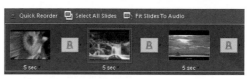

Figure 14.8 Click and drag a slide in the Slide Show Bin to move it to a different spot in your slide show (top). When you release the mouse button, the slide and its transition snap into place.

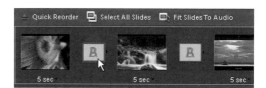

Figure 14.9 Click any transition to edit its properties.

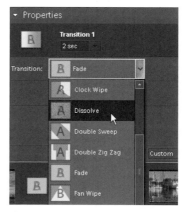

Figure 14.10 The Slide Show Editor offers a myriad of transitions.

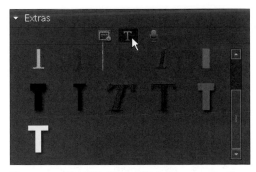

Figure 14.11 The Slide Show Editor offers a collection of type styles to choose from.

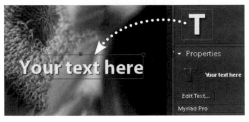

Figure 14.12 Drag to add a text placeholder to a slide.

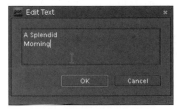

Figure 14.13 As you type, the text appears immediately in the Preview.

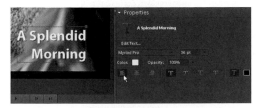

Figure 14.14 You can use the Slide Show Editor's default type styles, or use the type controls to customize your type manually.

To add text to a slide:

1. In the Slide Show Bin, click to select the slide onto which you want to apply text. The slide appears in the Slide Preview.

2. Click the Text button in the Extras pane to open the default text collection (**Figure 14.11**); then scroll to find the text style you would like to use.

3. Drag the selected text directly onto the slide in the Slide Preview (**Figure 14.12**).

4. Double-click the default text in the Slide Preview to open the Edit Text box.

5. Type the text you would like to appear on your slide and then click OK (**Figure 14.13**).

6. Use the controls in the Properties area of the Slide Show Editor to change the font, size, color, and orientation of the text (**Figure 14.14**).

7. You can reposition the type by clicking anywhere within its bounding box and dragging it to a new location.

✔ Tips

- If you want to add some whimsy to your slides, feel free to drag elements from the Graphics section of the Extras pane to the slide preview area.

- The Narration button in the Extras pane enables you to record audio narration that will accompany the currently selected slide.

MAKING YOUR OWN SLIDE SHOW

To save a slide show:

1. Click the Save Project button (you can also choose Save Slide Show Project from the File menu, or press Ctrl+S).

2. In the Save dialog, type a name for your slide show and click Save (**Figure 14.15**).

   Your slide show is saved to the Organizer's Photo Browser, where you can reopen it at any time to make revisions or to output it.

3. To close the Slide Show Editor, *do one of the following:*

   ▲ From the File menu, choose Exit Slide Editor, or press Ctrl+Q.

   ▲ Click the close button in the upper-right corner of the Slide Show Editor window.

   ▲ If you want to output a slide show right away, leave the Slide Show Editor open and proceed to the next task.

To output a slide show:

1. Click the Output button near the top of the Slide Show Editor (**Figure 14.16**).

   The Slide Show Output window opens.

2. To output a simple PDF slide show, first check that Save As a File is selected in the options column on the left side of the window (**Figure 14.17**).

3. Click the PDF File radio button in the center of the window, and then choose the settings you would like to apply to your slide show (**Figure 14.18**).

4. Click OK to close the Slide Show Output window. Then, in the Save As dialog, navigate to the location where you would like to save your slide show, rename it if you would like, and click Save.

   If you selected View Slide Show after Saving in the Slide Show Output dialog, Acrobat Reader will launch automatically and play your slide show.

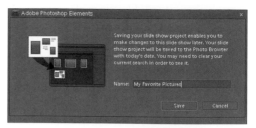

Figure 14.15 The Slide Show Editor has its own unique Save dialog.

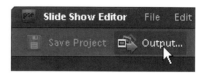

Figure 14.16 The Output button is the first step to creating a PDF.

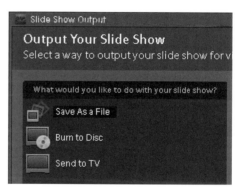

Figure 14.17 The Slide Show Output window offers several different ways to export your slide show.

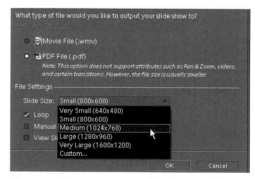

Figure 14.18 You can export a slide show as either a PDF or a movie file.

To view a slide show:

1. Make sure Adobe Acrobat Reader is installed on your computer.

   If it's not installed, install it from the Photoshop Elements installation disc, or download it free from www.adobe.com.

2. In Acrobat Reader, open the PDF slide show you created.

   The slide show appears, taking up the full screen. If the slide show is set to run automatically, each image will be displayed for the time you set in the Slide Show dialog.

3. To navigate through your slide show, use the following keyboard commands:

   ▲ Move forward one slide by pressing Enter or the right arrow key.

   ▲ Move back one slide by pressing Shift+Enter or the left arrow key.

   ▲ Exit Full Screen view and access Acrobat Reader's interface by pressing Ctrl+L.

✔ Tip

■ The transitions and auto advance features of the slide show will only work in Acrobat Reader 5.0 or later. The slide show will open and display with older versions of Acrobat, but you'll need to navigate through the slides manually using the keyboard commands listed above.

MAKING YOUR OWN SLIDE SHOW

Creating an Online Album

Preparing a gallery of photos for use on the Web can be repetitive, tedious work. You have to resize and format each image, one at a time—a lengthy process. Photoshop Elements eliminates this drudgework with its Online Album feature. When you create an Online Album, Elements guides you through the steps to building a Flash-based slideshow that can be published to Photoshop.com, to a CD or DVD, or uploaded directly to a Web server via FTP (File Transfer Protocol).

To create an Online Album:

1. In the Organizer, select one or more photos that will appear in the album.

2. In the Task Pane, click the Share tab.

3. Click the Online Album option (**Figure 14.19**); thumbnails of your selected photos appear in the Task pane.

   To add more photos, select the additions in the Catalog pane and then click the + (plus button) in the Task pane. To remove photos from the album, select them in the Task pane and then click the – (minus button) (**Figure 14.20**).

4. Give the album a title in the Album Name field.

5. Click the Share button to continue. Elements builds a preview of the album (**Figure 14.21**).

   If you'd like to change the album style, click the Change Template button (**Figure 14.22**), select a style, and click the Apply button. (Also see the sidebar on the next page.) At this stage, you can also edit the Album name. Then, click Next.

6. Choose where you'd like to share the album (Photoshop.com, CD/DVD, or FTP) by clicking one of the radio buttons the under Share To: heading.

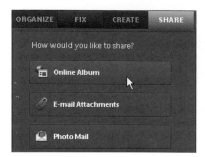

Figure 14.19 Choose Online Album from the Share tab.

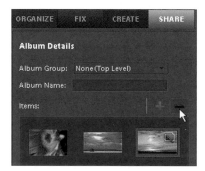

Figure 14.20 Easily remove items from the album in progress.

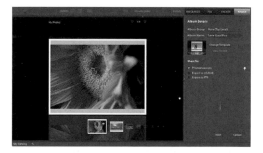

Figure 14.21 Elements displays an animated preview of the online album.

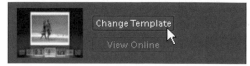

Figure 14.22 Click the Change Template button to view other design options.

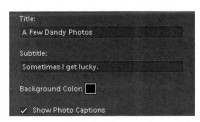

Figure 14.23 The Album Details pane lets you edit other information that appears.

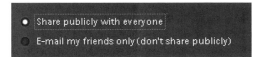

Figure 14.24 Will your album be viewable to the public, or just to select people?

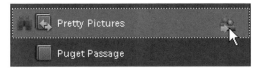

Figure 14.25 The Share button in the Album list is a speedy way to publish an album's photos online.

Interactive Album Layouts

Some online album templates can be modified while you're building them, with options to change effects, image sizes, or object placement. These options, if available, appear as a set of menus above the theme (**Figure 14.26**). In some layouts, you can also drag to reposition photos.

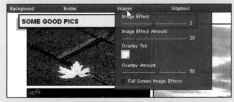

Figure 14.26 Some themes include customization options, such as this comic book style.

The rest of the steps on this page apply to publishing to Photoshop.com. If you choose Export to CD/DVD, Elements asks you to insert a blank disc and writes the necessary files to it. If you choose Export to FTP, you'll need to enter the server, login, and password information for your Web site.

7. Click the Next button to continue.

8. In the Album Details pane, type a title and (optionally) a subtitle that will appear with the album (**Figure 14.23**); these are separate from the title you set in the Album Name field.

   You can also click the Background Color box to change the backdrop, and choose to display captions by enabling the Show Photo Captions check box. If you make any changes here, click the Refresh button to view them in the preview area.

9. Click the Next button to continue. The Album Details pane expands to include sharing options; you can still change the template and album name at this point.

10. Click a radio button to determine how widely the album is to be shared (**Figure 14.24**). If you're sharing with just a few friends, mark the friends' names in the Send E-Mail To field.

    The Allow Viewers To options apply to both public and private shared albums.

11. Click the Share button to publish the album. Elements builds the album and uploads it to Photoshop.com.

✔ Tip

■ A faster method of creating an online album is to click the Share icon that appears to the right of an album (**Figure 14.25**). This approach skips steps 3 through 7.

CREATING AN ONLINE ALBUM

To edit a shared album:

1. Select the shared album in the Albums pane.

2. Add or remove photos by *doing one of the following*:

   ▲ Click the Edit Album button at the top of the pane to display the Album Details pane, then add or remove photos using the Add (+) or Remove (–) buttons.

   ▲ Add photos to the album by dragging them from the Catalog pane.

3. Click the Done button. Elements uploads new images if needed and modifies the slide show.

   Or, click the Share button to change the album name, template, or privacy options.

To stop sharing an album:

◆ Locate the shared album in the Albums pane and click the Stop Sharing button (**Figure 14.27**).

   Although the album will no longer be available as a published slide show, the photos will remain at Photoshop.com.

✔ Tip

■ The small thumbnail views of the different albums in the Task Pane aren't really big enough to give you a good idea of what the final album will look like, but you can click Apply to load one, check it out, and then click Cancel to return to the previous template.

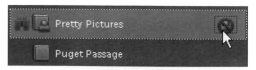

Figure 14.27 Click the Stop Sharing button to remove the album's online slide show.

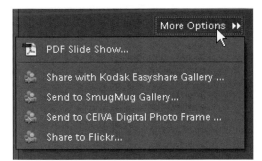

Figure 14.28 The More Options drop-down menu reveals options for uploading to other services.

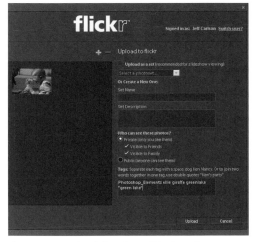

Figure 14.29 Upload directly to Flickr from Elements.

Start with Compatible Files

Elements won't convert your images when uploading to a third-party service, as it does for Photoshop.com. For example, Flickr accepts JPEG files but not camera raw files. If you typically shoot in raw, you'll need to first save your image as JPEG (choose File > Save As) before uploading to the service.

Uploading to a Photo Sharing Service

Photoshop.com is deeply tied into Photoshop Elements, but it wasn't the first photo sharing service on the scene. If you already have an account with another service, you can upload photos directly from within Elements. I'll use Flickr in my example below.

To upload to a photo sharing service:

1. In the Organizer, select one or more photos you wish to upload.

2. Click the Share tab of the Task Pane.

3. Click the More Options link to display a drop-down menu (**Figure 14.28**).

4. Choose Share to Flickr.

   The first time you do so, you'll need to authorize Elements as a legitimate sharing service within Flickr. Click the Authorize button in the Share to Flickr dialog, which takes you to Flickr's site on the Web. Return to the Share to Flickr dialog and click the Complete Authorization button. The Upload to Flickr interface appears (**Figure 14.29**).

5. The photos you selected appear in the Items field; click the Add (+) or Remove (−) buttons if you want to change which images are uploaded.

6. If you wish to include the photos in a set, click the Upload as a set checkbox and specify a photoset you've previously set up at Flickr or create a new one by typing its title in the Set Name field.

7. Specify the photos' privacy settings under the heading Who can see these photos?

8. Type keyword tags in the Tags field.

9. Click the Upload button to publish the photos.

Sending Images by E-mail

With the E-mail feature, Elements stream-lines the process of sending digital photos to family and friends. If your photo is too large or is in the wrong file format, Elements can automatically resize your image, if you prefer.

To attach a simple photo to e-mail:

1. In the Organizer, select the photo or image you want to send.

2. Click the Share tab in the Task Pane and click the E-mail Attachments button (**Figure 14.30**).

3. From the Maximum Photo Size drop-down menu, you can choose to change the size of your attachment or leave it unchanged.

   If you choose an option other than Use Original Size, use the Quality slider to control the size and download speed of your attachment (**Figure 14.31**).

   If the source image is not a JPEG file, you also have the option of converting the outgoing file. Click Next.

4. Type a personal note in the Message field.

5. Choose a name (or names) from the Select Recipients list.

   If you're using the E-mail function for the first time, your Select Recipients window will probably be empty, and you'll want to create a recipient list. See the steps on the next page.

6. Click Next. Elements converts the images and attaches them to an outgoing mes-sage in your default e-mail program (**Figure 14.32**).

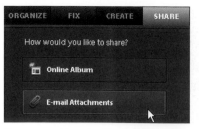

Figure 14.30 From the Share tab, choose E-mail Attachments.

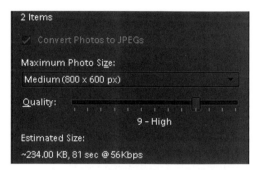

Figure 14.31 The Quality slider allows you to make size and quality adjustments to your image, just as you can in the Save for Web dialog.

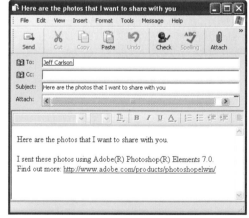

Figure 14.32 An e-mail message, with the attachment included, is automatically created for you.

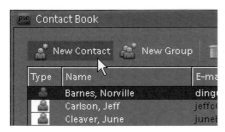

Figure 14.33 It's easy to add new contacts to your list.

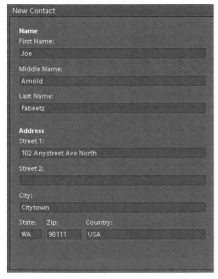

Figure 14.34 Create new contacts for later use.

To add or edit recipients:

1. To create a new contact/recipient, or to edit a recipient's contact information, click the Edit Contacts button at the recipients screen.

2. In the Contact Book dialog, click New Contact (**Figure 14.33**); or, select an existing contact, and then click the Edit button.

3. In the New Contact or Edit Contact window, add detailed telephone and mailing address information (**Figure 14.34**).

4. When you've finished adding or editing your contact information, click OK to close the window. Then click OK again to close the Contact Book dialog.

✔ Tips

- You can import contact information directly into your Photoshop Elements Contact Book. Click the Import button in the Contact Book dialog. In the Choose Contact Source dialog, select vCard Files or Outlook Express, and then click OK. If the former, you then locate a vCard file you've exported from another e-mail program or contact manager. If the latter, your Elements Contact Book will automatically be populated with your Outlook Express contacts.

- Do you send photos to the same people over and over? If so, as you're specifying recipients, click Yes under Save as Quick Share Flow? Enter a name and click Next; a new item appears in the Quick Share pane. When you drag photos to it (just as you would create an order for prints) and click the E-mail button, a new outgoing message is created with those recipients already filled-in.

To attach a photo on custom stationery to e-mail:

1. Open the photo or image you want to send, and then follow the steps in the previous procedure to select a list of recipients.

2. In the Share pane, click the Photo Mail button (**Figure 14.35**).

3. If you like, mark the Include Caption check box to add additional text later. Add or remove pictures using the plus or minus buttons. Click Next.

4. Type a message to your recipients and choose your recipients. Click Next to open the Stationery & Layouts Wizard.

5. From the Stationery pane on the left side of the Wizard window, choose a stationery layout on which you'd like to place your photo (**Figure 14.36**). Then click the Next Step button at the bottom of the Wizard.

6. If you like, use the various sliders, buttons, and drop-down menus to customize the look of your stationery (**Figure 14.37**).

7. Insert a message and caption into the placeholder text areas, and then click the Next button.

   Your default e-mail program opens automatically and places your photo on its special stationery into the body of your e-mail.

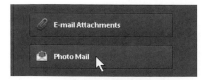

Figure 14.35 To create a graphical e-mail attachment, select Photo Mail.

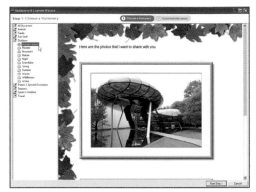

Figure 14.36 The Stationery & Layouts Wizard.

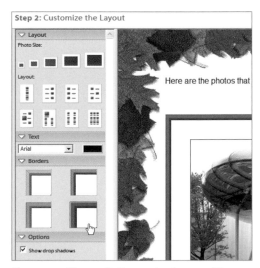

Figure 14.37 You can further customize any of the stationery templates to give them just the look you want.

EDITOR KEYBOARD SHORTCUTS

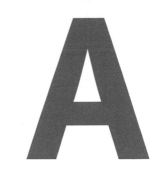

To choose a tool	
Tools	
Move	V
Zoom	Z
Hand	H
Eyedropper	I
Marquee	M
Lasso	L
Magic Wand	W
Magic Selection Brush	F
Selection Brush	A
Type & Type Mask	T
Crop	C
Cookie Cutter	Q
Straighten	P
Red Eye Removal	Y
Healing Brush	J
Clone Stamp	S
Eraser	E
Brush	B
Smart Brush	F
Pencil	N
Paint Bucket	K
Gradient	G
Shape	U
Blur	R
Sponge	O

To cycle through tools	
Marquee tools	M
Lasso tools	L
Type & Type Mask tools	T
Healing Brush tools	J
Clone Stamp tools	S
Eraser tools	E
Brush tools	B
Smart Brush tools	F
Shape tools	U
Blur & Sharpen tools	R
Dodge & Burn tools	O

Working with tools

MARQUEE TOOL

Draw marquee from center	[Alt]+drag
Constrain to square or circle	[Shift]+drag
Draw from center and constrain to	[Alt]+[Shift]+drag

MOVE TOOL

Constrain move to 45°	[Shift]+drag
Copy selection or layer	[Alt]+drag
Nudge selection or layer 1 pixel	Arrow key
Nudge selection or layer 10 pixels	[Shift]+arrow

LASSO TOOL

Add to selection	[Shift]+click, then draw
Delete from selection	[Alt]+click, then draw
Intersect with selection	[Alt]+[Shift]+click, then draw
Change to Polygonal Lasso	Click, then [Alt]+drag

POLYGONAL LASSO TOOL

Add to selection	[Shift]+click, then draw
Delete from selection	[Alt]+click, then draw
Intersect with selection	[Alt]+[Shift]+click, then draw
Draw using Lasso	[Alt]+drag
Constrain to 45° while drawing	[Shift]+drag

MAGNETIC LASSO TOOL

Add to selection	[Shift]+click, then draw
Delete from selection	[Alt]+click, then draw
Intersect with selection	[Alt]+[Shift]+click, then draw
Add point	Single click
Remove last point	Backspace or [Delete]
Close path	Double-click or [Enter]

MAGNETIC LASSO TOOL

Close path over start point	Click on start point
Close path using straight line segment	[Alt]+double-click
Switch to Lasso	[Alt]+drag
Switch to Polygonal Lasso	[Alt]+click

CROP TOOL

Rotate crop marquee	Drag outside crop marquee
Move crop marquee	Drag inside crop marquee
Resize crop marquee	Drag crop handles
Resize crop box while maintaining its aspect ratio	[Shift]+drag corner handles

(continued on next page)

Working with tools *(continued)*

SHAPE TOOLS	
Constrain to square or circle	`Shift`+drag
Constrain Line tool to 45°	`Shift`+drag
Transform shape	`Ctrl`+T
Distort	`Ctrl`+drag
Skew	`Ctrl`+`Alt`+drag
Create Perspective	`Ctrl`+`Alt`+`Shift`+drag
TYPE TOOL	
Select a word	Double-click in text
Select a line	Triple-click in text
Select a paragraph	Quadruple-click in text
Select all characters	`Ctrl`+A
Left align text	`Ctrl`+`Shift`+L
Center text	`Ctrl`+`Shift`+C
Right align text	`Ctrl`+`Shift`+R
Increase by 2 points	`Ctrl`+`Shift`+ . (period)
Decrease by 2 points	`Ctrl`+`Shift`+ , (comma)
Scroll through fonts	Select font in menu+up/down arrow
PAINT BUCKET TOOL	
Change color of area	`Shift`+click outside canvas
BRUSH AND PENCIL TOOL	
Decrease or increase size by 10 pixels	[(key) or] (key) (or by 1 pixel when size is less than 10 pixels)
SMUDGE TOOL	
Smudge using Foreground color	`Alt`+drag
EYEDROPPER TOOL	
Choose Background color	`Alt`+click

Display Shortcuts

CHANGE VIEW	
Zoom In	[Ctrl]+Spacebar+click/drag or [Ctrl]++(plus)
Zoom out	[Alt]+Spacebar+click/drag or [Ctrl]+–(minus)
Zoom to 100% / Actual pixels	Double-click Zoom tool or [Ctrl]+[Alt]+o
Zoom to fit window / Fit on screen	Double-click Hand tool or [Ctrl]+o
Show/hide edges of selection	[Ctrl]+H
Show/hide ruler	[Ctrl]+R
HAND TOOL	
Toggle to zoom in	[Ctrl]
Toggle to zoom out	[Alt]
Fit image on screen	Double-click tool
ZOOM TOOL	
Zoom out	[Alt]+click
Actual size	Double-click tool
MOVE IMAGE IN WINDOW	
Scroll up one screen	Page Up
Scroll down one screen	Page Down
Scroll left one screen	[Ctrl]+page up
Scroll right one screen	[Ctrl]+page down
Scroll up 10 pixels	[Shift]+page up
Scroll down 10 pixels	[Shift]+page down
Scroll left 10 pixels	[Ctrl]+[Shift]+page up
Scroll right 10 pixels	[Ctrl]+[Shift]+page down
Move view to upper left	Home key
Move view to lower right	End key

Menu Shortcuts

FILE MENU

New	`Ctrl`+N
Open	`Ctrl`+O
Open As	`Ctrl`+`Alt`+O
Close	`Ctrl`+W
Close All	`Ctrl`+`Alt`+W
Save	`Ctrl`+S
Save As	`Ctrl`+`Shift`+S
Save for Web	`Ctrl`+`Alt`+`Shift`+S
Page Setup	`Ctrl`+`Shift`+P
Print	`Ctrl`+P
Print Multiple Photos	`Ctrl`+`Alt`+P
Exit	`Ctrl`+Q

EDIT MENU

Undo	`Ctrl`+Z
Redo	`Ctrl`+Y
Cut	`Ctrl`+X
Copy	`Ctrl`+C
Copy Merged	`Ctrl`+`Shift`+C
Paste	`Ctrl`+V
Paste Into Selection	`Ctrl`+`Shift`+V
Color Settings	`Ctrl`+`Shift`+K
Preferences > General	`Ctrl`+K

IMAGE MENU

Free Transform	`Ctrl`+T
Image Size	`Ctrl`+`Alt`+I

ENHANCE MENU

Auto Smart Fix	`Ctrl`+`Alt`+M
Auto Levels	`Ctrl`+`Shift`+L
Auto Contrast	`Ctrl`+`Alt`+`Shift`+L
Auto Color Correction	`Ctrl`+`Shift`+B
Auto Red Eye Fix	`Ctrl`+R
Adjust Smart Fix	`Ctrl`+`Shift`+M
Adjust Lighting > Adjust Levels	`Ctrl`+L
Adjust Color > Adjust Hue/Saturation	`Ctrl`+U
Adjust Color > Remove Color	`Ctrl`+`Shift`+U

(continued on next page)

EDITOR KEYBOARD SHORTCUTS

Menu Shortcuts *(continued)*

LAYER MENU

New > Layer	`Ctrl`+`Shift`+N
New > Layer via Copy	`Ctrl`+J
New > Layer via Cut	`Ctrl`+`Shift`+J
Group with Previous	`Ctrl`+G
Ungroup	`Ctrl`+`Shift`+G
Arrange > Bring to Front	`Ctrl`+`Shift`+]
Arrange > Bring Forward	`Ctrl`+]
Arrange > Send Backward	`Ctrl`+[
Arrange > Send to Back	`Ctrl`+`Shift`+]
Merge Down	`Ctrl`+E
Merge Visible	`Ctrl`+`Shift`+E

SELECT MENU

All	`Ctrl`+A
Deselect	`Ctrl`+D
Reselect	`Ctrl`+`Shift`+D
Inverse	`Ctrl`+`Shift`+I
Feather	`Ctrl`+`Alt`+D
Nudge selection marquee 1 pixel	Arrow key
Nudge selection marquee 10 pixels	`Shift`+Arrow key

FILTER MENU

Last Filter	`Ctrl`+F
Adjustments > Invert	`Ctrl`+I

LIQUIFY FILTER

Warp tool	W
Turbulence tool	A
Twirl Clockwise tool	R
Twirl Counterclockwise tool	L
Pucker tool	P
Bloat tool	B
Shift Pixels tool	S
Reflection tool	M
Reconstruct tool	E
Zoom tool	Z
Hand tool	H
Reverse direction for Shift Pixels	`Alt`+tool and Reflect tools
Increase/decrease brush pressure by 1	Up/down arrow key
Increase/decrease brush size by 1	Up/down arrow key

ORGANIZER KEYBOARD SHORTCUTS

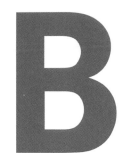

Menu Shortcuts	
FILE MENU	
Get Photos and Videos > From Camera or Card Reader	`Ctrl`+G
Get Photos and Videos > From Scanner	`Ctrl`+U
Get Photos and Videos > From Files and Folders	`Ctrl`+`Shift`+G
Catalog	`Ctrl`+`Shift`+C
Make a CD/DVD	`Ctrl`+`Alt`+C
Copy/Move to Removable Disk	`Ctrl`+`Shift`+O
Backup Catalog	`Ctrl`+B
Duplicate	`Ctrl`+`Shift`+D
Rename	`Ctrl`+`Shift`+N
Move	`Ctrl`+`Shift`+V
Export As New File(s)	`Ctrl`+E
Page Setup	`Ctrl`+`Shift`+P
Print	`Ctrl`+P
Exit	`Ctrl`+Q
EDIT MENU	
Undo	`Ctrl`+Z
Redo	`Ctrl`+Y
Copy	`Ctrl`+C
Select All	`Ctrl`+A
Deselect	`Ctrl`+`Shift`+A
Delete from Catalog	`Del` key
Rotate 90° Left	`Ctrl`+Left
Rotate 90° Right	`Ctrl`+Right
Auto Smart Fix	`Ctrl`+`Alt`+M
Auto Red Eye Fix	`Ctrl`+R
Adjust Date and Time	`Ctrl`+J

(continued on next page)

Menu Shortcuts *(continued)*

Add Caption	Ctrl+Shift+T
Update Thumbnail	Ctrl+Shift+U
Set as Desktop Wallpaper	Ctrl+Shift+W
Visibility > Mark as Hidden	Alt+F2
Stack > Automatically Suggest Stacks	Ctrl+Alt+K
Stack > Stack Selected Photos	Ctrl+Alt+S
Stack > Reveal Photos in a Stack	Ctrl+Alt+R
Stack > Collapse Photos in Stack	Ctrl+Alt+Shift+R
Color Settings	Ctrl+Alt+G
Preferences > General	Ctrl+K

FIND MENU

Set Date Range	Ctrl+Alt+F
Clear Date Range	Ctrl+Shift+F
By Caption or Note	Ctrl+Shift+J
By Filename	Ctrl+Shift+K
All Version Sets	Ctrl+Alt+V
All Stacks	Ctrl+Alt+Shift+S
By Media Type > Photos	Alt+1
By Media Type > Video	Alt+2
By Media Type > Audio	Alt+3
By Media Type > Creations	Alt+4
By Media Type > Items with Audio Captions	Alt+5
By Media Type > PDF	Alt+6
Items with Unknown Date or Time	Ctrl+Shift+X
Untagged Items	Ctrl+Shift+Q

VIEW MENU

Refresh	F5
Media Types > Photos	Ctrl+1
Media Types > Video	Ctrl+2
Media Types > Audio	Ctrl+3
Media Types > Projects	Ctrl+4
Media Types > PDF	Ctrl+5
Details	Ctrl+D

WINDOW MENU

Timeline	Ctrl+L
Properties	Alt+Enter

HELP MENU

Photoshop Elements Help	F1

DISPLAY DROP-DOWN MENU

Thumbnail View	Ctrl+Alt+1
Import Batch	Ctrl+Alt+2
Folder Location	Ctrl+Alt+3
Date View	Ctrl+Alt+D
View Photos in Full Screen	F11
Compare Photos Side by Side	F12

EDITOR DROP-DOWN MENU

Full Edit	Ctrl+I

Navigating in the Photo Browser

Move Selection up/down/left/right	Up/Down/ Left/Right
Show full-size thumbnail of selected photo	Enter

Viewing Photos in Full Screen mode

Start slide show	Spacebar
Show next slide	Right/Down
Show previous slide	Left/Up
Pause slide show	Spacebar
End slide show	Esc

ORGANIZER KEYBOARD SHORTCUTS

INDEX

INDEX

INDEX

INDEX

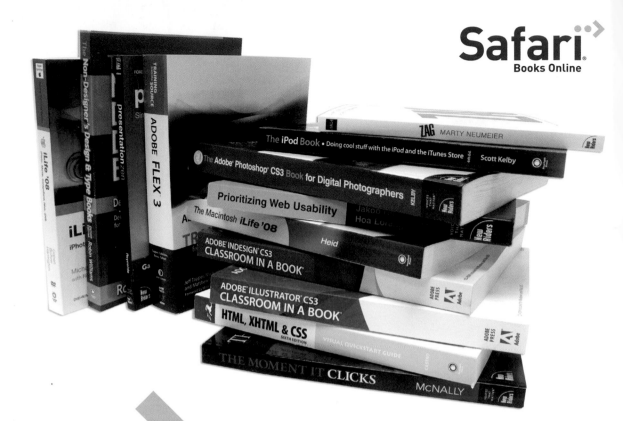